YOUR RIGHT
to Be
RICH

YOUR RIGHT

to Be

RICH

———

NAPOLEON HILL

JEREMY P. TARCHER/PENGUIN
An imprint of Penguin Random House
New York

JEREMY P. TARCHER/PENGUIN
An imprint of Penguin Random House LLC
375 Hudson Street
New York, New York 10014

Originally published in 1961 (Brilliance Audio)
This is the first print edition.

Editorial direction: Francine Huss

Most Tarcher/Penguin books are available at special quantity discounts for
bulk purchase for sales promotions, premiums, fund-raising, and educational needs.
Special books or book excerpts also can be created to fit specific needs.
For details, write: SpecialMarkets@penguinrandomhouse.com

Library of Congress Cataloging-in-Publication Data

Hill, Napoleon, 1883–1970.
Your right to be rich / Napoleon Hill.
pages   cm
"Originally published in 1961 (Brilliance Audio)."
Includes index.
ISBN 978-0-399-17321-9
1. Success.   2. Success in business.   3. Wealth.   I. Title.
HF5386.H5784 2015
332.024'01—dc23
2015016532

Printed in the United States of America
1 3 5 7 9 10 8 6 4 2

Book design by Gretchen Achilles

CONTENTS

YOUR RIGHT
to Be
RICH

INTRODUCTION
to the LECTURE
SERIES,

from the Publisher

Your Right to Be Rich by Napoleon Hill was originally presented as a lecture series to a Chicago audience in spring 1954. Courtesy of The Napoleon Hill Foundation, this publication makes this series of lectures available to you and grows the illustrious works of Napoleon Hill, an American icon of successful living.

Your Right to Be Rich can truly help you achieve your every goal and dream. It will inspire new goals and dreams whereby riches are not restricted to such narrow parameters as fortune and fame. You deserve to be rich in every way— personally, spiritually, and financially. Dr. Hill discovered that those who attained only financial rewards from life, no matter how great those rewards may have been, were the least happy and satisfied people in the world. To be truly rich, you must be rich in all aspects of life.

While Dr. Hill refers to this philosophy as a science of personal achievement—a science of success—you may wonder how success can follow science. Can the steps to riches be synthesized, quantified, and made to work without fail, like a trusted experiment in the laboratory? Dr. Hill defines science as the art of organizing and classifying facts. Like all sciences, the science of success is only useful in its application toward some goal. Dr. Hill presents factual, proven principles so carefully organized and explained that they will, if you follow them carefully and without fail, lead you to the riches you so earnestly desire.

These outstanding lectures represent a unique opportunity to long-devoted students as well as newcomers to Napoleon Hill's work. From this material, based on his live lecture recordings, we experience Dr. Hill's personal presentation of his outstanding philosophy as never before, in a remarkable, effective, and dramatic manner. This lecture series gives us Napoleon Hill's seventeen principles of success, the culmination of decades of study and research.

To more closely achieve the same experience as his students, consider following these three points Dr. Hill strongly emphasized when he gave these lectures:

1. **Take notes.** Keep a notebook handy and take generous notes, starting now. Writing down the information you learn will help to imprint Dr. Hill's philosophy

more strongly on your conscious and subconscious mind, putting it to work more immediately and effectively. You may choose to write or record your ideas.

2. **Add your own ideas.** As you progress through the material, expand your notes, constantly adding to them your own original thoughts as well as relevant thoughts from newspapers, magazines, radio, and TV.

3. **Use repetition to make these ideas yours.** Don't just read these ideas once. Review this material over and over and over again, emphasizing through the power of repetition their messages of thought and action. The more you work with this course, the more it will work for you.

THE SEVENTEEN PRINCIPLES OF SUCCESS

1. **Definiteness of Purpose.** All achievement starts with setting your major objective and making specific plans for obtaining it.

2. **Mastermind.** This process lets you reap the full benefits of the experience, training, education, and specialized knowledge and influence of others.

3. **Applied Faith.** Turn faith into action so that the power of the soul through which your aims, desires, plans, and purposes are developed may be translated into reality.

4. **Going the Extra Mile.** Rewards multiply when you render more service and better service than you are paid to render.

5. **Pleasing Personality.** Develop the mental, spiritual, and physical traits that will help you make the most of yourself and lead you to success.

6. **Personal Initiative.** Taking action is the principle that is necessary for leadership in any walk of life.

7. **Positive Mental Attitude.** The right attitude creates a path to success and the means by which this philosophy can be implemented.

8. **Self-Discipline.** Emotions must be managed in order to balance your head and your heart to achieve a coordination of reason and emotion.

9. **Enthusiasm.** This dynamo of all individual achievement helps you develop self-confidence and overcome negative thoughts, worries, and fears.

10. **Controlled Attention.** Organize your mind. Focus on success. Coordinate and control the powers of your mind. Use the powerful tool of autosuggestion.

11. **Accurate Thinking.** Gather facts, weigh their relative importance, use your own judgment, and think a matter through in order to make the right decision based on thought vs. opinion or emotion.

12. **Learning from Adversity and Defeat.** Understand and circumvent the causes of failure, turning the inevitable setbacks, failures, and opposition into positive benefit.

13. **Cooperation.** Coordinate your efforts with others and work together to achieve a common goal. Use teamwork and tact to your advantage in your personal and business endeavors.

14. **Creative Vision or Imagination.** Let the powerful workshop in your mind reveal the ways to express the purpose of your brain and ideals of your soul.

15. **Sound Health.** Physical well-being is essential to cultivating the energy, vitality, attitudes, and habits for a truly healthy, happy, and successful life.

16. **Budget Time and Money.** Make and get the most out of your physical resources.

17. **Law of Cosmic Habit Force.** Understand and apply the dynamics and power of the controlling force and the natural laws that govern the universe (including human relationships).

THE INCREMENTAL POWER OF ALL
PRINCIPLES WORKING TOGETHER

Each of these seventeen principles, in and of itself, is of tremendous value. However, this is a synergistic philosophy in which all the elements working together have an overall effect greater than the sum of their individual effects. As Dr. Hill discusses each principle, he frequently refers to one or more of the other principles. His repetition is a purposeful and constant reminder that all these principles are interrelated, each one drawing from and building upon every other one. Much like baking a cake, each ingredient is necessary to get the desired results. You can't make a cake only from flour or baking powder or shortening or flavoring; you need all the ingredients in the recipe.

You will notice one particular word Dr. Hill uses often. The word is *transmute*. A dictionary defines it as changing one form, condition, nature, or substance into another. To transform or convert, this thought is essential to your understanding and application of this philosophy.

Transmutation means that you have the ultimate control over your thoughts and feelings. If they are negative, you can make them positive. If they are restrictive, you can make them expansive. If you have held yourself back, you can set yourself free. You have the capacity to transmute or change the habits and patterns that have defeated you.

You will also notice Dr. Hill's reference to the nine basic motives, also called (in other works) the alphabet of success. They are important to understand because emotions and desires inspire all voluntary actions that become individual achievements. As the basic building blocks of human character, motives are the foundation on which this philosophy rests. They are vital to your understanding of other people and of yourself, for they are part of us all.

THE NINE BASIC MOTIVES

1. The emotion of love.

2. The emotion of sex.

3. The desire for material gain.

4. The desire for self-preservation.

5. The desire for freedom of body and mind.

6. The desire for self-expression and recognition.

7. The desire for life after death.

8. The desire for revenge.

9. The emotion of fear.

As you can see, this list truly mirrors human nature, with motives that are positive and motives that are negative.

To achieve the riches we want, we must understand these forces and how to work with them.

The principles of this philosophy and the basic dynamic forces of humanity hint at the exciting and inspiring journey that awaits you. In the following pages, you will learn from the man who developed this philosophy, and who has motivated more men and women to achieve success than anyone else in history. Napoleon Hill, America's greatest millionaire-maker, will share his secrets of success with you in this never-before-published series of powerful lectures. Take a front-row seat as one of his students. Welcome the wisdom that will change your life. Prepare for the adventure of a lifetime. Accept your right to be rich.

DEFINITENESS
of PURPOSE

Let's break down the lesson on Definiteness of Purpose and see exactly what it means and why it's the starting point of achievements—because it truly is the starting point of all individual achievements. A "definite purpose" must be accompanied by a definite plan for an objective followed by appropriate action.

PREMISE #1: A PLAN FOR ACTION

You have to have a purpose, you have to have a plan, and you have to start putting that plan into action. It's not too important that your plan be sound because, if you find that you've adopted a plan that's not sound or not working, you can always change your plan. You can modify your plan, but it is very important that you be definite about it. What it is that you're going after, and your purpose for getting it—that must be very definite. There can be no ifs, ands, or buts about it. You'll see before you get through this lesson why it's got to be definite.

Now, just to understand this philosophy—to read it or hear me talk about it—wouldn't be very much value to you. The value will come when you begin to form your own patterns out of this philosophy and put it into work in your daily life, your business, your profession, your job, or your human relations. That's where the benefits will really come.

PREMISE #2: MOTIVE DETERMINES EVERY ACTION AND ALL ACHIEVEMENT

The second premise is that all individual achievements are the results of a motive or a combination of motives. I want to impress upon you that you have no right to ask anybody to do anything, at any time . . . without what? Without giving that person an adequate motive. Incidentally, that's the measure of good salesmanship, the ability to plant in the mind of the prospective buyer an adequate motive for his buying. Learn to deal with people by planting in their minds adequate motives while they're doing the things that you want them to do. There are a lot of people who call themselves "salesman" who have never heard of the nine basic motives. They do not know that they have no right to ask for a sale until they have planted a motive in the mind of the buyer for his buy.

PREMISE #3: THE POWER
OF THE SUBCONSCIOUS

The third premise is that any dominating idea, plan, or purpose which is held in the mind through repetition of thought, and which is emotionalized with a burning desire for its realization, *will be taken over by the subconscious section of the mind and acted upon through whatever natural and logical means available.* That last sentence contains a tremendous lesson in psychology. If you want the mind to pick up an idea and to form a habit so that the mind will automatically act upon that idea, you've got to tell the mind what you want, over and over and over again.

"Day by day, in every way, I'm getting better and better," is the phrase originated from Emile Coue, the famous French psychologist. It encapsulates his formula for curing thousands of people, in fact a great many more than he didn't cure. I wonder if you would know why. After all, there was no desire or feeling in his statement (and you may as well blow into the wind as to make any statement without feeling in it).

The important thing about any statement is whether or not you believe it. If you tell yourself anything often enough, you'll get to where you will believe it. Even a lie. It's funny but it's true, that there are people who tell little white lies (and sometimes not so "white"), until they get to where they believe them. The subconscious mind doesn't know the difference between right or wrong. It doesn't know the difference between positive or negative. It doesn't know the difference between a penny or a million dollars. It doesn't know the difference between success and failure. It'll accept any statement that you keep repeating to it, by thoughts, or by words, or by any other means. It's up to you (in the beginning) to lay out your definite purpose, write it out so it can be understood, memorize it, and repeat it day in and day out, until your subconscious mind picks it up and automatically acts upon it.

This is going to take a little time. You can't expect to undo overnight what you've been doing to your subconscious mind through the years by allowing negative thoughts to get into it. But you will find that if you emotionalize any plan that you send over to your subconscious mind, repeat it in a state of enthusiasm, and back it up with a spirit of faith, the subconscious mind not only acts more quickly, it also acts more definitely and more positively.

PREMISE #4: THE POWER OF FAITH

The fourth premise is that any dominating desire, plan, or purpose which is backed by that state of mind known as faith is taken over by the subconscious section of the mind and acted upon immediately. Faith is the only state of mind that will produce immediate action in the subconscious mind. By faith, I'm not making reference to wishing, or hoping, or mildly believing, or any of those things. I'm making reference to a state of mind wherein whatever it is that you're going to do, you can see it already in a finished act before you even begin it. That's pretty positive, isn't it?

I can truthfully tell you that not ever in my whole life have I undertaken to do anything that I didn't actually do, unless I got careless in my desire to do it, backed away from it, or changed my mind or my mental attitude. I have never failed to do anything that I made up my mind to do. You can put yourself in a frame of mind to do whatever you make up your mind to do, unless you weaken as you go along (as so many people do).

I don't know for sure, but I suspect that there are a relatively small number of people in the world at any one time who understand the principle of faith—who really understand it and know how to apply it. Even if you do understand it, if you don't back it up with action and make it a part of your habit life, you might just as well not understand it. Faith without deeds is dead, faith without action is dead, and faith without absolute, positive belief is dead. You won't get any results through believing unless you put some action back of that belief.

If you tell your mind often enough that you have faith in anything, the time will come when your subconscious mind will accept that, even if you tell your mind often enough that you have faith in yourself. Have you ever thought what a nice thing it would be if you had such complete faith in yourself that you wouldn't hesitate to undertake anything you wanted to do in life? Have you ever thought what a benefit that would be to you? Do you know how many people sell themselves short all the way through life because they don't have the right amount of confidence, let alone faith? Give a guess as to the percentage. It's somewhere between 98 and 100. The percentage that does is so small that I wouldn't begin to guess just exactly what it is. But judging by the good many thousands of people that I have come into contact with (and you know without my telling you that my audiences and my classes are always above average), I would say that well over 98 percent of the people never in their whole lives develop a sufficient amount of confidence in themselves to go out and to undertake and to do the things they want to do in life. They accept from life whatever life hands them.

Isn't it strange how nature works? She gives you a set of tools; everything that you need to obtain all that you can use or aspire to have in this world. She gives you tools for your every need and she rewards you bountifully for accepting and using those tools. That's all you have to do, just accept them and use them. She penalizes you beyond compare if you don't accept them and use them. Nature hates vacuums and idleness. She wants everything in action, and she especially wants the human mind to be in action. The mind is not different from any other part of the body. If you don't use it or rely on it, it atrophies, withers away, and finally gets to where anybody can push you around. Anybody. Sometimes, you don't have the willpower to even resist or protest when people push you around.

PREMISE #5: THE POWER OF THOUGHT

The fifth premise is the power of thought, the only thing over which any human being has complete and unquestionable means of control. This is so astounding that it connotes a close relationship between the mind of man and Infinite Intelligence. There are only five known things in the whole universe and out of those five is shaped everything that's in existence, from the smallest electrons and protons of matter on up to the largest suns that float out there in the heavens, including you and me. Just five things. There's time, space, energy, and matter, and those four things would be no good without the fifth thing. They'd be nothing. Everything would be chaos. You and I wouldn't have, never could have existed without that fifth thing. What do you think it is? Universal Intelligence.

It reflects itself in every blade of grass, everything that grows out of the ground, and in all of the electrons and protons of matter. It reflects itself in space and in time, in everything that is. There's intelligence—intelligence operating all the time—and the person who is the most successful is the one who finds the ways and means to appropriate most of this intelligence through his brain and put it into action. This intelligence permeates the whole universe: space, time, matter, energy, and everything else. Every individual has the privilege of appropriating to his own use as much of this intelligence as he chooses. He can only appropriate it by using it. Just understanding it or believing in it is not enough. You've got to put it into specialized use, in some form, and the responsibility of this course is mainly to give you a pattern, a blueprint, by which you can take possession of your mind and put it into operation. All you have to do is to follow the blueprint. Don't just pick out that part of it which you like best and discard the others. Take it all as is.

PREMISE #6: SUBCONSCIOUS LINK TO INFINITE INTELLIGENCE

The sixth premise states that the subconscious section of the mind appears to be the only doorway of individual approach to Infinite Intelligence.

I want you to study that language very carefully. I said it *appears* to be. I don't know if it is, I doubt if you do, and I doubt if anyone knows definitely. A lot of people have a lot of different ideas about it. But from the best intelligence that I have been able to use, from the best observations that I have been able to make through thousands of experiments, it appears true. The subconscious section of the mind is the only doorway of individual approach to Infinite Intelligence

16

and it is capable of influence by the individual through the means described in the subject of this lesson. The basic approach is faith based upon definiteness of purpose. This one sentence gives you the key to this premise: faith based upon definiteness of purpose.

Do you have any idea why it is that you don't have as much confidence in yourself as you should have? Have you ever stopped to think about that? Did you ever stop to think why it is, when you see an opportunity coming along or what you believe to be an opportunity, you begin to question your ability to embrace and use it? Haven't you had that happen to you many times? Doesn't it happen every day?

If you've had a chance to be close to people who are very successful, you'll know that is one thing that they're not bothered by. If they want to do something, it never occurs to them that they can't do it. I hope that in your association with Napoleon Hill Associates, you've come to know my distinguished business associate, Mr. W. Clement Stone. If I ever saw a man that knows the power of his mind and is willing to rely upon that mind, Mr. Stone is that man. I don't think Mr. Stone has any worries. I don't believe he would tolerate a worry. I think it would be an insult to his intelligence if he recognized that anything worried him. Why? Because he has confidence in his ability to use his mind and to make that mind create the circumstances that he wants to be created. That's the condition and the operation of mind—any successful mind—and that's going to be the condition of your mind when you get through with this philosophy. You're going to be able to project your mind into whatever objective you choose and there'll never be a question in your mind as to whether you can do what you want to do or not—never a question in the world.

PREMISE #7: BRAIN AS THOUGHT TRANSMITTER

The seventh premise is that every brain is both a receiving set and broadcasting station for the vibrations of thought. This explains the importance of moving with definiteness of purpose instead of drifting. A brain thoroughly charged with the nature of one's purpose will begin to attract the physical or material equivalents of that purpose. Get it into your consciousness that the first radio broadcasting set is the one that exists in the brain of man. Not only does it exist in the brain of man, it also exists in a great many animals. I have a couple of Pomeranian dogs and they will know exactly what I'm thinking, sometimes before I know. They're so smart, they can tune in on it. They know when we start off for an automobile ride whether they're going along or whether they're not. I don't have to say a word—not a word—because they're in constant attunement with us.

Your mind is sending out vibrations constantly. If you're a salesman and you're going to call on a prospective buyer, the sale ought to be made before you ever come into the presence of the buyer. If you're going to do anything requiring the cooperation of other people, condition your mind so that you know the other fellow's going to cooperate. Why? Because the plan that you're going to offer is so fair, honest, and beneficial to him that he can't refuse it. In other words, you have a right to his cooperation. What a change there will be in people when you come sending out positive thoughts instead of thoughts of fear over this broadcasting station of yours.

Here's a good illustration of how this broadcasting station works. Maybe you need a thousand dollars very badly. You go down to the bank because you've got to have that thousand by day after tomorrow or else they're going to take back your car, or the furniture, or something else. You just have to have that thousand dollars. The banker can tell the moment you walk inside the door that you just have to have it. The funny thing is, he doesn't want you to have it. Actually it's not funny, it's tragic. It's like carrying matches around in your pocket all the time and being surprised when you eventually set your own house on fire. You broadcast your thoughts. They precede you. And, when you get there, you find that instead of getting the cooperation you went after, the other person reflects back to you that state of doubt, that state of mind that you sent out ahead.

While I was doing the research on this philosophy, I made my living teaching salesmanship. I taught over thirty thousand salesmen, many of them now life members of the coveted million-dollar round table in the life insurance field. If there is one thing in this world that has to be sold, it's life insurance. Nobody ever buys life insurance. It has to be sold. The first thing I taught people under my direction was that they must make the sale to themselves before they try to make it to the other fellow. If they don't do that, they're not going to make a sale. Somebody might buy something from him or her, but they'll never make a sale unless they first make it to themselves.

Every brain is a broadcasting station and a receiving set and you can attune that brain so that it'll attract the positive vibrations released by other people. This is the point I'm coming to and I want you to get. There are myriad vibrations floating out there constantly. You can train your own mind to pick up, and to attract, only the vibrations that are related to what you want most in life. How do you do that? You keep your mind on what you want most in life—your definite major purpose—so that, by repetition, by thought, and by action, the brain will eventually only identify vibrations related to your definite purpose. What a marvelous thought. You can educate your brain so that it will absolutely refuse to pick up any vibrations except those related to what you want. When you get your brain under control like that, you will be on the path—really and truly on the beam.

BENEFITS OF DEFINITENESS OF PURPOSE

What are some of the benefits of definiteness of purpose? First, definiteness of purpose automatically develops self-reliance, personal initiative, imagination, enthusiasm, self-discipline, and concentration of effort. All of these are vital and important prerequisites for success, which you develop through definiteness of purpose. This requires knowing what you want, having a plan for getting it, and having your mind mostly occupied with carrying out that plan.

PUT INFINITE INTELLIGENCE TO WORK

Unless you're an unusual person, you're almost sure to adopt some plans that are not going to work so well. When you find out that your plan is not right, immediately discard it and get another one. Keep at it until you find one that will work. In the process, remember that Infinite Intelligence, with all Its wisdom, might have a plan for you better than the one you had for yourself. Have an open mind, so that if you adopt a plan to carry out your major purpose (or a minor purpose) and if it doesn't work well, you can dismiss that plan and ask for guidance from Infinite Intelligence. You may get that guidance, and what can you do to be sure that you'll get it? You can believe that you'll get it. It's not even going to hurt if you say out loud orally that you believe it. I suspect that the Creator knows your thought, but I've found that if you express yourself with a lot of enthusiasm, it stirs your belief and arouses your subconscious mind.

When I wrote *Think and Grow Rich*, the original title was *The Thirteen Steps to Riches*. Both the publisher and I knew that was not a box office title. We had to have a million-dollar title. They set the book in type, and the publisher kept prodding me every day to give him the title I wanted. I wrote five or six hundred titles but none of them were any good. Not any of them. One day, my publisher called me and scared the dickens out of me by saying, "Tomorrow morning I've got to have that title, and if you don't have one, I have one that's a humdinger." "What is it?" I asked. He said, "We're going to call it *Use Your Noodle and Get the Boodle*." I replied, "My goodness, you'll ruin me! This is a dignified book and that flippant title will ruin the book, and me too!" "Well," he said, "that's the title unless you give me a better one by tomorrow morning." Now, I want you to follow this incident because it's potent food for thought. That night, I sat down on my bed and I had a talk with my subconscious mind and I said, "Now, you and I've gone a long way together. You've done a lot of things for me, and some things to me (thanks to my ignorance). But, I've got to have a million-dollar title and I've got to have it tonight, do you understand?" I was talking so loudly that the man in the apartment above me thumped on the floor. I don't blame him because he probably thought I was quarrelling with my wife. I really gave the subconscious mind no doubt as to what I wanted. I didn't tell the subconscious mind exactly what kind of a title, I only said it's got to be *a million-dollar title*. I went to bed only after I had tried my subconscious mind and I reached that physiological moment where I knew it was going to produce what I wanted. If I hadn't gotten to that point, I'd still be there sitting there on the side of that bed, talking to my subconscious. There is a physiological moment you can feel when the power of faith takes over whatever you're trying to do and says, "All right, now you can relax. That's it."

I went to bed, and about two o'clock in the morning, I woke up as if somebody had shaken me. As I came out of my sleep, *Think and Grow Rich* was in my mind. I let out a whoop, jumped to my typewriter, wrote it down, grabbed the telephone, and called the publisher. He answered, "What's the matter, is the town on fire?" I said, "You bet it is, with a million-dollar title: *Think and Grow Rich!*" He immediately said, "Boy, you've got it!" and I'd say we got it. That book grossed over twenty-three million dollars already and probably will gross over a hundred million dollars before I pass on. There's no end to it. A million-dollar title is already a multimillion-dollar title. After the thrashing I gave my subconscious, I'm not surprised.

Why didn't I use that method in the first place? After all, I know the law. Why didn't I go directly to the source and get my subconscious mind heated up instead of sitting down at my typewriter, writing out five or six hundred titles? I'll tell you why. It's the same reason that you will oftentimes know what to do but won't do it. There's no explaining the indifference of mankind toward himself. Even after you know what the law is, you'll fool around until the last minute before you do anything about it. It's the same with prayer. When a time of great need comes and you're scared to death, you don't get any results from prayer. To get results from prayer, you must condition your mind so that your life is a prayer. Day in and day out, every minute of your life is a constant prayer. Prayer is based on belief in your dignity— your right to tune into Infinite Intelligence to have the things that you need in this world.

So it is with this human mind. You've got to condition the mind as you go along from day to day, so that when any emergency arises, you'll be right there ready to deal with it. Also, the definiteness of purpose induces one to budget one's time and to plan day-to-day those endeavors that lead to the attainment of one's major purpose. If you compare an hour-by-hour account of the actual work you put in each day for one week against an hour-by-hour account that you waste (but could devote to anything you want to, if you wanted to badly enough), you'd get one of the shocks of your life. We're not efficient. You only have three sets of hours: about eight hours to sleep, about eight hours to earn a living, and about eight hours of free time to do anything that you want.

OPPORTUNITY APPEARS WHEN YOU LOOK FOR IT

Definiteness of purpose makes us more alert in recognizing opportunities related to the object of our major purpose. It inspires the courage to embrace and act upon those opportunities. It lets us see opportunities almost every day of our lives that could benefit us if only we embraced them and acted upon them. Unfortunately, there's something in us we call prostration, which is a lack of will, alertness, or determination to embrace opportunities when they come along. If you condition your mind with this philosophy, you'll not only embrace opportunities but you'll do something better. What could you do better than embrace an opportunity? Make the opportunity.

The day before an attack, one of Napoleon's generals told him that the conditions (the circumstances) were not just right for the planned morning attack. Napoleon responds, "Circumstances not right? Hell, I *make* circumstances! Attack!" I have never seen a successful man yet in any business that didn't say attack when somebody says it can't be done. Attack where you are. And when you get to that curve in the road that you can't see until you get there, you'll always find that the road keeps going around. Attack. Don't procrastinate and don't stand still. Attack.

PURPOSE INSPIRES CONFIDENCE

Definiteness of purpose inspires confidence in one's integrity and character. It attracts the favorable attention of other people. Have you ever thought about that? I think the whole world loves to see a person walking with his chest sticking out, with an atmosphere that tells the whole doggone world that he knows what he's doing and he is proud in doing it. People will get out of the way on the sidewalk and let you go by if you are determined to get by. You don't even have to whistle at them, or holler at them, or anything of that kind. You just have to send your thoughts ahead, with determination that you're going ahead proudly, and believe me, they stand aside and let you go through. The world's like that.

The man who knows where he is going and is determined to get there will always encounter willing helpers to cooperate with him. The greatest of all the benefits of the definiteness of purpose is that it opens the way for the full exercise of that state of mind known as faith. It makes the mind positive and frees the mind from the limitations of fear, doubt, discouragement, indecision, and prostration. When you know what you want and you know what you're going to do, at that very minute all of the negatives that have been bothering you will pick up their baggage and move out. They can't live in a positive mind.

Can you imagine a negative and a positive frame of mind occupying the same space at the same time? No, you can't, because it can't be done. Did you know that the slightest bit of negative mental attitude is sufficient to destroy the power of prayer? Did you know that the slightest bit of a negative mental thought is sufficient to destroy your plan, whatever it is? You have to move with courage, faith, and determination in carrying out your definiteness of purpose.

THE CONSCIOUSNESS OF SUCCESS

Definiteness of purpose also makes one success conscious. Do you know what I mean by "success conscious"? If I said it makes one health conscious, you'd probably know that I mean your thoughts are predominantly about health. With success consciousness, your thoughts are predominantly about success: the can-do part of life, not the no-can-do. Ninety-eight percent of the people (the ones we were talking about a while ago) never get anywhere because they are no-can-do people. No matter what circumstance is before them, they fasten their attention upon the no-can-do part, the negative part.

As long as I live, I'll never forget when Mr. Carnegie surprised me and gave me the chance to organize this philosophy. I tried every way in the world to give him all the reasons I could think of that I couldn't do it. I think I had six reasons why I couldn't do it: I didn't have sufficient education, I didn't have the money, I didn't have the influence, I didn't know what the word *philosophy* meant. Two other reasons immediately popped into my mind as I was trying to get my mouth open to thank Mr. Carnegie for the compliment he'd paid me. In my mind, I doubted Mr. Carnegie was as good a judge of human nature as he was reported to be because he was picking me to do this job. However, something over my shoulder was telling me, "Go ahead. Tell him you can do it. Spit it out." I said, "Yes, Mr. Carnegie, I'll accept the commission and you can depend upon it, sir, that I will complete it!" He reached over and grabbed me by the hand and said, "I not only like what you said, I like the way you said it. That's what I was waiting for." He said that my mind was on fire with a belief that I could do it, even though I hadn't the slightest asset to give me a beginning, other than my determination that I would gain the assets necessary to create this philosophy. If I had wavered in the slightest and said, "Yes, Mr. Carnegie, I'll do my best," I am sure (though I never asked him) that he would have taken the opportunity away from me instantly. It would have indicated that I wasn't too determined to do it. "Yes, Mr. Carnegie, you can depend upon me, sir, to complete it!" Although Mr. Carnegie's long since gone, you are my witness that Mr. Carnegie didn't pick wrongly. You know what he was about. He had found something in the human mind, and in my mind, that he'd been searching for years for. He found it. I didn't know its value but I found out the value of it, and I want you to recognize the value of it. You have that same thing in your mind, that same capacity to know what you want and to be determined that you'll get it, even though you don't know where to make the first start.

What makes a great man? Do you have any idea what greatness is? Greatness is the ability to recognize the power of your own mind—to embrace it and use it. That's what makes greatness. In my book of rules, every man and every woman can become truly great by the simple process of recognizing his or her own mind, embracing it, and using it.

STEPS FOR CREATING YOUR DEFINITENESS OF PURPOSE

Here are instructions for applying the principle of a definite major purpose. These instructions are to be carried out *to the letter*. Don't overlook any part of them.

1. Write out a clear statement of your major purpose.

    Sign it, commit it to memory, and repeat it orally at least once a day in the form of a prayer, or an affirmation, if you choose. You can see the advantage of this because it places your faith in your creator squarely back of you. I've found from experience that this is the weakest spot in the students' activities. As they read this, they say, "Why, that's simple enough. I understand it and what's the use going to the trouble of writing it out?" You might just as well not have this lesson if you're going to take that attitude to it. You must write it out, you must go through the physical act of translating a thought into words and onto paper. You must memorize it and start talking to your subconscious mind about it.

    Give that subconscious mind a pretty good idea of what it is you want. It won't hurt if you remember the story I told you about what I did to get my million-dollar book title. It won't do a bit of harm if you command your subconscious mind to understand that, from here on out, you're the boss and you're going to do something about it. You can't expect the subconscious mind, or anything else, to help you if you don't know what it is you want and if you're not definite about it. In a general cross-section of humanity, ninety-eight out of every hundred people do not know what they want in life and, consequently, never get it. They take whatever life hands them.

In addition to your definite major purpose, you can have minor purposes. You can have as many as you want, provided that they are related to or lead you in the direction of your major purpose. Your whole life should be devoted to carrying out your major purpose in life. Find out what it is you want. It's all right to be modest like I am when you ask for what you want. Don't be too modest. Reach out and ask for a bounty. Ask for the things that you are sure you are entitled to, but don't overlook the subsequent instructions I'm going to give you about what it is you're going to give in return for what you expect.

2. Write out a clear, definite outline of the plan (or plans) by which you intend to achieve the object of your purpose.

State the maximum time within which you intend to attain your purpose. Describe in detail precisely what you intend to give in return for the realization of the object of your purpose. Make your plan flexible enough to permit changes any time you are inspired to do so. Remember that Infinite Intelligence may present you with a better plan than yours, and oftentimes will, if you are definite about what you want.

Have any of you ever had a hunch that you couldn't describe or you couldn't explain away? Do you know what a hunch is? It's your subconscious mind trying to get an idea over to you, though you're often too indifferent to let the subconscious mind talk to you for a few moments. I've heard people say, "Well, I've had the darnedest fool idea today." That "darn fool idea" might have been a million-dollar idea if you would have listened to it and had done something about it. Have great respect for these hunches that come to you because there's something outside of yourself trying to communicate with you. Undoubtedly. I have a great respect for these hunches that come to me, and they come to me constantly. I find them always related to something that my mind's been dwelling upon, something that I want to do, and something that I'm engaged in.

Write out a clear, definite outline of the plan or plans and state the maximum of time within which you intend to attain it. That timing is very important. Don't write out as your definite major aim that

"I intend to become the best salesman in the world" or that "I intend to become the best employee in my organization" or that "I intend to make a lot of money." That's not definite. Whatever it is that you consider your major objective in life, write it out clearly and time it. "I intend to attain within blank number of years so-and-so." Describe what so-and-so is. In the following paragraph, write, "I intend to give so-and-so in return for the thing that I request." Now describe that, too.

As for the business of timing, nature has a system of timing everything. If you're a farmer and you want to plant some wheat in the field, you prepare the ground. At the right season of the year, you sow the wheat, and the very next day, you go back with a harvester and start harvesting.

Did you notice the business of timing on that one? Before you can sow the wheat, you must wait for nature to do her part. Infinite Intelligence (or God, or whatever you want to call it) does Its part, if you do your part first. Intelligence is not going to direct you to, nor attract to you, the object of your major purpose unless you know what it is and unless you properly time it. It would be quite ridiculous if you started out with only a mediocre talent and said that you're going to make a million dollars within the next thirty days. You must make your major purpose within reason of what you know you're able to accomplish and deserve.

3. Keep your major purpose strictly to yourself.

You will receive further instructions on this subject in the lesson on the mastermind. Meanwhile, there's an important reason that you don't disclose your major purpose to other people. There are a lot of idle, curious people who like to stand on the sidelines and stick their toes out when you go by, especially if you've got a high head and look like you're going to accomplish more in life than they are. They do this for no other reason than to just see you fall. They'll throw monkey wrenches in your machinery and sand in your gearbox. They will slow you down because they harbor the envy of mankind. Therefore, the only way to speak about your definite major purpose is in action— after the fact, not before. Speak about it after you've achieved it. Let it speak for itself. The only way anybody can afford to boast or brag about himself is not by words but by deeds. If the deeds are already engaged, you don't need words because the deeds speak for themselves.

4. Make your plan flexible.

Don't become determined that the plan you worked out is perfect just because you worked it out. You'll make a mistake if you do that. Leave your plan flexible, give it a good trial, and if it's not working properly, change it.

5. Engage your conscious mind.

Call your major purpose into your conscious mind as often as may be practical. Eat with it, sleep with it, and take it with you wherever you go, keeping in mind the fact that your subconscious can thus be influenced to work for its attainment while you sleep. Your conscious mind is a very jealous mind. It stands guard and doesn't want anything to get by (to the subconscious), except for the things that you are afraid of and the things that you are enthusiastic about.

6. Add enthusiasm.

Generally speaking, if you want to plant an idea in your subconscious, you have to do it with a tremendous amount of faith and a tremendous amount of enthusiasm. You've got to rush the conscious mind with so much enthusiasm and faith that it steps aside and lets you go through to the subconscious.

7. Apply repetition.

Repetition is a marvelous thing. As you say a thing over and over and over, the conscious mind finally gets tired of hearing you say it. It says, "All right, if you're bound to repeat that, I can't stand here and watch you forever. Go on in there and take it into sub. See what he'll do with it." That's the way it works.

This conscious mind is a very contrary thing. Do you know it learns all of the things that won't work? Do you know it has a tremendous stock of things that won't work and things that are not right? It has a tremendous stock of useless trash that it's gathered and that you don't need: old pieces of string, horse-shoes, nails like the ones misers gather up. It has a whole stock of those things lying around and that's the kind of stuff that it's feeding to your subconscious mind.

8. Put your subconscious to work.

Just before you go to bed each night, you should give your subconscious mind some sort of order for the night: what it is you want done. Maybe your order is for the healing of your body, because certainly the body needs repairing every day. When you lay your carcass down for sleep, your request will put your sub-conscious mind to work with Infinite Intelligence to heal every cell and every organ. By morning, it will give you a perfectly conditioned body in which the mind may function. Don't go to bed without giving orders to your subconscious mind. Get in the habit of telling it what you want. If you keep on long enough, it'll believe you and deliver what you've asked for. Therefore, you'd better be careful about what you ask for, because if you keep on asking for it, you're going to get it.

I wonder if you would be surprised if you knew right now what you've been asking for back through the years. You've been asking for it. Everything that you have that you don't want, you've been asking for it, maybe by neglect. Maybe you didn't tell the subconscious mind what you really wanted and stocked up on a lot of stuff you didn't want. It works that way.

9. Include your life purpose.

Here are some important factors in connection with your definite major purpose. First of all, it should represent your greatest purpose in life—the one single purpose which above all others you desire to achieve and the fruits of which you are willing to leave behind as a monument to yourself. That's what your major purpose should be. I'm not talking about your minor purposes. I'm talking about your major, overall purpose—your lifelong purpose. Believe me friends, if you don't have an overall lifelong purpose, you're wasting the better portion of your life. The wear and tear of living is not worth the price you pay for it unless you really are aiming for something, unless you're going somewhere in life, unless you're doing something with this opportunity here on this plane. I imagine you were sent over here to do something. I imagine you were sent over here with a mind capable of hewing out and attaining your destiny. If you don't attain that, if you don't use that mind, I imagine that your life to a large extent will have been wasted . . . from the viewpoint of the one who sent you over.

10. Engage the power of your mind.

Take possession of your mind. Aim high. Don't believe because you may not have achieved much in the past that you can't achieve in the future. Don't measure your future by your past. If you do, you're sunk. A new day is coming. You're going to be born again. You're setting up a new pattern. You're in a new world and you're a new person. I intend that every one of you shall be born again—mentally, physically, and maybe spiritually. You shall be born to a new aim, a new purpose, a new realization of your own individual power, and a new realization of your own dignity as a unit of mankind.

If you ask me what I believe to be the greatest sin of mankind, I bet you'd be surprised at what my answer would be. What would yours be? What do you think the greatest sin of mankind is? I believe the greatest sin of mankind is neglecting to use his greatest asset—because if you'll use that greatest asset, you'll have everything you want and you'll have it in abundance. Notice that I didn't say you'll have everything within reason. I said *you'd have everything you want and have it in abundance*. I didn't put any qualifying words in there. You're the only one that can put qualifying words in there as to what you want. You're the only one that sets up limitations for yourself. Nobody can do it for you unless you let them.

11. Let your purpose grow.

Your major purpose, or some portion of it, should remain a few jumps ahead of you at all times. It should be something to which you may look forward with hope and anticipation. Now, if you ever catch up with your major purpose and attain it, then what are you going to do when you get there? Get another one, of course. You will have learned by having attained the first one that you *can* attain a major purpose. Chances are, when you select the next one, you'll make it a bigger objective than you did for your first one. If your objective is to acquire riches, don't aim too high for the first year. Work out a twelve-month plan within reason, watch how easily you can attain it, and then next year, double it. And then the next year, double that. One's major purpose should keep a few jumps ahead of him. Why? Why not allow a definite purpose that you can catch up with by tomorrow? Obviously, if you do that, your definite major purpose is not going to be very extensive, is it?

A bigger purpose is going to have the fun of pursuit. Pursuit is a great thing. After you've found success, or after you found your objective, there's no fun in it until you turn around and start after something else. Life is less interesting when one has no definite purpose to be obtained other than that of merely living. **The hope of future achievement of a major purpose is among the greatest of man's pleasures.** Indeed, sorry is the man who has caught up with himself and no longer has anything to do. I've found a lot of them and they're all miserable. You've got to keep active, keep doing something, keep working, and keep an objective ahead of you.

One's major purpose may (and it generally does) consist of that which can be attained only by a series of day-to-day, month-to-month, and year-to-year steps. It is something that should be so designed as to consume *an entire lifetime of happy endeavor*. It should harmonize with one's occupation, business, or profession, because each day's work should enable one to come one day nearer to the attainment of his major purpose in life. I feel sorry for the individual who is just working day in and day out in order to have something to eat, some clothes to wear, and a place to sleep. I feel sorry for anyone who has no aim beyond having just enough to exist on. I can't imagine anybody in this lecture class being satisfied by existence alone. I think you want to live. I think you want abundance. I think you want everything that's necessary for you to do the thing you want to do in life, including money.

One's major purpose may consist of many different combinations of lesser aims, such as the nature of one's occupation, which should be something of your own choice when you come to write out your definite major purpose. Write it out like planks in a platform: number one so-and-so, number two so-and-so.

HARMONIOUS RELATIONSHIPS

Be sure that you include in your major purpose perfect harmony between yourself and your mate. Do you know of anything more important than that? Do you know of anything, any human relationship more important than that of a man and his wife? I'll answer that one for you: of course you don't. Nobody does. Have you ever heard of a relationship of man and wife where there was not harmony? I'll answer that for you too: I know you have. It's not pleasant to even be around people who are not in step with one another. You *can* be harmonious and that is where you ought to be applying your mastermind relationship first. Your wife or your husband should be your first mastermind ally. Maybe you'll have to go back and court him or her over again, but that's nice, too. I don't know of anything I ever did in my life that I enjoyed as much as courting. It's a wonderful experience. Go back and court the gal over again (or the man).

If you're not on the right kind of terms with your business, or your fellow worker, or the people you work with every day, go back and rededicate yourself to the business of striking off on a new basis. You'll be surprised at what a little confession on your part will do. Wonderful thing the confession is. Most people claim they have too much pride to confess their weaknesses. I tell you it's a good thing to get that out and to get some of your weaknesses out of your system by confession. Acknowledge that maybe you're not perfect, nigh perfect, but not entirely perfect. Maybe the other fellow will say, "Come to think about it, neither am I," and then you're off to the races. Rededicate yourself to a better relationship with the people that you come in contact with every day, whoever they may be. What a wonderful thing it is. You can do that. You can handle it. I know you can. Most inharmonious human relationships are due to the neglect of people. Maybe you've neglected to build up your human relationships, but you could change that if you wanted to.

Part of your definite major purpose should be the budgeting of income and expenses—to provide for the accumulation of a definite security now, for old age, for the security of loved ones, and so forth. Include the budgeting of time so as to provide whatever income is necessary to support one's plan for the attainment of a definite major purpose.

Write out your platform for life and include under these minor purposes the things that are related to your major purpose. Include the things that you're going to have to get in order to have a step-by-step movement up toward your major purpose. Make a definite plan for developing harmony in all of your relations, especially in the home where you work, play, or relax. The human relationship plank is the most important one in connection with one's major aim, since the aim is attainable very largely through the cooperation of others. Have you ever thought of that? The things that you do in life, if they're worthwhile, have to be done through harmonious cooperation with other people. And, how are you going to get that harmonious cooperation if you don't cultivate people, understand them, and make allowances for their weaknesses? Did you ever have a friend that appreciated your trying to reform him or change his mind about something? Do you like to have a friend come around and try to reform you? No, nobody does. But, there are certain things that you can do for a friend *by example*— that's a mighty effective way of doing it.

Tell a man where he's wrong and chances are that he'll have business to attend to right around the corner from you, and when he sees you coming, he'll get on the other side of the street. In your human relations you can develop a marvelous relationship, but you can't do it by criticizing people or harping upon their faults, because we all have faults. A better thing to do is to talk upon a person's virtues and his good qualities. I have never seen a person so low that he didn't have *some* good qualities. If you'll concentrate upon those good qualities, that person on whom you're concentrating will go out of his way and lean over backward to make sure that you're not disappointed.

One should not hesitate to choose a major aim that may be out of his reach . . . for the time being. This prepares one to attain pretty much *any* desired purpose in life. When I chose as my definite major purpose *the organizing and taking to the world of the first practical philosophy of individual achievement*, it was way beyond my reach.

What kept me being brought down throughout twenty years of unproductive effort of research? What kept me striving and struggling while the majority of people I knew were criticizing me? I had to have an abundance of faith, and I had to keep that faith alive by moving as if I knew in advance that I was going to complete the task Mr. Carnegie assigned to me. There were times when it looked as if what my friends and relatives were saying about me was absolutely true. In a sense it was; I was wasting my time. From their viewpoint and their measuring stick and their standards, I was wasting twenty years of my time. But, from the viewpoint of the millions of people who *have* benefited and *will* benefit by my work during those twenty years, I was *not* wasting my time. You can't fail, unless you think you can. If you think you can fail, then you can. If you stay around me long enough, you'll know you're not going to fail.

NATURE OPERATES WITH PURPOSE

Our greatest demonstration of the universal application of the principle of definiteness of purpose is evidenced by nature. If there is anything in this universe that's definite, it's the laws of nature. They don't deviate, they don't temporize, and they don't subside. You can't go around them, and you can't avoid them, but you *can* learn their nature and adjust yourselves to them and benefit by them. Nobody ever heard of the law of gravitation being suspended by even one fraction of a second. It never has been done and never will be. Throughout the whole universe (perhaps even throughout systems of universes), nature is so definite that everything moves with precision, like clockwork. If you want an example of the necessity of moving with definitiveness, you only need a smattering of understanding of the sciences to see how nature does things. That's your example: the orderliness of the universe, the interrelation of all of the natural laws, and the fixation of the stars and planets in the immovable relationship to one another. It's a marvelous thing to know that the astronomers can sit down with a pencil and a few pieces of paper and predetermine hundreds of years in advance the exact relationship of given planets and stars. They can determine in advance exactly where they'll be with relationship to one another. They couldn't do that if there was not a purpose or a plan under which we're working. We want to find out what that purpose is as it relates to us as individuals. That's what I'm teaching you. I'm giving you that little bit that I've picked from life, from the experiences of men, and from my own experience, so that you will learn how to adjust yourself to the laws of nature in order that you may *use* those laws instead of allowing yourself to be abused by your *neglect* in using them.

One of the most horrible things I could contemplate is the possible cessation of natural laws. Imagine all the chaos: all of the stars and planets running together. It would make the H bomb look like a firecracker if nature allowed her laws to be suspended. But she doesn't do that. Nature has definite laws and if you would check these seventeen principles, you'd find that they check perfectly with all of the laws of nature. When you get to the principle of going the extra mile, you find that nature is *profound* in her application of the principle of going the extra mile. When she produces blooms on the trees, she doesn't produce just *enough* to fill the tree. Nature produces enough to take care of all of the damages, winds, and storms. When she produces fish in the sea, she doesn't produce *enough* to perpetuate the fish, she produces enough to feed the bullfrogs, the snakes, the alligators, and all the other things and *still* have enough left to carry out her purpose. She has an abundance of things—an *overabundance*. Also, she forces man to go the extra mile or else he'll perish. He would perish in one season if he didn't go the extra mile. If nature didn't compensate a man when he goes out and puts a grain of wheat in the ground by giving him back five hundred grains to compensate him for his intelligence, we would starve to death in one season.

If you'll do your part, nature does her part. She does it in abundance—in *super*abundance. One of the strange things about nature is that if you keep your mind focused on the positive side of life, it becomes greater than the negative side. Always. If you keep your mind on the positive side, it becomes greater than all of the negatives that may try to penetrate your mind and influence your life. Look around and you'll find examples—living examples—of people that you want to emulate and people you do not want to emulate. You'll see people that are failing and you'll be able to tell why they're failing. I dare say that from this time on, you'll be able to use this philosophy as a measuring stick: wherever you find a success or failure, you'll be able to lay your finger right on the cause of it!

MASTERMIND

The second principle of *Your Right to Be Rich* is the Mastermind. It has been referred to as the very hub or axis of the entire philosophy. This principle consists of an alliance of two or more minds working in perfect harmony for the attainment of a definite objective. According to Dr. Hill, no one has ever attained outstanding success in any calling without applying this principle. This is because no mind is complete by itself. Every mind needs association and contact with other minds in order to grow and expand. The achievements that can result from that contact and association are truly awe inspiring.

PREMISE #1: TAPPING OTHERS CREATES NEW POSSIBILITIES

The first premise is that the mastermind principle is the medium through which one may procure the full benefits of the experience, the training, the education, and the specialized knowledge and influence of others as completely as if their minds were in reality one zone. Isn't that a marvelous state to contemplate? **Whatever it is that you lack in education, or knowledge, or influence, you can always obtain it through somebody who has it. Exchange of favors and exchange of knowledge is one of the greatest exchanges in the world.** It's a very nice thing to engage in business where the exchange of money makes you a profit, but I would much rather exchange *ideas* with somebody. Give me an idea I didn't have before, and in which I receive in return more than I had before, and I will do it.

Thomas A. Edison was perhaps the greatest inventor the world had ever known. He was dealing all the time with science and yet he knew nothing at all *about* science. It would seem impossible for a man to succeed in any undertaking unless he was educated in that field. I was astounded when I first talked to Andrew Carnegie, and he told me that he personally didn't know anything about the making or the marketing of steel. I was so astounded at that statement, I said, "Well, Mr. Carnegie, that probably isn't your part here. What part *do* you play?" He said, "I'll tell you the part that I play. My job is to keep the members of my mastermind allegiance working in a state of perfect harmony." And, I asked, "Is that all you have to do?" He replied, "Have you ever tried to get any two people to agree on anything for three minutes at a time in your life? Try it someday and see just what kind of job it is to get people to work together in the spirit of harmony. It is one of the greatest of human achievements." And, then Mr. Carnegie elaborated on his mastermind group, describing each one individually and telling me what part each one played. One was his metal jurist, one was his chief chemist, one was his plant's work manager, one was his legal advisor, one was the chief of his financial staff, and so on. There were over twenty men working together whose combined education, experience, and knowledge constituted all that was known about the making and marketing of steel at that time. Mr. Carnegie said it wasn't necessary for him to know about it because he had men all round him who *did* understand the making and marketing of steel, and that it was his job to keep them working in perfect harmony.

PREMISE #2: A COMMON GOAL CREATES ENERGY

The second premise proves that an active allegiance of two or more minds in a spirit of perfect harmony for the obtainment of a common objective actually stimulates each individual mind to a higher degree of courage than that which would ordinarily be experienced. This prepares the way for that state of mind known as faith. In driving an automobile, sometimes the battery runs down. Maybe you have to go somewhere, but when you step on the starter, nothing happens. I know people who get out of bed in the morning and do the same thing. Nothing happens, except they feel badly. They don't want to put on their shoes, they don't want to get dressed, and they don't even eat breakfast. What do they need? They need their batteries charged, of course, and fortunately, they have to have a source for doing it. It's a mighty fine thing if a man gets up in the morning feeling like that, and if he can have a little talk with his wife and she's a good communicator, she helps to charge his batteries. The change appears when he comes home that night with all of the rabbit skins that he went out to get.

PREMISE #3: LOYALTY BUILDS CONFIDENCE

The third premise states that a mastermind allegiance properly conducted stimulates each mind in the allegiance to move with enthusiasm, personal initiative, imagination, and courage to a degree far above that which the individual experiences when moving without such an allegiance.

In my own early beginning, I had a mastermind allegiance of three people: Mr. Carnegie, my stepmother, and me. We three people nursed this philosophy through the stages when everybody else was laughing at me and making fun of me for undertaking to serve the richest man in the world for twenty years without any compensation. There was a lot of logic to what they were saying because at that time I wasn't getting very much compensation out of it—in the way of money at least. There came a time, however, when the laughing was on the other side of the fence, but that took a long time. I assure you there were plenty of blood and tears before I got to the point when I could laugh back when people laughed at me. Nonetheless, the relationship among us three people, my stepmother, Mr. Carnegie, and myself, enabled me to offset all the fun-making that was thrown at me by my relatives and my friends and everybody who knew what I was engaged in.

If you undertake anything above mediocre, you're going to meet with opposition. You're going to meet with people who'll charge you and poke fun at you. Most of them will be right there close to you, perhaps even your own relatives. You need some source to which you can turn when you are going to aim above mediocre, to get your batteries charged and to keep them charged, so that you won't quit when the going is hard and so you won't pay any attention when somebody criticizes you.

Criticism falls off my back just like water off of a duck's back, or more like a bullet off of a rhinoceros's hide. I'm absolutely immune to all forms of criticism, whether it's friendly or unfriendly. It makes no difference to me whatsoever. I'm just immune to it, that's all. I became immune because of my relationship with certain people to whom I built up immunity under my mastermind allegiance. If it had not been for the relationship with my stepmother and Mr. Carnegie, I wouldn't be standing here talking to you, you wouldn't be here as students in the philosophy, and this philosophy would not be spread all over the world—helping millions of people. I had at least a million opportunities to quit, and every one of them looked very alluring, and sometimes it seemed I was stupid if I *didn't* quit.

I could always go back to Mr. Carnegie. I could always run to my stepmother; we'd sit down, have a little chat, and she'd say, "You'll come out on top, I know you will." At a time when I didn't have two nickels to rub together (at least that's what my enemies were saying about me), my stepmother said, "You are going to be the richest member of the Hill family. I know it because I can see it in the future." Well, if you would take all of my riches and put them together, I suspect that I do have more riches than all of my relatives put together for three generations back, on both sides of the house. My stepmother could see that. She could see what I was doing. It was bound to make me rich, and I'm not making reference only to monetary riches. I'm referring to those higher and broader riches, which let you render services to so many people.

PREMISE #4: ACTION HARMONIZES POWER

The fourth premise of an effective mastermind allegiance is that it must be active. Don't just form an allegiance and say, "That's it, we've got it. I'm lined up with this person, that person, and the other person, and we've got a mastermind allegiance." It amounts to absolutely nothing until you become active. Every member of the allegiance has got to step right in and start pitching—mentally, spiritually, physically, financially, and in every way that is necessary. They must engage in the pursuit of a definite purpose and they must move with perfect harmony.

Do you know the difference between perfect harmony and ordinary harmony? How many of you have ever had a relationship of perfect harmony with anybody? I suspect I have had good harmony with about as many people as, maybe more people than, any person living today. However, *perfect harmony* in a relationship is a rare thing in this world. I could count on the fingers of my two hands all of the people that I now know with whom I have a relationship of perfect harmony. I have a speaking acquaintance, actually a very nice polite speaking acquaintance, with a lot of the people, but that's not perfect harmony. I have a working allegiance with a lot of people, but that's not perfect harmony.

Perfect harmony exists only when your relationship to the other fellow is such that if he wanted everything you have, you'd willingly turn it over to him. It takes a lot of unselfishness to put yourself in that frame of mind. Mr. Carnegie stressed time and time again the importance of this relationship of perfect harmony. He said if you don't have perfect harmony in a mastermind allegiance, it's not a mastermind allegiance after all. It's just a cooperation or coordination of effort. Without this factor of harmony, the allegiance may be nothing more than ordinary cooperation, or friendly coordination, of effort. *The mastermind gives one full access to the spiritual powers of the other members of the allegiance.* I want you to underscore that part in your notes.

The mastermind gives one full access of the other members of his allegiance. I'm not talking about just the mental powers or the financial powers but *the spiritual powers*. I'm referring to that feeling you have when you begin to establish permanency in your mastermind relationship, that this is going to be one of the most outstanding and pleasant experiences of your entire life. When you're engaged in the mastermind activity, I want to tell you that you have so much faith, you know that you can do anything that you start out to do. You have no doubts, you have no fears, and you have no limitations. It's a marvelous frame of mind to be in.

PREMISE #5: THE SUM IS GREATER THAN ITS PARTS

It is a matter of established record that all individual successes based upon any kind of achievement above mediocre are attained through the mastermind principle and not by individual effort alone. Just imagine how little you could accomplish if you didn't have the cooperation of other people. Suppose that you're a dentist, or a lawyer, or a doctor, or anybody in a profession. Suppose that you didn't understand how to convert each one of your clients or patients into a salesman for yourself. Imagine how long it would take to build up a clientele or a following. Outstanding professional men understand how to make a salesman out of every person they serve. They do it by going the extra mile, going out of their way to be of unusual service—they make salesmen out of all of their clients. Most successes are the result of personal power of sufficient proportions to enable one to rise above mediocre. This is not possible without the application of the mastermind principle.

During the first term of Franklin D. Roosevelt, I had the privilege of visiting the White House and working with him as a confidential advisor. It was I who laid out the skeleton of the propaganda plan that took the words "business depression" out of the headlines of the papers and instead substituted "business recovery." Some of you may remember what happened on that Black Sunday, when we had a meeting at the White House, and the banks closed the following Monday morning. Do you remember what a stampede there was in this country? People were lined up in front of the banks all over the country to draw out their deposits. They were scared to death. They had lost confidence in their country, in their banks, in themselves, and in everybody else. I suppose they still had some confidence in God, but they didn't show much sign of it. It was a scary time, I tell you.

We sat down there and worked out a skeleton of a plan (a procedure) that created one of the most outstanding applications of the mastermind that this nation has ever seen. I doubt if any nation on earth has ever had the equal of it. It was only a matter of weeks until we had taken all that fear out of people. It was only a matter of days until salesmen on the road who had run out of funds, who couldn't get money, were laughing about it, and not in any way scared about it. My own funds were closed. I must tell you something funny. I got very smart when I found out what was coming, and I ran down to the bank and got a thousand-dollar bill. I might just as well have had only ten cents. It wasn't even worth a nickel, not a nickel. I wasn't scared because everybody else was in the same boat that I was in.

But something had to be done about it. Franklin D. Roosevelt was a great leader. He had great imagination. He had great courage. Here's what we did. First, we got both houses of Congress working in harmony with the president. It was the first time in the history of this nation that both houses of Congress, Democrats and Republicans alike, got behind the president and forgot about what their political faiths happened to be. In other words, there were no Democrats and there were no Republicans. There were just Americans backing the president, allowing everything he needed in order to stop that stampede of fear. I have never seen anything equal to it in my life. I never hope to see it again. I would wish I could see that spirit of cooperation, but I don't hope to experience another depression for it. There was a great emergency and something had to be done about it.

Second, everything that we sent out to the American newspapers was published, and they gave it marvelous space. The radio station operators gave us marvelous help despite their political beliefs. All denominations of churches showed one of the most beautiful things I've ever seen in this country: Catholics and Protestants, Jews and Gentiles, and all of the rest pulling together as Americans. It was a wonderful sight. A wonderful sight! What a wonderful thing it was, everyone getting behind the president, everyone making some sort of a contribution toward reestablishing faith in the people of this country.

During these hectic days, I want to tell you that whether there was any doubt in the minds of the majority of the people, I don't know. I didn't come into contact with anybody who didn't think that Mr. Roosevelt was the only man, the finest man, that could possibly have handled that chaotic condition. Don't get me wrong. Politically, I'm just talking about a great man who did a great job at a time when it needed to be done, and he did it because he had a mastermind alliance that was unbeatable.

Let's take up the different kinds of mastermind alliances that you may have. First of all, there are alliances for purely social or personal reasons, consisting of one's relatives, friends, and religious advisors, where no material gain is solved. The most important of this type is the mastermind alliance that exists between a man and his wife. I can't overemphasize the importance to you who are married of immediately working on and rededicating that marriage to a master-mind alliance based upon this lesson tonight. It'll bring joys into your life that you never dreamed of. It'll bring success into your life that you've never dreamed of. It'll bring health into your life that you've never dreamed of. It's a perfectly marvelous thing when a real mastermind alliance exists between a man and his wife. I don't know of anything that equals it.

And then there are alliances for business or professional advancement, consisting of individuals who have a personal motive of a material or a financial nature connected with an object of their alliances. I imagine that the majority of you will be forming your first mastermind alliances for purely economic or financial advancement purposes and that's perfectly legitimate. That's one of the reasons you're learning this philosophy. If you want to improve your economic and financial condition, you should start immediately to form a mastermind alliance for that purpose. If you can begin with one person, that's all right, just start out with one. Then, look around until the two of you select another. When you go to select the third party, be sure the first one and the second one that you've already formed your mastermind alliance with are in accord with the selection. This is very important. When you go to select the fourth, the three of you then will pass on the fourth and you'll go over the matter very carefully before you make him or her a member of the alliance. When you go to select the fifth, the four of you will select the fifth. In a mastermind alliance, there's no such thing as one person dominating except in the respect that generally speaking one person is the leader. He's the coordinator and the leader but in no way undertakes to dominate his associates. The very moment you start to dominate anybody, you will find resistance and rebellion, and even though it may not be an open rebellion, it's rebellion nevertheless. **The mastermind alliance must be one continuous spirit of perfect harmony, where you move and act as if you were only one mind.**

The American system of free enterprise is another example of efficiency through the mastermind principle. This system is the envy of the world because it has raised the standard of living of the American people to an all-time high level. Despite the fact that there's perfect harmony, there is motive in the American system of free enterprise to inspire every individual to do his best. There is a motive there.

More and more industry and business is coming to understand that they can go a step further, and instead of just having cooperation or coordination of effort between management and the workers, they can have the mastermind principle by sharing the management problems, sharing the profits—sharing everything. Where I have been successful in influencing any business to adopt that policy, the business has made more money than it's ever made before. The employees have received more wages and everybody's happy.

INSTRUCTIONS ON FORMING AND MAINTENANCE OF A MASTERMIND ALLIANCE

1. **Adopt a definite purpose.** Adopt a definite purpose as an objective to be obtained by the alliance.

2. **Choose members.** Find individual members whose education, experience, and influence make them the greatest value in achieving the purpose. Students often ask me what is the most favorable number for a mastermind alliance, and how do you go about selecting the right sort of people for your mastermind alliance? The nearest answer that I can give you is that the procedure is exactly the same as if you were starting a business and you were choosing employees. What kind of an employee would you choose?

    Dependability is at the top of the list. If a person is not dependable, I don't want any part of him in a business transaction, no matter how brilliant he may be and no matter how well educated he may be. In fact, the more educated he is, the more dangerous he may be if he's not dependable. If he's not **loyal**, I would say the same thing. If an individual is not loyal to those to whom he owes loyalty, then to me he has no character whatsoever and I want no part of him. **Ability** to do the job is the third step. I'm not interested in a man's ability until I find out whether he's dependable and whether he's loyal. Number four is a **positive mental attitude**. After all, what good is a negative wet blanket around you? I think if you'd pay him to stay away, you'd be ahead of the game. Number five, what would that be? **Going the extra mile**, that's right. And number six, what would you say that is? **Applied faith**.

When you find people that come up to all of those six traits, you've really found somebody. You're in the presence of royalty. If you're only running a peanut stand or two, you may need only one person, but if you're running a chain of peanut stands, you might need a hundred people.

The six qualifications for your mastermind group are: dependability, loyalty, ability, positive mental attitude, willingness to go the extra mile, and applied faith. Those are the qualifications of your mastermind allies. Don't settle for anything less. If you find a man that has five of those qualities and doesn't have all six of them, beware of him before you start. Because they are all essentials of the mastermind relationship, check very carefully to see if they're there. You can't have perfect harmony unless you're working with somebody who checks 100 percent on all six fronts. You might have a working arrangement, like so many people do, but it wouldn't embrace all of the potential values of the mastermind.

3. **Determine motive and compensation.**

What's appropriate for each member to receive in return for his cooperation in this alliance? Remember, nobody ever does anything for nothing. They never do. You say when you give love to somebody you don't get anything out of that. But you get plenty out of that. Love is a great privilege and even when the love is not returned, you still had the benefits of that state of mind known as love. You enjoyed the development and growth as a result of it. There's no such thing as something for nothing. Nobody works without some sort of compensation.

There are very many different forms of compensation. Don't expect that your mastermind allies are going to jump in and help you make a fortune or help you do anything unless they are equally participating in the benefit that comes out of that mastermind alliance. That's the criteria. Each individual must approximately benefit equally with yourself, whether it's a monetary benefit, a happiness benefit, a peace of mind benefit, a social benefit, or whatever it happens to be. Never ask anybody to do anything (if you want to be sure of his doing it) unless you give him an adequate motive for doing it.

If I went down to the bank and wanted to borrow ten thousand dollars, what would be an adequate motive for the bank lending me that money? Two of their motives come under the heading of desirable financial gain. The bank would be delighted to loan me as much as I could take away if I give them three things. They'll want security. They'll want collateral. And they'll want to profit on that loan. That's what they're in business for.

There are other transactions not based upon the monetary motive. For instance, when a man asks the girl of his choice to marry him, what's the motive? Sometimes, theatrically, love, yes. I bet out of all the people sitting here, everyone would have a different idea or definition as to what the motive is when a man asks the girl of his choice to marry him. And if she accepts, why does she accept him?

When my father brought my stepmother home, he was just a farmer. He never had a white shirt or a tie. He wouldn't. He was afraid of white shirts and ties, and wore blue cotton shirts. My stepmother was a college woman. She was well educated. They were as different as the North Pole and the South Pole, and I wondered all of my life how he was able to sell himself to her. Of course, she cleaned him up and put a white shirt on him and made him look like somebody, but nevertheless it took her quite a little while to do it. She eventually got him into the money and he became an outstanding man. I remember what he used to look like and how he used to talk. He abused the Queen's English. He said, "I seen him coming," "I done my duty," and that sort of thing. So I asked her, "How in

YOUR RIGHT TO BE RICH

the world did my father ever sell himself to you? What was the motive?" She said, "I'll tell you. First of all, I recognized he had good blood in his veins. Secondly, he had possibilities, and I believed that I could bring them out." She did bring them out.

Mrs. Henry Ford and Mrs. Thomas A. Edison are two of the outstanding examples that I use time and time again to show what a woman can do to make her husband successful. Had it not been for Mrs. Ford's understanding of the mastermind principle (although she didn't call it by that name), Mr. Ford would never have been known, the Ford automobile would never have been made, and I doubt if the automobile industry would have been ushered in as it has been. It was Mrs. Ford more than Mr. Ford that kept him going, kept him alert, and kept him filled with confidence in himself when the going was hard. People were criticizing him in connection with his contraption that they said was only designed to scare horses. Remember that I, too, was criticized for fooling away my time with the richest man in the world, working for nothing. Mrs. Ford sustained him through those trying hours when the going was hard. All of you will experience that period in your life. The going is hard at some time with everybody.

Frequently, a woman will marry a man because she sees that he has possibilities, that she can do something with him, and make something out of him.

Sometimes it's monetary consideration, sometimes it's love, sometimes it's one thing, and sometimes another. Nevertheless, anytime anyone engages in any transaction, there is a motive in back of it, you may be sure of that. Whatever you want anybody to do, pick out the right kind of motive, plant it in his or her mind under the proper circumstances, and you'll become a master salesman.

Establish a definite plan through which each member of the alliance will make his contribution in working toward achieving the object of the alliance. Arrange a definite time and place for the mutual discussion of the plan. Indefiniteness will bring defeat. Keep a regular means of contact between all members of your alliance. Have you ever heard of a great friendship, or have you ever *had* a great friendship with somebody, that suddenly grew cold and finally died? Certainly, most of us have had that experience, and do you know the reason for it? Neglect. By far, neglect. If you have very close and very dear friends, the only way you can keep them is to keep in contact constantly, even if it's only by an occasional postcard.

I have one student who was a member of my class in 1928 in New York City. She never has missed a single one of my birthdays to send me a card. One time she was off on her vacation and she forgot it until the midafternoon of my birthday and she sent me a telegram congratulating me on my birthday. In other words, she has been the most constant student that I have ever had out of the many thousands all over the country. As a result of that close attention that she's given me, there have been times when I have been able to help her in a business way, too. The last time I got her a promotion that amounted to about four thousand dollars a year, which is quite a little bit of payoff for the business of keeping in contact. To keep in contact with your master-mind allies, you have to have regular meeting places, and you have to keep them active. If you don't, they grow cold and grow indifferent, and finally they are of no value to you.

APPLIED FAITH

The third principle of *Your Right to Be Rich* is Applied Faith. This principle, along with definiteness of purpose and the mastermind, are the big three of the seventeen principles.

This principle is not steeped in any particular religious doctrine or denomination. As defined here, *faith* means an active state of mind in which there is a relating of the mind to the great eternal force of the universe. Faith is human beings sensing the powers that surround them in the world and trying to harmonize their lives with those powers as they feel them. In the final analysis, faith is the activity of individual minds discovering themselves and establishing a working association with the power referred to as the Universal Mind, the Divine Mind, or God. Dr. Hill refers to this power as Infinite Intelligence, the source of all life energy, the cosmic force of the universe we inhabit.

> The word *applied* indicates action. This is an active, not a passive principle. The faith referred to is applied to the achievement of a definite major purpose in life. With faith applied, achievement will be the result.

If you had a definite major purpose, knew exactly what you wanted to do, had a mastermind alliance of people that could help you do it, and then had the sufficient faith to keep you going while you did it, that would be about all you would need.

Why do you suppose we need the fourteen additional principles? We need fourteen additional principles to induce you to make use of these three. You need personal initiative. You need imagination. You need enthusiasm. In other words, this philosophy is like baking a cake. When you bake a cake, you don't put in just one ingredient. You put in a pinch of this, a pinch of that, a dash of the other thing, and then you put it in the stove and bake it. If you took out any one of those ingredients, you wouldn't end up with the same kind of cake. It's the same way with this philosophy. You can't leave out any one of these seventeen principles. It would be like taking a link out of a chain. You wouldn't have a chain anymore, you'd have two parts of a chain, but not a whole chain. The other fourteen principles are supporting principles of these three.

Faith is a state of mind that has been called the mainspring of the soul, to which one's aims, desires, plans, and purposes may be translated into their physical or financial equivalent. There are the fundamentals of faith, but by applied faith, I'm talking about something vastly different from mere belief. The word *applied* means what? Action. It's the action part of faith. Without action, faith is nothing but just daydreaming. There are a lot of people who believe in things but don't do anything about them, engaging only in daydreaming. Applied faith is an active faith.

FAITH AND THE FIRST THREE PRINCIPLES OF SUCCESS

1. **Definiteness of Purpose.** Purpose is supported by a personal initiative and action, action, action—the more action, the better. That means continual action, not only on your part but also on the part of those that may be cooperating with you or your mastermind allies.

2. **Positive Mental Attitude.** A positive mind, free from all negatives such as fear, envy, hatred, jealousy, and greed, is essential. Mental attitude determines the effectiveness of faith. It's a fact. The frame of mind that you are in when you pray will determine what

happens as a result of that prayer. There's no two ways
about it. You can test it for yourself and find out.

I have no doubt that you have had the experiences that I've had, sending out prayers that didn't
produce anything but a negative result. Do you suppose there is anybody that *didn't* have that experience
at one time or another? When you pray, unless you
have such absolute faith that whatever you are going
after you're going to acquire, and that you can see it in
advance in your possession before you start asking for
it, chances are the effect of your prayer is going to be
negative.

3. **Mastermind Alliance.** A mastermind alliance con-
   venes one or more other people who radiate courage
   based on faith and are suited mentally and spiritually
   to one's needs in carrying out a given purpose.

ELEMENTS OF APPLIED FAITH

1. **Every adversity carries with it the seed of an
   equivalent benefit; temporary defeat is not failure
   until it has been accepted as such.** Do you know
   where the majority of people fall down in connection with their application of their faith? It's when
   they're defeated and they accept that defeat as being
   something they can't do anything about. Instead of
   beginning immediately to search for that seed of an

equivalent benefit that's in *every* defeat, they become moody and broody, discouraged, and build up inferiority complexes. Instead, they could reverse the order and *use* defeat as nothing more than a temporary point from which to make another effort.

My saying that every adversity carries with it the seed of an equivalent benefit, that every defeat and every failure carries the seed of an equivalent benefit, wouldn't mean anything to you unless I made application of it, and gave you illustration after illustration. If you examine enough illustrations in your own experience, you'll see that it always works out that way. That's why I want you to look closely at the adversities that come to you.

Do you know that your adversities are often your greatest blessings? Do you know the greatest blessing that ever came into my life? Of course, it was the loss of my mother. Ordinarily, the greatest catastrophe that could overtake a child would be to lose his mother at the age of nine years. Why do I say that was the greatest, greatest blessing? Because it brought me a new mother to take her place, one who is responsible for everything that I've achieved and everything that I shall achieve. Without her influence, I'd still be fighting rattlesnakes, drinking mountain liquor, and fighting feuds. My relatives are still doing that same thing, so there's no reason to expect that I wouldn't be. I've had a lot of other adversities, and I want to tell you that without some twenty major adversities I've gone through, I would never have been able to pursue the soundness of this philosophy—that there is a seed of equivalent benefit in every adversity.

Can you imagine any worse adversity to a man than to be informed that his son was born without any signs of ears and would be a deaf and dumb mute all of his life? Can you imagine anything worse than that? I'll always be thankful that because of my contact with Infinite Intelligence, my deaf son was provided with a sort of hearing system that gave him 65 percent of his normal hearing and eventually 100 percent with a modern hearing aid. He learned to live a normal life and I got the greatest demonstration of my entire experience in the power of faith. I couldn't have gotten it any other way. I couldn't have gotten it secondhand, I had to get it firsthand.

I never accepted that affliction of that child, not even before I saw him, and not even after I saw him. I never accepted it. His relatives accepted it. They wanted to put him in the school of underprivileged where he'd learn sign language and lip reading. I didn't even want him to know there *were* such things. When he was old enough to go to school, I had a fight with the school authorities every year just as regular as a clock, because they wanted to send him to a school for underprivileged children, to mix with the other children and see their afflictions. I didn't want him to know there were such things. I taught him from the very beginning that his not having any ears was a great blessing—and he believed it. Compassion led people to do things for him they wouldn't have done otherwise. He got a job as a salesman for the *Saturday Evening Post* and he led every salesman throughout the United States. He'd often go out with five dollars' worth of merchandise and come back with ten dollars in cash. He did that many times. People would look at him and say, "Why that poor little fellow with no ears is out selling papers. I guess his parents are poor." They'd give him a dollar bill and when he'd try to give them their change, they'd say, "Oh, sonny, you just keep that." So he'd often get a dollar apiece for the *Saturday Evening Post*. Not at all conscious today of any affliction, he's living a perfectly normal life because I taught him that an affliction, *any kind of an affliction,* can be transmuted into a benefit.

2. **Applied faith requires the habit of affirming one's definite major purpose in the form of a prayer at least once daily.** The subconscious mind only knows what you tell it, or what you allow other people to tell it, or what you allow the circumstances of life to tell it. It doesn't know the difference between a lie and the truth. It doesn't know the difference between a penny and a million dollars. It accepts the things that you send over, and if you send over predominating

thoughts on poverty and ill health and failure, that's exactly what'll you get. No matter how much faith that you may have later on, you'll find out the subconscious responds to the mental attitude that you're maintaining during the day. It's necessary for you to affirm over and over again the objects that you are going to attain in life until you educate your subconscious mind to automatically attract to you the things that are related to what you're aiming to attain in life. You'll find that your mind is like an electrode magnet and once you charge it with a clear picture of what you want, it'll attract to you from the highways and the byways the things that you need to carry out that purpose.

3. **Recognition of the existence of an Infinite Intelligence that gives order to the vast, entire universe**. You are a minute expression of this intelligence and as such your mind has no limitation except those accepted or set up in your own mind. Let me repeat that statement. Your mind has no limitations whatsoever, except those that you allow to be established there or that you deliberately set up in your mind or accept. That's a pretty broad statement. However, the achievements of men like Mr. Edison, Mr. Ford, Mr. Carnegie, and Napoleon Hill (if you please) definitely support the idea that there is no limitation except that which you set up in your mind.

If I had ever wavered for one second in my belief of what I would do, from the time that I started with Mr. Carnegie up until the time I gave this philosophy to the world, I would never have done it. How did I do it? Do you have any idea what played the strongest part in what I've achieved? It wasn't my brilliancy and it wasn't my outstanding intelligence. I have no more brilliance than the average person and no more intelligence than the average person. But, I believed that I could do it and I never stopped believing it. The harder the going was, the more I believed I would do it. If you can take that attitude toward yourself, throwing yourself over on the side of yourself when you're overtaken by adversity, or when people are against you, and not go *against* yourself, then you're using applied faith. You've got to do that.

Do you know there are testing times for people? Nobody is permitted to attain a high state in life and stay there without being tested. Nobody is allowed to go into a well-managed business or go to a high position and stay there without being tested at lower positions until, step-by-step, he earns the right to be up on the top. I don't know how the Creator runs his business entirely, but I can catch a pretty good idea of how he does it from observing that part which I can understand. Of course, there's much more that I *can't* understand, but I can definitely see that he allows nobody to attain to a higher stage of life without giving him severe testing.

One of the most outstanding things that I found in my research was that the men of great achievement in all walks of life, and throughout the ages, were great only in proportion as they had been defeated and as they met with opposition. What an outstanding thing. It couldn't be a coincidence that every one of these outstanding men was exactly great in proportion as he had been small and as he had been opposed and as he had had to struggle.

I used to tell of my early struggles and tell some of my defeats. My business manager said it wasn't a good idea. I think it's a fine idea, because if you knew the amount of the major defeats that I have met, recognizing how I still kept my head above water and still live to deliver this philosophy, you'd say, "If Hill can do it, I can do it too." That's the only reason I ever spoke of it.

I don't mind what terms you use: God, Jehovah, Buddha, or Muhammad. You can call it anything you want to. No matter what you call it, we're all talking about one first cause. There aren't two first causes, there's only one. There couldn't be two. There's one first cause that's responsible for this great universe we're living in—for you and for me and for everything that's in the universe. I call it Infinite Intelligence because I have students of all faiths and all religions all over the world and Infinite Intelligence happens to be a neutral term nobody can object to.

But unless you not only believe in that, unless you can prove to yourself, and absolutely put down on paper evidence that there is first cause that you can draw upon, you're not going to be able to make the fullest use of a definite plan.

One of my students asked me about my concept of Infinite Intelligence and if I meant the same thing as God. I said, "Yes I do." "Well," he said, "can you prove the existence of your concept of God?" I replied, "Everything in the universe is the finest evidence of Its existence, because of the orderliness of the universe." Everything's orderly, from the electrons and protons in the smallest part of the matter, up to the largest suns that float through the heavens. Everything's in orderliness: no chaos, no running together of the planets. There's more evidence of a first cause than there is of anything that I know of. And, if you don't believe that, if you don't accept it, if you don't see it, if you don't feel it, and if you don't know it, then you won't know that you are a minute part of that Infinite Intelligence being expressed through your brain. If you recognize that, then you recognize the truth of what I said—that your only limitations are those which you set up in your mind, or permit

somebody to set up there, or let circumstances establish there for you.

Careful inventory of your past defeats (and adversities
from it) shows that all such experiences do carry the seed of
an equivalent benefit.

GOING *the* EXTRA MILE

The fourth principle of *Your Right to Be Rich* is Going the Extra Mile. This means rendering more and better service than you're being paid to render, and doing it all with a pleasant mental attitude. It's a principle that many people have questioned in the past and seem to question even more deeply today, "Why should I give my company, my boss, one more minute's work than I'm being paid for? What's in it for me?" Here's what's in it for you: if you go the extra mile, sooner or later you'll receive compensation exceeding the service you render. You will exhibit greater strength of character, maintain a positive attitude, and experience the thrill of courage and self-reliance. You will achieve these things, and more. Let Dr. Napoleon Hill prove that this is so and explain how you can do it.

Going the extra mile means rendering of more service and better service than you're paid to render, doing it all the time, and doing it with a pleasant, pleasing mental attitude.

One of the reasons why there are so many failures in the world is that the majority of people do not even go the first mile, let along the second one. If they do go the first mile, they usually gripe as they go along and make themselves a darned nuisance to people around them. I suppose you know the type. But it doesn't apply to any of you, because if you were like that before you got into this philosophy, you're going to get over it very fast.

I don't know of any one quality or trait that can get a person an opportunity quicker than to go out of his or her way to do somebody a favor, or do something useful. It's the one thing you can do in life without having to ask anybody for the privilege of doing it. Unless you form the habit of going the extra mile and make yourself as indispensable as you possibly can, the only other way you'll ever be free, and independent, and self-determining, and financially independent in old age will be by a stroke of good luck, a rich uncle or rich aunt dying, or something of that sort. I don't know of any way anybody can make himself or herself indispensable *except* by going the extra mile, by rendering some sort of service that you're not expected to render, and rendering it in the right sort of a mental attitude.

Mental attitude is important. If you gripe about going the extra mile, chances are that it won't bring you very many returns. Where do you suppose I get my authority for empha-sizing this principle of going the extra mile? Experience.

I've watched the way nature does things, because you won't go wrong if you follow the way or the habits of nature. Conversely, if you fail to recognize and follow the way nature does things, you'll get into trouble sooner or later—it's just a question of time. There is an overall plan in which this universe operates, no matter what you call the first cause of that plan, or the operator of it, or the creator of it. There's just one set of natural laws, and it's up to every indi-vidual to discover them and adjust himself favorably to them. Above all, nature requests and demands that every living thing go the extra mile in order to eat, in order to live, and in order to survive. Man wouldn't survive one sea-son if it were not for this law of going the extra mile.

Don't render a million dollars' worth of service today and expect to get a bank check for it tomorrow. If you start out to render a million dollars' worth of service, you might have to render it a little bit at a time. You're going to have to get yourself recognized for doing it and you'll have to go the extra mile for a little while before anybody takes notice of you. However, be careful not to go the extra mile *too* long without somebody taking notice of you. If the right fellow doesn't take notice, look around until you find the right fellow who will. In other words, if your present employer doesn't recognize you, fire the employer sooner or later and let his competitor know what kind of service you're rendering. I assure you it won't hurt your chances a bit. Have a little competition as you go along.

Nobody ever accepts a rule or does anything without a motive, and I have a great variety of reasons why you should go the extra mile.

THE LAW OF INCREASING RETURNS

The law of increasing returns means that you'll get back more than you give out, whether it's good or bad, whether it's positive or negative. That's the way the law of nature works. **Whatever you give out, whatever you do to or for another person, or whatever you give out from yourself, comes back to you greatly multiplied in kind.** No exception whatsoever. It doesn't always come back very quickly; sometimes it takes longer than you expect. But you may be sure that if you send out some negative influence, it's going to come back to you sooner or later. You may not recognize what caused it, but it'll come back. It won't overlook you.

The law of increasing returns is eternal, automatic, and it's working all the time. It's just as inexorable as the law of gravitation. Nobody in the world can circumvent it, go around it, or have it suspended for one moment. It's operating all the time. The law of increasing returns means that when you go out of your way to render more service and better service than you're paid to render, it's impossible for you *not* to get back more than you really did, because the law of increasing returns takes care of that. If you're working for a salary, the law takes care of it in additional wages, greater responsibilities, promotions, or opportunities to go into business for yourself. In a thousand and one different ways, it'll come back.

THE LAW OF COMPENSATION

It doesn't always come back from the source to which you rendered the service. Don't be afraid to render service to a greedy buyer or a greedy employer. It makes no difference to whom you render service. If you render it in good faith and in good spirit, and keep doing it as a matter of habit, it's equally impossible for you *not* to be compensated as it is to *be* compensated. Therefore, you don't have to be too careful about the person to whom you render it. In fact, apply this principle with *everybody*, no matter who it is—strangers, acquaintances, business associates, and relatives, too. Make it your business to render useful service to everyone, regardless of the shape, form, or fashion in which you touch them.

The only way you can increase the space that you occupy in the world—and I don't mean just the physical space, but also the mental and the spiritual space as well—will be determined by the quality and the quantity of the service that you render. In addition to the quality and the quantity, is the mental attitude in which you render it. Those are the determining factors as to how far you'll go in life, how much you'll get out of life, how much you'll enjoy life, and how much peace of mind you'll have.

SELF-PROMOTION

Self-promotion elicits the favorable attention of other people. If you're alert-minded and take notice, you'll find in any organization those people that are going the extra mile. You'll find out very quickly. And if you watch the procedure and the records of those people who are going the extra mile, you'll see that when there are promotions around, they're the ones that get them. They don't have to ask for them; it's not necessary at all. Employers *look* for people who will go the extra mile. It permits one to become indispensable in many different human relationships. It enables one to command more than the average compensation.

GIVING FEEDS THE SOUL

I want you to know that it also does something to your soul inside of you; it makes you feel better. And if there were no other reason in the world why you should go the extra mile, I'd say that would be adequate. There are a lot of things in life that cause us to have negative feelings or cause us unpleasant experiences and feelings. However, this is one thing that you can do for yourself that'll *always* give you a pleasant feeling. And if you'll go back through your own experiences, I'm sure you'll remember that you never did a kind thing for anybody without getting a great deal of joy out of it. Maybe the other fellow didn't appreciate it, but that's unimportant.

It's like love. To have loved, that alone is a great privilege. It makes no difference whatsoever whether your love was returned by the other person. You've had the benefit by the emotion of love itself. So it is by the principle of going the extra mile. It'll do something *to you*. It'll give you greater courage. It'll enable you to overcome inhibitions and inferiority complexes that you've been storing through the years. There is so much benefit available to stepping out and making yourself useful to somebody.

If you do something courteous or useful for somebody who is not expecting it, don't be too surprised when they look at you in a quizzical sort of way, as much as to say, "Well, I just wonder why you're doing that." Some people will be a little bit surprised when you go out of your way to be useful to them.

MENTAL AND PHYSICAL BENEFITS

Going the extra mile in all forms of service will lead to mental growth and physical perfection across all areas as well as greater ability and skill in one's chosen vocation. Whether you're delivering a lecture or making up your notebook, or filling your job, if it's something that you're going to do over and over again in your life, make up your mind that every time you do it, you will excel beyond all previous efforts on your part. In other words, become a constant challenge to yourself. See how quickly and how rapidly you will grow if you'll go at it in that way.

I have never delivered a lecture in my life that I didn't intend to deliver better than I did previously. I don't always do it, but that's my intention. It makes no difference what kind of an audience I have, whether I have a big class or a small class. I don't often have small classes, but when I do, I put just as much into a small class as a big one, not only because I want to be useful to my students, but because I want to grow and I want to develop. Out of effort, out of struggle, and out of the use of your faculties comes growth. It enables one to profit by the law of contrast. You won't have to advertise that one very much—it'll advertise itself—because the majority of people around you are *not* going to be going the extra mile, and that's all the better for you.

If everybody went the extra mile this would be a grand world to live in, but you wouldn't be able to cash in on this principle as definitely as you can now because you'd have a tremendous amount of competition. Don't worry. I can assure you you're not going to have it. You'll be in a class by yourself. There will be cases where people you work with or are associated with will be shown up for *not* going the first mile, let alone the second one, and they won't like that. Are you going to cry about that one and quit and go back to your old habits, just because the other fellow doesn't like what you're doing? Of course not.

It's your individual responsibility to succeed. That's your sole responsibility. You can't afford to let anybody's ideas, idiosyncrasies, or notions get in the way of your success. You can't afford to do that. You should be fair with other people, but beyond that, you're under no obligations to let anybody's opinions or ideas stop you from being successful. I'd like to see the person that could stop me from being successful. I'd love to see what he looks like, and I want you to feel that way about it, too. I want you to make up your mind that you're going to put these laws into operation and that you're not going to let anybody stop you from doing it. It leads to the development of a positive, pleasing mental attitude, which is among the more important traits of a pleasing personality— actually, not *among* the more important; it *is* the most important one. A positive mental attitude is the first trait of a pleasing personality.

It's a marvelous thing to know what you can do to change the chemistry of your brain so that you're positive instead of negative. Do you know how easy it is? It's as easy as getting in that frame of mind where you want to do something useful for the other fellow, without rendering service on the one hand and picking his pocket with the other. You're doing it just because of the goodness that you get *out* of doing it. You know that if you render more service and better service than you're paid to render, sooner or later you'll be paid for more than you do and you'll be paid willingly. That's the way the law works. That's the law of compensation. It's an eternal law, it never forgets, and it has a perfectly marvelous bookkeeping system. You may be sure that when you are giving out the right kind of service with the right kind of a mental attitude, you are piling up credits that'll come back to you multiplied, sooner or later.

UNLIMITED BENEFITS

Going the extra mile tends to develop a keen, alert imagination because it is a habit that keeps you continuously seeking new and more efficient ways of rendering useful service. The reason that's important is that, as you begin to look around to see how many places, and ways, and means there are in helping the other fellow to find *himself*, you find *yourself*.

One of the most outstanding things that I discovered in my research was that when you have a problem or an unpleasant situation you don't know how to solve, when you've done everything you know, and when you've tried every source you know of, and you're still at a stalemate, there is always one thing that you can do. I want to tell you that if you'll do that one thing, the chances are that you not only will solve your problem, but you'll also learn a great lesson. That one thing is to find somebody who has an equal or a greater problem and start where you stand, then and there, to help that *other* person. Lo and behold, it unlocks something in you. It unlocks cells of the brain, unlocking cells that permit Infinite Intelligence to come into your brain and give you the answer to the solution of your problem.

I don't know why that works, but do you know how I know that it *does* work? Do you know why I can make that statement so positive and not qualify it? I arrived at that decision by experience, by trying it out hundreds and hundreds of times myself, and by seeing it tried out hundreds and hundreds of times by my students to whom I have recommended that same thing. What a simple thing that is! I don't know *what it does* and I don't know *why it works*. There are a lot of things in life I don't know and there are a lot of things you don't know. There are also some things that you do know that you don't do much about. This is one of those things that I don't know anything about but I do something about.

I follow the law because I know that if I need my own mind to be opened up to receive opportunity, the best way in the world to open it up is to start looking around to see how many other people I can help.

PERSONAL INITIATIVE

Personal initiative gets you into the habit of looking around for something useful to do and going out and doing it without somebody telling you to do it. That old man Procrastination is a sour old bird and he causes a lot of trouble in this world. People put off things until the day after tomorrow that they should have done the day before yesterday. Every one of us is guilty of it. I know I'm not free of it and I know you're not, either. But I can tell you I'm freer of it than I was a few years back. I can find a lot of things to do now and I find them because I get joy out of doing them. Anytime you're going the extra mile, you're going to get joy out of what you're doing; otherwise, you won't go the extra mile. It will help you develop the quality of personal initiative and help you overcome the quality of procrastination.

Going the extra mile also serves to build the confidence of others on one's integrity and general ability, and it aids one in mastering the destructive habit of procrastination. It develops definiteness of purpose, without which one cannot hope for success. That alone would be enough to justify it. It gives you an objective, so that you don't go around and around in circles like a goldfish in a bowl, always coming back to where you started with something that you didn't start out with. Definiteness of purpose comes out of this business of going the extra mile. It also enables you to make your work a joy instead of a burden—you get to where you love it. If you're not engaged in a labor of love, you're wasting a lot of your time.

One of the greatest joys in the world is being permitted to engage in the thing that you would rather do than all other things. When you're going the extra mile, you're doing just exactly that. You don't have to do it, nobody expects you to do it, and nobody asks you to do it. Certainly no employer would ask his employees to go the extra mile. He might ask for extra help once in a while, but he wouldn't do it as a regular thing. It's something that you do on your own initiative, and it gives a dignity to your labor. Even if you're digging a ditch, you're *helping* somebody, and there's a certain dignity to that which takes the fatigue and the unpleasantness out of the labor.

Going the extra mile often gives the greatest amount of joy. You might think you go the extra mile being married, but what about before you get married? Believe me, I spent a lot of time burning midnight oil and I didn't consider it hard work at all. It was my own idea and I used my initiative, but I also got a lot of joy out of doing it and I made it pay off. When you're courting the girl of your choice (or being courted by the man of your choice), it's marvelous how much sleep you can lose and still not be seriously hurt by it. Wouldn't it be a wonderful thing if you could put the same attitude into your relations with people professionally or in the business that you put into courtship? We're going to start sparking again. It's going to start at home, with our own mates. I couldn't begin to tell you the number of married couples that I've started in on a new sparking spree. They're getting a lot of joy out of it. It saves a lot of friction and a lot of argument. It cuts down expenses. Go ahead and laugh, but it will do you good.

I don't mean to be facetious. I'm very serious when I say that there is one of the finest places in the world to start going the extra mile. When you start going the extra mile with somebody that you haven't seen, sit down and have a little sales talk with them. Tell them that you've changed your attitude and you want a mutual agreement for both parties to change the attitude so that from here on out, *all* of us are going the extra mile. We're going to relate together on a different basis, where we'll all get joy out of it, more peace of mind, and more happiness in living. Wouldn't it be a wonderful thing if you went home tonight and had that kind of speech with your mate? It wouldn't hurt; it might help. Your mate might not be impressed by it, but you will be. Nothing will hinder you from enjoying it.

What about that person in business that you haven't been getting along so well with? Why not go in tomorrow morning with a smile and walk over to him or her and shake his hand and say, "Now look here and listen up, pal. From here on out, let's you and I enjoy working together." What would he say? It wouldn't work, huh? Oh, yes, it would. You try it and see. There's another thing that we have called pride, and if there's one thing that does more damage in this world than any other one, it's that little thing called pride. Don't be afraid. Don't be afraid to humiliate yourself if it's going to build better human relations with the people that you have to associate with all the time.

"Those final remarks are not in my notes, but I'll tell you where they were: they were in my heart. [Applause.] Thank you. And one of the reasons why you and I get along so well is that very often I deviate from my notes and go down into my heart and dig up things for you that I want you to have—little morsels of food for your soul that I want you

*to have, because I know they're good. I know they're good,
because I know where I got them and what they've done for
me through the years."*

ESTABLISH OBLIGATION

Going the extra mile is the only thing that gives one the right
to ask for promotions or more pay. Did you ever stop to think
about that? You don't have a leg to stand on if you go to the
purchaser of your services and ask for more money or for promotion to a better job unless, for some time previously, you
have been going the extra mile and doing more than you're
paid for. Obviously, if you're doing no more than you're paid
for, then you're being paid for all you're entitled to, aren't you?
Certainly, you are. So you have to first start going the extra
mile and put the other fellow under obligation to you before
you can ask any favors of him. And if you have enough people
whom you have put under obligations to you by going the
extra mile, when you need some favor, you can always turn in
one direction or other and get it. It's a nice thing to know that
you have that kind of credit hanging around, isn't it? I want
you to have that kind of credit with other people and I want
to teach you the technique by which you can do that.

NATURE GOES THE EXTRA MILE

We get our cue as to the soundness of the principle of going
the extra mile by observing nature, and there's quite a bit of

illustration regarding that. You will see that nature goes the extra mile by producing not only enough of everything for her needs but also a surplus for emergencies and waste. It shows this by the blooms on the trees and the fishes in the seas. She doesn't just produce enough fish to perpetuate the species; she produces enough to feed the snakes and the alligators and everything else. She produces those that die of natural causes, and even more, so there's enough to perpetuate the species. Nature is most bountiful in her business of going the extra mile, and in return, she is very demanding in seeing that every living creature goes the extra mile. Bees are provided with honey as compensation for their services in fertilizing the flowers in which the honey is attractively stored. But they have to perform the service to get the honey, and it must be performed in advance.

You've heard it said that the birds of the air and the beasts of the jungle neither weave nor spin, but they always live and eat. If you observe wildlife at all, you'll see they don't eat without performing some sort of service, without working or doing something before they can eat. Take a flock of common old cornfield crows, for instance. They have to be organized in order to travel in flocks. And they have sentinels to protect them and codes by which they warn one another. In other words, they have to do a lot of educating before they can even eat safely.

Nature requires man to go the extra mile if he's going to have food. All food comes out of the ground, and if he's going to have food, he's got to plant seed. He can't live entirely on what nature plants (at least not in civilized life). On islands where they're not civilized, I suppose they depend on eating raw coconuts and what have you, but in civilized life, we have to plant our food in the ground. We have to clear the ground first before we plow it, harrow it, fence it, protect it against predatory animals and so forth. All of that costs labor and time and money. All of that has to be done in advance or you're not going to eat. I wouldn't have any trouble at all selling this idea that nature makes everybody go the extra mile to a farmer, because he already knows it beyond any question of a doubt. He knows every minute of his life that if he doesn't go the extra mile, he doesn't eat and he doesn't have anything to sell. A new employee can't start going the extra mile and immediately demand top wages or the best job in the place. It doesn't work out that way. You have to establish a record, a reputation. You have to get yourself recognized and received before you can begin to put the pressure on to get compensation back. If you go the extra mile in the right sort of mental attitude, chances are a thousand to one you'll never have to ask for compensation for the service you render, because it'll be tendered to you automatically, in the way of promotions or increased salary.

LAW OF COMPENSATION

Throughout the whole universe, everything has been so arranged through the law of compensation (and so adequately described by Emerson) that nature's budget is balanced. Everything has its opposite equivalent in something else. Positive and negative in every unit of energy, day and night, hot and cold, success and failure, sweet and sour, happiness and misery, man and woman. Everywhere and in everything, one may see the law of action and reaction in operation. Everything you do, everything you think, and every thought that you release causes a reaction, on somebody else or on you as the person releasing the thought. Because when you release a thought, you're not through with it. Every thought that you express, silently even, becomes a definite part of the pattern of your subconscious mind.

If you store in that subconscious mind enough negative thoughts, you'll be predominantly negative. And if you follow the habit of releasing only the positive thoughts, your subconscious pattern will be predominantly positive, and you will attract to you all of the things that you want. If you're negative, you'll repel the things that you want and attract only the things you don't want. That's a law of nature, too. Going the extra mile is one of the finest ways that I know to educate your subconscious mind to attract to you the things you want and to repel the things you don't want.

It's an established fact that if you neglect to develop and apply this principle of going the extra mile, you will never become personally successful, and you will never become financially independent. I know it's sound because

I've had a great privilege that you haven't had yet, but you will have, in time. I've had the privilege of observing a great many thousands of people, some of whom applied the principle of going the extra mile and some of whom did not. I've had the privilege of finding out what happened to those who did and those who didn't. **And I know beyond any question of a doubt that nobody ever rises above the ordinary stations in life or mediocrity without the habit of going the extra mile.** It just doesn't happen. If I had discovered one case, just one case where somebody went on to the top without going the extra mile, I would say then that there are exceptions, but I am in a position to say there are no exceptions because I have never found that one case. I can definitely tell you from my own experiences that I have never had a major benefit of any kind in the world that I didn't get as the result of going the extra mile.

I want you to become self-determining, so you can do these things without the help of anybody. The payoff will come to you when you can go out and do anything in this world that you want to do, and regardless of whether anybody wants you to do it or whether they want to help you or whether they don't, you can do it on your own. That's one of the grandest, most glorious feelings that I know—that whatever I want to do, I can do it. I don't have to ask anybody, not even my wife. But if I had to ask her, I would, because I'm on good terms with her.

PEACE OF MIND

Here's a little item now that's not to be sniffed at: peace of mind that I got out of all those twenty years of going the extra mile. Do you have any idea how many people there are in the world at any one time who are willing to do anything for twenty years in succession without getting something back out of it? Do you have any idea how many people there are in this world who are willing to do something for only three days in succession without being sure they're going to get something out of it? You'd be surprised at how few there are.

We're looking at one of the grandest opportunities that a human being could possibly have, especially here in this country where we really can create our own destiny and where we can express ourselves any way we want. Speech is free, activities are free, and education is free. There's wonderful opportunity to go the extra mile in any direction you want to travel in life. And yet, most people are not doing it. I have seen a time when there were not so many people interested in the philosophy because they were prosperous. They were doing all right and they had no troubles to speak of. Today, almost everybody has troubles, or they think they do.

Do you know what I do instead of finding out what's wrong with the rest of the world? Do you know how I put in my time? I try to find out what I can do to correct this guy here. I have to eat with him, sleep with him, shave his face every morning, wash his face, and give him a bath now and then. You have no idea how many things I have to do for him! I have to live with the guy, twenty-four hours a day.

I put in my time trying to improve myself, and, through myself, I try to improve my friends and my students, by writing books, by delivering lectures, and by teaching in other ways. It pays off very much better than it would if I sat down and took the old newspapers and read all of the murder stories and all of the divorce scandals and everything that's blazoned across the pages every day. I'm still talking about this fellow Napoleon Hill, who didn't have sense enough to decline Andrew Carnegie's offer to work twenty years for nothing. His declining years will be years of happiness because of the seeds of kindness and help he has sown in the hearts of others.

If I had my life to live over again, I'd live it just exactly the way I have. I'd make all the mistakes I made. I'd make them at the time in life when I made them, early on so I'd have time enough to correct some of them. And that period during which I would come into peace of mind and understanding would be in the afternoon of life, not in the forenoon, because I couldn't take it. When you're young, you can take it. But when you pass the noon hour and you go into the afternoon, your energies are not as great as they were before. Your physical energy, and sometimes your mental capacity, is not as great. You can't take as much trouble as you can in your days of youth. And you haven't got so many years left to correct the mistakes that you made.

To have the tranquility and the peace of mind that I have today, in the afternoon of life, is one of the great joys that has come out of this philosophy. If you ask me what has been my greatest compensation, I would say that's it. There are so many people at my age, and even much younger than I, who haven't found peace of mind and never will. They never will, because they're looking for it in the wrong place. They're not doing anything about it; they're expecting somebody else to do something about it for them. Peace of mind is something that you've got to get for yourself. First of all, you've got to earn it. As to how anybody can get peace of mind, a few of you would be surprised where you have to really start looking for it. It's not where the average person is looking for it. It's not out there in the joys of what money will buy or out there in the joys of recognition and fame and fortune. You'll find peace of mind in the humility of the one individual's own heart.

Dr. Hill's "inner wall" that appears next is part of his system of walls that he describes in the lecture on Principle #8: Self-Discipline. To help you understand his words here, he is referring to his inner spiritual sanctuary. The "wall" keeps all else from entering this sanctuary, which is reserved for him and God alone.

I get peace of mind mostly through an "inner wall," **a place I go within** where the wall is as high as eternity. I go into meditation many times each day and there's where I get my real peace of mind. I can always withdraw into that inner wall area, cut out every earthly influence, and commune with the higher forces of the universe. Anybody can do that. You can do that. When you get through with this philosophy, you'll be able to do anything you want to do, just as well or better than anything I can do. I'm hoping that every student that I turn out will eventually excel me in every way that I know possible. Maybe through writing books, you'll take up where I left off and write better books than I wrote. Why not? I haven't said the last word in my books nor in my lectures, or in anything else. As a matter of fact, I'm just a student, a fairly intelligent student, I think, but just a student on the path. The only state of perfection that I have achieved (and which cannot be surpassed by anyone) is that I have actually found peace of mind, and how to get it.

Engage in at least one act of going the extra mile every day. You can choose your own circumstance, even if it's nothing more than telephoning an acquaintance and wishing him good fortune. You'll be surprised what'll happen to you when you begin to call up your friends that you have been neglecting for some time and just say, "You were on my mind. I was thinking about you, and I just wanted to call and say how do you do, and I hope you are feeling as good as I am." You'd be surprised at what that'll do to you and what it'll do to your friend, too. It doesn't have to be a close personal friend. It just has to be somebody you know. Or, maybe relieve a friend from duty for half an hour or so, or have a neighbor send over his children while he attends the movies, or do a little babysitting for one of your neighbors. If you're going to be at home anyway, with children of your own, maybe you know a neighbor who would like to get off and go down to the movies but can't get away from her children. The children may be noisy, and they'll probably fight with your children, but if you're a real diplomat, you'll keep them apart. She'll be under obligation to you, and you'll feel that you've really been kind by helping out somebody who otherwise wouldn't have had a little freedom. It'd be a nice thing for some of you people who don't have any children to say, "Why don't I come over and baby-sit for you while you go out? You and your husband can go on a little courtship. Let me come over and babysit for you while you go out to the movie or go to a show." You'll have to know your neighbors pretty well in order to do that. Certainly, most of you would have some neighbor that you could approach on some such basis, and they wouldn't think you were crazy.

It's not so much what you do to the other fellow. It's what you do to yourself by finding ways and means of going the extra mile in little ways. Did you know that both the successes in life as well as the failures are made up of little things? So little that they're often overlooked, because the things that make success are such small and seemingly insignificant things.

I know people who are so popular they couldn't have an enemy. One of them is my distinguished business associate, Mr. Stone. He always goes the extra mile and look how prosperous he is. Look how many people are going the extra mile for him. There are a lot of people who, if they didn't make good money working for Mr. Stone, they'd pay him a salary just to work for him. I've actually heard one say that he's become immensely wealthy himself working for Mr. Stone. He said, "If I didn't make money out of working for him, I'd pay him if I had to, just for the association with him." Mr. Stone's not different from you or me or anybody else, except in his mental attitude toward people and toward himself. He makes it his business to go the extra mile. Sometimes, people take advantage of that. They don't act fairly with him. I've seen that happen, but he doesn't worry about that too much. In fact, he doesn't worry about anything at all, period. He's learned to adjust himself to life in such a way that he gets great joy out of living and gets great joy out of people. Write a letter to some acquaintance, offering him encouragement. In your job, do a little more than you're paid to do, stay a little longer on the job, or make some other person a little happier.

PLEASING PERSONALITY

Who are you? How do you appear to others? Do the people you meet seem to like you, dislike you, or perhaps even worse, do they seem not to care one way or the other? The fifth principle of *Your Right to Be Rich* is a Pleasing Personality. Remember that no matter who you are or what you do, every time you meet someone, explain an idea, talk on the telephone, or give an opinion, you are selling your most valuable asset: you. When you become your best, you will achieve the most. Developing a pleasing personality will enable you to put yourself forward in a positive, dynamic, and appealing way. Fully utilizing this principle will make the difference between a salesman and an order-taker, between a successful leader and an ordinary worker, and between a person who is well liked and one who is detested.

As Dr. Hill stresses, that phrase, "fully utilized," is important. The traits that make up a pleasing personality will be of little value to you unless you use them at all times.

Dr. Hill's seminars were conducted like a test. He asked students to grade themselves on each of the twenty-five traits. May we suggest that you use this lecture as a starting point, as a way of understanding the key elements of a pleasing personality? Grade yourself from 0 to 100 percent on each trait. Here's how to tally your score: if you feel you're perfect or nearly so on any single trait (a rare achievement), give yourself an A-plus. If you are above average, give yourself an A. If you are fair or average, give yourself a B. If you are poor or below average, that's a C. And if you feel you're unsatisfactory in any given trait, mark down a D. Be brutally honest. Scoring yourself higher than you deserve will only foster a kind of self-deception that will keep you from attaining your goals. Then test yourself again a month from now, and keep testing yourself to track your improvement.

I want to introduce you to the most wonderful person in the world—the person sitting in your seat right now. When you break down that person by the twenty-five factors that go into making a pleasing personality, you'll find out just exactly where you're wonderful, and why. I'm going to ask you to give yourself the rating you think you're entitled to, and it can be anything from 0 to 100 percent. When you get through, add up the total and divide it by the twenty-five traits and that will give you your average rating on the pleasing personality. If you rate a 50 percent, you're doing fine, but I hope some of you will rate much higher than that.

TRAIT #1: POSITIVE MENTAL ATTITUDE

The first trait of a pleasing personality always is a positive mental attitude, because nobody wants to be around a person who's negative. No matter what other traits you may have, if you don't have a positive mental attitude (at least in the presence of other people), you're not going to be considered to have a pleasing personality. Now, rate yourself on that anywhere from 0 to 100, and if you can rate yourself 100, you'll be in the same class as Franklin D. Roosevelt. That's pretty high.

TRAIT #2: FLEXIBILITY

The next trait is flexibility, which is the ability to bend and adjust to the varying circumstances of life without going down under them. A lot of people in this world are so staid in their habits and in their mental attitude that they cannot adjust to anything that's unpleasant, or anything they don't agree with. Do you know why Franklin D. Roosevelt was one of the most, if not *the* most, popular presidents we've had in our generation? He could be all things to all people. I have been in his office when senators and congressmen would come in there ready to cut his throat but go out singing his praises—all because of his mental attitude. In other words, he adjusted himself to *their* mental attitude. He didn't get mad at the same time the other fellow did. That's a mighty good way of adjusting: be flexible enough not to get mad when the other fellow's mad. If you want to get mad, do it on your own account, when the other fellow's in a good humor, and you'll have a much better chance of not getting hurt.

I've seen presidents of the United States come and go, I've been associated with several of them, and I know what this factor of flexibility can mean in the highest office in the world. Herbert Hoover was probably one of the best all-around business executives we've ever had in the White House, and yet he couldn't sell himself to the people a second time. It was because he was inflexible, he couldn't bend, he was too static, and he was too fixed. Calvin Coolidge was the same way. Woodrow Wilson was also the same way to some extent. He was too austere, too static, too fixed, and too correct. In other words, he wouldn't allow anybody to slap him on the shoulder, call him "Woody," or take any personal liberties with him at all. Of course, there are so many things in this life that you have to adjust yourself to. If you're going to have peace of mind and good health, you might just as well learn how to do it now. And if you're not flexible, you can become flexible.

TRAIT #3: PLEASING TONE OF VOICE

A pleasing tone of voice is an important thing that you can experiment with: a lot of people have harsh tones, or they have nasal tones, or something in their tone of voice that irritates other people. A monotonous speaker, for instance, who does not have personal magnetism and does not know how to fine-tune the pitch and tone to his voice, will never get his audience in a million years. If you're going to teach, or lecture, or do any public speaking (or even command good conversation), you've got to learn to give a pleasant, pleasing tone to your voice. You can do it with a little bit of practice. Just simply lowering your voice, and not talking too loudly, can give it that something that is pleasing to the ear. I don't think anybody can teach another person how to make his tone of voice pleasing. I think you have to do it yourself by experimenting.

First, you have to *feel* pleasing. How could you use a pleasant tone of voice when you feel angry or when you don't like the person that you're talking to? You can, but it's not effective unless you really *feel* the way you want to express yourself.

All of these are carefully studied techniques that you have to acquire if you're going to make yourself pleasing, but I don't know of anything that'll pay off better than to be pleasing in the eyes of other people. It's just one of those things you can't get along without.

TRAIT #4: TOLERANCE

A lot of people don't understand the full meaning of tolerance, but it means an open mind on all subjects toward all people at all times. An open mind means that your mind's not closed against anybody or anything; you're always willing to hear the last word or hear an additional word about anything. You'd be surprised at how few people there are in this world with open minds. Some of them have closed so tight you couldn't open them with a crowbar. You couldn't get a new idea in there if you tried. Did you ever see anyone who had a closed mind and was also pleasing? You never did and you never will. To have a pleasant mental attitude, you've got to have an open mind. The very minute people find that you have prejudices that involve them, or their understanding of religion, or politics, or economics, or anything else that affects them they're going to back away from you.

I get along well with the people in my classes of all different religions: Catholics and Protestants and Jews, and

Gentiles. In fact, I get along with all races and all creeds because, to me, they're all one brand. I get along with them because they're my fellow beings, my brothers and sisters. I never think of anybody in terms of what he believes politically or religiously or economically. I think of him in terms of what he's trying to do to better himself and to better somebody else. Those are the terms that I think of people in, and that's why I get along so well with them.

An open mind is a marvelous thing to possess. If you don't keep it open, you're not going to learn very much. If you have a closed mind, you'll miss out on a lot of information and facts that you need, but wouldn't get, without an open mind.

It does something inside to have your mind closed up, against anybody or anything. The very moment you close your mind on any subject and say, "That's the last word. I want no more information on it," you cease to grow.

TRAIT #5: SENSE OF HUMOR

A keen sense of humor means you have to have a good disposition—if you don't have it, you have to cultivate it—so that you can adjust to all the unpleasant things that come along in life, without taking them too seriously.

I think I told you about the motto that I saw in the office of Dr. Frank Crane once. It impressed me very much, especially because it was in the office of a preacher. It said,

"Don't take yourself too damn seriously." And he explained that the word *damned* meant just exactly what it said. If you take yourself too seriously, you are *damning* yourself. It wasn't a profane word after all. I think it's a good motto for anybody: not to take himself too seriously.

One of the finest tonics that you can take is to have a good, hearty laugh at least several times a day. If you don't have anything to laugh at, cook up something. Look at yourself in a glass, for instance, because you can always get a laugh out of that. You'll be surprised at how it'll change the chemistry of your mind while you're doing it. If you've got troubles, they'll melt away and they won't seem near as big when you're laughing as when you're crying. A keen sense of humor is a marvelous thing. I don't know if my sense of humor is what you'd call keen, but it's alert. I can get some fun out of almost any circumstance in life. I used to get a lot of punishment out of some circumstances that I now get fun out of. My sense of humor is a little more alert than it used to be.

TRAIT #6: FRANKNESS

A frank manner and speech ensures discriminate control of the tongue at all times and creates the habit of thinking before you speak. Most people don't do that. They speak first and think afterward, or have regret afterward. It's a wonderful thing if, just before you utter *any* kind of an expression to anybody, you figure out whether it's going to *benefit* the person that's listening or *damage* him. Consider, too, whether it's going to benefit you or damage you. Following those two simple rules will stop you from saying half of the things that you *do* say that you wish you *hadn't*. Do a little weighing and a little thinking before you open your mouth and start speaking. There are a lot of people who get their mouths going and forget what they said because they weren't thinking. These people are almost always in difficulty with somebody.

Frankness of manner and speech doesn't mean that you have to tell everybody exactly what you think of him. If you do that, you'll have no friends. But frankness means not being evasive and not engaging in double-talk. Nobody likes a double-talker. Nobody likes a person who's always evasive or never expresses an opinion about anything.

TRAIT #7: PLEASING FACIAL EXPRESSION

If you study your facial expression in the mirror, it's a marvelous thing to see how much more pleasing you can make it when you try than when you don't try. Try smiling a little bit. Learn to smile when you're talking to people. You'd be surprised at how much more effective what you say is when you're smiling than when you're frowning, or when you're looking serious. It makes a tremendous difference on the person who's listening. I hate to talk to a person who's got a serious expression on, as if the whole world is on his shoulders. It makes me fidgety. I just wish that whatever he's saying, he'd get through with it and go on. If only he'd limber up, like Franklin D. Roosevelt. When he gives you that million-dollar smile, even the most trivial thing that he says sounds like music, and sounds like wisdom because of what his smile does to you psychologically. That smile is a marvelous thing. Don't grin at people when you don't mean it, because monkeys can grin. Learn to smile because you feel it. But where does a smile take place first—on your lips or face, or where? It starts in your heart, where you feel it. That's where it takes place.

You don't have to be pretty, you don't have to be handsome, but a smile will decorate you and embellish you no matter who you are. It makes your facial expression much more beautiful.

TRAIT #8: KEEN SENSE OF JUSTICE

What do you think about being just with another person, even when it's to your disadvantage to do so? It's a wonderful thing that endears you to other people, because they know very well that your being just with them is costing you something to do it. There's no particular virtue in being just with the other fellow when you're benefiting by it. Do you have any idea how many people there are that are fair, and just, and honest only when they know it's going to come back to them in one way or another? How quickly they'd be dishonest if it was profitable to them to do it. I can't give you the percentage; I'd hate to tell you what I think it is, but I'm sure it's much too high. Too many people are like that.

TRAIT #9: SINCERITY OF PURPOSE

Nobody likes a person who is obviously insincere in what he says and does, who's trying to be something that he's not, or who's saying something that doesn't represent his inner thoughts. It's not as bad as out-and-out lying, but it's the first cousin to it, lacking sincerity of purpose.

TRAIT #10: VERSATILITY

Versatility comes from a wide range of knowledge of people and world events outside of one's immediate personal interests. A person who doesn't know anything except about one thing is a person who will be boresome the moment he gets out of that field. It doesn't take much imagination to think of somebody that you know who's got his nose so closely to the grindstone in one thing that he doesn't know what's going on about anything outside of that. He won't be interesting as a conversationalist, nor in any other way, if he doesn't have a wide enough range of things to talk about so that it includes things that interest you. You know the best way in the world to make yourself liked by other people? Talk to them about the things that interest them. If you talk to the other fellow about things that interest *him*, when you start talking about the things that interest *you*, he'll be a receptive listener.

TRAIT #11: TACT

Your speech doesn't have to reflect *everything* in your mental attitude. You don't have to speak everything that goes on in your mind. If you do, you'll be an open book for everybody to read at will. Sometimes they'll read you when you wish they hadn't. Be tactful in your speech and in your attitude toward other people. You can always be tactful.

You know those drivers on the road—the other fellow that skins your fenders? You know how tactful they are when they jump out and run around to see how much damage is done. Maybe ten cents' worth of paint's been knocked off, but they do a hundred dollars' worth of damage cussing one another out. One of these days, I'm going to have an experience of seeing two fellows collide on the highway, and they're going to jump out and apologize, each one claiming it was his fault and wanting to pay the bill. And when I do, I don't know what's going to happen to me, but I'm going to see that, one of these days.

You'd be surprised how much you can do with people if you're just tactful with them. Instead of telling people to do things, or asking, or requesting, or demanding that they do things, it might be very tactful and helpful if you requested them, or asked them if they would *mind* doing things. Even though you're in authority to give them an instruction, it's still better to ask if they would mind doing certain things. One of the most outstanding employers I ever knew never gave his employees direct instructions. That was Andrew Carnegie. He always asked his associates and his employees in even the humblest positions if they would mind doing something for him, if it would be convenient, or if it would be suitable. He never ordered them to do anything, he always asked them. No wonder he got along so well with people. No wonder he was so successful.

TRAIT #12: PROMPTNESS OF DECISION

Nobody can be truly well liked and have a truly pleasing personality who always puts off making a decision when he has all of the facts before him and ought to make the decision on the spot. I don't mean they should go off half-cocked or render snap judgments. But when you have all of the facts and the time has arrived for a decision, get in the habit of making those decisions.

If you make a decision that's wrong, you can always

reverse it. Don't be too big or too little to reverse yourself when you find out that you should reverse yourself. There's a great advantage in being fair enough with yourself and with the other fellow to reverse yourself if you've made the wrong decision.

TRAIT #13: FAITH IN INFINITE INTELLIGENCE

I don't need to make much comment on faith in Infinite Intelligence. You know what your faith is there, and you should rate very high if you're faithfully following your religion, whatever it is.

You'd be surprised how many people give lip service to this question of faith in Infinite Intelligence and don't do very much about it outside of lip service. This lip service is not so loud that you can hear it very far away. They don't indulge in very outstanding acts, backing up their alleged belief in Infinite Intelligence. I don't know how the Creator feels about it, but I believe that an ounce of a good act is worth a million tons of good intentions or belief. Just one act.

TRAIT #14: APPROPRIATE USE OF WORDS

Appropriateness of words means your words are free from slang, wisecracks, and profanity. I never saw an age when the people indulged in so many wisecracks, slang statements, double-talk, and all that sort of thing as now. It may seem smart to the fellow who's doing it, but it's not smart to the fellow who's listening. He may laugh at it, but he's not going to be impressed with a fellow that's engaged in wisecracks and smart sayings.

Our English language is not the easiest thing in the world to conquer or to master, but it is a beautiful language and has a wide range of words and meanings. It's wonderful to be able to control the English language so that you can convey to the other fellow precisely what you have in your mind, what you want him to think you have in your mind, or what you want him to know.

TRAIT #15. CONTROLLED ENTHUSIASM

Why control enthusiasm? Why not turn it loose and let it run riot? Letting your enthusiasm run loose can get you into trouble. Your enthusiasm ought to be handled very much like you handle your electricity. Electricity is indeed a wonderful thing. It washes dishes, washes your clothes, runs the toaster, and maybe cooks your food on the stove. It does a lot of things, but you handle it with care. You turn it on when you want it and then turn it off when you don't want it. Your enthusiasm should be handled with just as much care. You turn it on when you want to turn it on, and then you can just as quickly turn it off. If you're not able to turn it off as quickly as you turn it on, somebody will come along and get you all enthused over something that you ought not to be enthused over. What a sucker you will be at that time, prey to whatever he wants you to do.

You can also be too enthusiastic with the other fellow and wear him out so that he'll pull down his mental shades and resist you. I've met salesmen so enthusiastic that I wouldn't let them in my place a second time, because I didn't want to go to the trouble of defending myself against them. I have heard some speakers and preachers like that, too. I wouldn't want to follow them because I'd have too much trouble resisting them. I'm talking about the kind of fellow that turns his enthusiasm battery loose, and all you can do is to run away from it or try to turn it off. A man who does that is not going to be popular. But the man who can turn on his enthusiasm at the right time, and in the right amount, and can turn it off at the right time, is a man that's going to be considered to have a pleasing personality.

If you're not able to exude enthusiasm when you want to, you are not going to be considered a pleasing person-ality, because there are times when you definitely need it. Teaching, lecturing, speaking, ordinary conversation, or selling, almost anything that involves human relationships requires a certain amount of enthusiasm. Enthusiasm is one of those things you can cultivate. It's just like all these other qualities. There's only one quality in here that you can't cultivate. See if you can find it. Andrew Carnegie said he could give you every one of the other traits except one: personal magnetism. You've got just so much of that, and it is subject to control and to transmutation, but it's just something one person can't give to another.

Be a sportsman about everything. You're not going to win all the time in life. Nobody can do that. There are going to be times when you lose, and when you do, lose gracefully and graciously. Lose and say, "I lost, but maybe it's the best thing that I did, because I'm going to start looking immediately for that seed of an equivalent benefit, and next time, I'm going to let somebody else lose. I'm going to wise myself up."

TRAIT #16: DON'T TAKE ANYTHING TOO SERIOUSLY

Don't take it too seriously, no matter what it is. During the Depression, I had four of my friends commit suicide. Two of them jumped off of tall buildings, one shot himself, and another one took poison. They did it because they lost all their money. I lost twice as much as they did, but I didn't jump off any building, I didn't shoot myself, I didn't poison myself. What did I do? I said, "It's a blessed fine thing, because losing this amount of money, now I'll have to start in and earn some more, and in earning some more, I'll learn some more." My mental attitude toward it was to start immediately looking for that seed of improvement. It didn't disturb me in the least. I said to myself, "If I lose every penny that I have, the last suit I have, even my BVDs, I can always get a barrel from somebody and start over again. Wherever I can get a bunch of people together to listen, I'll be able to start making money." How can you put down a person with that kind of attitude? No matter how many times he's defeated, he comes right up again. Just like a cork; you can put him down under the water, but he can bounce up the moment you take your hand off of him. If you don't take your hand off, he'll make you take it off.

TRAIT #17: COMMON COURTESY

Common courtesy is common, ordinary, garden-variety courtesy toward everybody. Treat people courteously, especially people on a lower plane (socially, economically, or financially) than yourself. It's a wonderful thing to be courteous to the person to whom you don't have to be courteous. It does something to the other fellow and it does something to you.

I hate to see anybody lording it over another person. Nothing upsets me more quickly than to go into a restaurant and have some newly rich people come in and start ordering the waiters around and abusing them. They may deserve it but I have never learned to like that. I think anybody who abuses another person in public, with or without a cause, has something wrong with his machinery. You may be sure that there is something he's missing in his life.

I remember when I was staying at the Bellevue-Stratford Hotel in Philadelphia, on that famous trip when I went there to meet my publisher the first time. One of the waiters spilled some hot soup right on the back of my neck and it burned me. The headwaiter ran over, and right behind him was the hotel manager, who wanted to call a doctor. I said, "Well, it's not that serious. The waiter spilled a little soup." "Well," he said, "we'll have your suit cleaned, and we'll do this, we'll do that and . . ." I said, "No, I'm not upset about it." Later, when that waiter got off duty, he came up to my room and said, "I want to tell you how much I appreciate what you said. You could have had me fired, because I was as good as fired. If you hadn't talked about it the way you did, I'd have been out, and I can't afford to be fired." I don't know how much good it did the waiter, but it did me a lot of good to know that there was a man I could have humiliated. As far as I know, never in my whole life have I intentionally humiliated anybody for anything whatsoever. I may have done it unintentionally, and I feel good to be able to say that.

I feel good to have that attitude toward people, and it comes back to me, because the people have that attitude toward me, too. They don't want to humiliate me, because you get back from people what you send out. You're a human magnet, and you're attracting to you the sum and substance of what goes on in your heart and soul.

TRAIT #18: APPROPRIATENESS
OF PERSONAL ADORNMENT

Appropriateness of personal adornment is important to anybody in public life. I've never been too fussy about that. I've never used formal clothes, except on very few occasions when it's perfectly appropriate. Ordinarily, use good taste. The best-dressed person is the one that's dressed so that if you were told to describe how he or she was dressed later on, you couldn't do it. They'll say, "All I know was, he looked nice," or, "She looked nice."

TRAIT #19: GOOD SHOWMANSHIP

You've got to be a showman if you're going to sell yourself in any walk of life. You've got to be a good showman and know when to dramatize words and when to dramatize circumstances. If you were to describe the history of the most outstanding man in the world, for instance, using the bare facts and without dramatizing them as you went along, you'd fall down flat. You've got to dramatize these things that you're talking about and these people that you're doing business with. You've got to learn the art of showmanship as you go along, and it's something you can learn.

TRAIT #20: GOING THE EXTRA MILE

I don't need to mention to you that you should have the habit of going the extra mile. There's a whole lecture on that and you can rate yourself on it.

TRAIT #21: TEMPERANCE

You should also apply temperance in eating, drinking, work, play, and thinking. Temperance means displaying not too much or not too little of anything. You can do yourself just as much damage with eating as you can with drinking liquor. The rule that I go by in everything is that I don't allow anything to take charge of me. When I was smoking and I got to the point where the cigars were smoking me, I quit. I can take a cocktail or two, or even three (I don't remember ever having taken more than that in a social evening, but I could if I wanted to). However, if I ever found them taking me, or if I ever found myself being unable to resist them, I'd part company with them in a hurry. I'd follow the same rule if I were still smoking. When I got to the point where the cigars were smoking me, I quit right off. I want to be in possession of Napoleon Hill all the time. Temperance means not too much or not too little. There's nothing so very bad in life, if you don't overdo it.

TRAIT #22: PATIENCE

Under all circumstances, patience is something you have to have in this world we're living in. It's a world of competition. You're constantly being called upon to use your patience and, by using patience, you learn to time these things so that you get action out of other people when the time is more favorable. If you don't have patience and try to force the hand of other people, you'll get a no or you'll get a turndown or a knockdown when you don't want it. You require patience in order that you may time your relationships with people. You have to have a lot of patience. You have to be able to control yourself at all times. Most people don't have much patience, you know. You take the average person, probably the majority of people, and you can make them mad in two seconds. All you've got to do is say the wrong thing, or do the wrong thing. Why, I don't need to get angry because somebody says or does the wrong thing. I could if I wanted to, but it's my choice and I can choose not to get mad.

TRAIT #23: GRACEFULNESS IN POSTURE AND CARRIAGE

Another important trait of a pleasing personality is gracefulness in posture and carriage of the body. If I came in with a relaxed body, I might be more comfortable and it might be easier. But it's finer of me to stand up straight without leaning on anything. To slump around and be careless in your posture marks you as one who is not very particular about your own personal appearance (and other things too). It's a good idea to have gracefulness in posture and carriage of the body.

TRAIT #24: HUMILITY AND MODESTY

I don't know of anything as wonderful as having true humility of the heart. There are times when I do have to criticize people, even some of the people I'm working with. If it's necessary for me to express disapproval of anything anybody does, I silently say to myself so they don't hear it, "God pity us all." I know that but for the grace of God, I'd be the man that I'm criticizing. Maybe I've done things ten times as bad as the thing I'm criticizing him for. In other words, I try to maintain that sense of humility in my heart. Regardless of what happens to me that's unpleasant, and regardless of how successful I become, I observe this feeling of humility of the heart. After all, whatever success I have is due entirely to the friendly, marvelous love, affection, and cooperation of other people. I could never have spread myself over the world the way I have, I could never have benefited the people that I have, and I could never have grown the way I have grown, had it not been for the love, affection, marvelous and friendly cooperation of other people. I couldn't have gotten that cooperation if I hadn't adjusted myself to other people in a state of friendliness.

TRAIT #25: PERSONAL MAGNETISM

Personal magnetism makes reference to the sex emotion, an inborn trait and the only personality trait that cannot be cultivated. It can be controlled and directed to beneficial usage. As a matter of fact, the most outstanding leaders, salesmen, speakers, clergymen, lawyers, lecturers, teachers, and the most outstanding in any field of endeavor, are people who have learned to transmute sex emotion.

To transmute sex emotion is to convert that great creative energy into doing the thing that you want to do most at that time. The word *transmute* is something to look up in the dictionary to make sure you understand what it means.

DISCOVERING STRENGTHS
AND WEAKNESSES

You've got a lot of thinking to do about this and in doing so, you're going to make discoveries about yourself. You're going to find out that when you really come down to answering these questions and giving yourself a rating, you have certain weaknesses that you didn't know you had, and you also have certain strengths and certain good qualities that perhaps you had undervalued. Let's find out about ourselves, to see just where we stand, and to see what it is that makes us tick. Why do people like us, and why do people dislike us?

I can sit down with any one of you, and by asking you no more than twenty questions, I could lay my finger right on what's keeping you from being popular (if you are not popular). I want you to do the same thing. I want you to learn to analyze people, starting with yourself. Find out what it is that makes people popular, what makes them tick, and when you do that, you'll have one of the greatest assets that you could possibly imagine.

PERSONAL INITIATIVE

The sixth principle of *Your Right to Be Rich* is Personal Initiative. In its simplest terms, this is the action-producing aspect of this philosophy. Consider the analogy of a car: the tires are properly inflated, the oil's been changed, it has a full tank of fuel, and the battery is at full charge. You even washed it so it sparkles like new. There's only one problem: the starter motor doesn't work, which means you aren't going anywhere.

Personal initiative is like a dynamo that not only starts all physical action but also sparks the faculty of your imagination into action. It is part of the process of translating your definite major purpose into physical or financial terms. Personal initiative also sparks the critical element of completing any action you've undertaken.

Dr. Hill points out that there are two types of people who never amount to anything. One is the person who never does what he is told to do. The other is the person who only does what he is told to do. Therefore, personal initiative is the twin brother of the principle of going the extra mile.

This principle, like that of a pleasing personality, is presented as a self-evaluative test. Be prepared to grade yourself openly and honestly on how much you possess of the qualities that comprise this vital principle of success.

This is a great lesson because it's the action-producing portion of this philosophy. It wouldn't make very much difference whether you understood all of the other principles or not if you didn't do something about it, now would it? In other words, the value that you're going to get out of this philosophy will not consist of anything I teach in these lectures. **The important thing is what you will do about all of this, and the action you will take to start using this philosophy on your own personal initiative.**

There are certain attributes of initiative and leadership that I want you to start in and grade yourself on. There are many attributes, and I'll comment here on the ones that I consider of the greatest importance. Grading yourself on these qualities will be the first step toward making those qualities your own.

ATTRIBUTE #1: DEFINITE MAJOR PURPOSE

There's no need to comment further on having a definite major purpose. Obviously if you don't have an objective in life—a major overall purpose—you haven't very much personal initiative. One of the most important steps to take is to find out what it is you want to do. If you're not sure what you want to do over a lifetime, let's find out what you're going to do the remainder of this year. Let's not set our goal too high or too far in the distance.

If you're in a business or a profession or a job, your definite major purpose could enable you to step up your income from your services, whatever your services may be. At the end of the year, you can review your record, reestablish your definite major purpose, and step it up to something bigger. Create a one-year plan or maybe a five-year plan. That's the starting point of personal initiative. Find out where you're going, why you're going there, what you're going to do after you get there, and how much you're going to get out of it financially. The majority of people in this world could be very successful if they would just make up their minds how much success they want and on what terms they want to evaluate success. There are a lot of people in this world who want a good position and plenty of money, but they're not quite sure just what kind of a position they want, how much money they want, nor when they want to get it. Let's do a little thinking on that subject, and grade ourselves on number one.

ATTRIBUTE #2: ADEQUATE MOTIVE

Adequate motive inspires continuous action in pursuit of the object of one's definite major purpose. Study yourself carefully and see if you have an adequate motive or motives. It will be much better if you have more than one motive for wanting to attain the object of your major purpose, whatever your motive or whatever your immediate purpose. Nobody ever does anything without a motive. Let me restate that. No one outside of the insane asylum does anything without a motive. A person who is off balance may do a lot of things without any motive whatsoever. But normal people move only on motive, and the stronger the motive is, the more active they become and the more apt they are to act upon their own personal initiative.

You don't have to have an awful lot of brains in this world. You don't have to be very brilliant. You don't have to have such a wonderful education. You can be an outstanding success if you will only take what little you have, whether it's little or much, and start using it, putting it into operation, doing something about it, and doing something *with* it. And, of course, that calls for initiative.

ATTRIBUTE #3: MASTERMIND ALLIANCE

A mastermind alliance is friendly cooperation through which to acquire the necessary power for noteworthy achievement. Take the initiative now and find out just how many friends you have that you can count on or call on if you were to need something in the way of cooperation. Make a list of the people that you could really and truly turn to if you needed some favor, an endorsement, an introduction, or maybe even a loan of money. Incidentally, unless you have all the money lying around that you need, the time might come when you need to take a loan. Wouldn't it be very nice to know someone that you could turn to in case of need and get the money you need? You can always go to a bank. All you have to do is to give four-for-one security (government bonds) and you can get all the money you want. But there are times when you want medium sums, perhaps, or you want something other than money. At that time, you need to have the acquaintance of somebody you have already cultivated, so that when you turn to them for favors, you can get them. Above all, if you're aiming at anything above mediocrity, you need to have a mastermind alliance of one or more people besides yourself, who not only will cooperate with you, but who will go out of the way to help you and assist you, and who have the ability to do something that will be a benefit to you.

It's up to you to take the initiative to build those mastermind allies. They don't just come along and join you because you're a good fellow. You have to lay out a plan, have an objective, and find people suitable to make up your mastermind alliance. You also have to give them an adequate motive for becoming a mastermind ally of yours.

I happen to know that the vast majority of people do not have a mastermind alliance with other people. Don't be afraid to grade yourself zero on this if you don't have one, but the next time you come to grade, make sure you grade yourself higher than that. And the only way you can grade higher later if you grade zero now is to start in and find at least one mastermind ally that you can attach yourself to right now, as you are beginning.

ATTRIBUTE #4: SELF-RELIANCE

You want to find out just exactly how much self-reliance you have in proportion to the nature of your major purpose.

When you check yourself on self-reliance, you may need some help from other people. You may need some help from your wife, your husband, your closest friend, or somebody who knows you really well. You may *think* you have self-reliance, but do you know how you can tell how much self-reliance you have? You can check your self-reliance accurately by first evaluating your definite major purpose to see just how big it is (if you *have* a definite major purpose, that is). If you don't have one, or if it's not outstanding, or it's not above anything that you've attained up to the present, then you don't have very much self-reliance, and you should grade yourself very low on that.

If you have the proper amount of self-reliance, you'll step your definite major purpose up beyond anything you have ever achieved before, and you'll become determined to attain it.

ATTRIBUTE #5: SELF-DISCIPLINE

Success requires self-discipline sufficient to ensure mastery of the head and the heart, and to sustain one's motives until they are realized. Where and when do you need self-discipline most? When you're on the way up, when everything's rosy and going well, and you're succeeding? No. You need self-discipline when things are tough, when the going is hard, and when the outlook is not favorable. And the kind of self-discipline you need at that point is discipline over your mind. You need to know where you're going, that you have a right to go there, and that you're determined to go there regardless of how hard the going may be or how much opposition you may meet with. You'll need at least enough self-discipline to sustain you through the period when the going is hard, instead of quitting or complaining.

ATTRIBUTE #6: PERSISTENCE

Persistence is based on the will to win. Do you know how many times the average person fails before he quits or decides he wants to do something else? Once? Once would be generous! The fellow that fails before he starts thinks there's no use in starting because he knows he can't do anything. He didn't even start once. You might be interested in knowing that the vast majority of people fail before they start. They actually never make a start. They think of things that they *might* do, but they never do anything about it. Did you also know that among the vast majority of the people who *do* start, at the first opposition, they quit or allow themselves to be diverted over to something else?

People who have been close to me (when I've taken my hair down and talked frankly) know that my most outstanding asset, in addition to my persistence and the will to win, is self-discipline. I stick to a thing hard, in fact, all the harder when the going is the hardest. *That's* my outstanding quality—always has been and always will be. I want to tell you that without those traits, I never would have completed this philosophy. I never would have been able to have it introduced as widely as it has been and I wouldn't be standing here talking to you tonight.

Do you think that trait is something you're born with, or is it something that you can acquire? You can acquire it, and it's not very difficult.

Burning desire is what makes people persistent. I never think of persistence and a burning desire that I don't think of my courtship. I put more persistence and more burning desire into my courtship than anything else in my life. I don't think you get very far in a courtship without that. What if you could transmute as much emotional feeling about attaining success in your business, or your profession, or your job as you could about selling yourself to the one of your choice? If you haven't tried it, start now. The next time you feel moody or discouraged, change that over into an emotion of courage and faith. A marvelous thing will happen. It'll change the whole chemistry of your whole brain and your whole body, and you'll be much more effective.

ATTRIBUTE #7: DIRECTED IMAGINATION

A well-developed faculty of the imagination is one that is controlled and directed. These distinctions are important, because an imagination that is *not* controlled and directed might be very dangerous. I once did a survey for the Department of Justice in which I made an analysis of all of the men in the federal penitentiaries of the United States. I found that the majority of the men in the penitentiary were there because they had too much imagination. But their

imagination was not controlled and directed in a constructive direction. Imagination is a marvelous thing, but if you
don't have it under control, and if you don't direct it to definite and constructive ends, it may be very dangerous to you.

ATTRIBUTE #8: DECISIVENESS

Do you form definite and prompt decisions when you have
all of the facts in hand with which to make decisions? If you
do not have the habit of making clear-cut decisions promptly
and definitely, you're loafing on the job, procrastinating, and
destroying this very vital thing called personal initiative.
One of the finest places to start practicing personal initiative
is to learn to make decisions firmly and definitely and
quickly, once you have all the facts that are available to you.
I'm not talking about opinions or snap judgments based
upon half-baked evidence. I'm talking about all of the facts
on a given subject which are in your hands and available.
Once you have them, you should then do something with
those facts. You should make up your mind about exactly what
you're going to do and not dilly-dally around, as so many
people do. Otherwise, you'll be in that habit of dilly-dallying
in connection with everything. In other words, you will not
be a person who acts upon his own personal initiative.

ATTRIBUTE #9: FACT-BASED OPINIONS

Get in the habit of basing opinions on facts instead of relying on guesswork. Do you know how many times you act on guesswork in comparison with the number of times that you act upon facts in forming your opinions? It is important to make it your business to get at facts before you form an opinion about anything. Do you know why you shouldn't form an opinion about anything—any time or anywhere—unless it's based upon facts or what you believe to be facts? Because doing so can get you into trouble or cause you to fail. You can go ahead and have opinions. We all do that. You can even give them to somebody else without them asking for them, and we all do that, too. But before you really and truly can safely express an opinion (or have one), you must do a certain amount of research in order to base your opinion upon facts, or what you believe to be facts.

ATTRIBUTE #10: CONTROLLED ENTHUSIASM

Attribute ten is the ability to generate enthusiasm at will and control it. Before you start doing anything with enthusiasm, you have to feel it, don't you? You have to feel the emotion. You have to be quickened, and your mind has to be alerted with some definite objective, or purpose, or motive in order to do something about that motive. You express emotional enthusiasm with your words, with the expression of your face, or by some other form of action.

That word *action* is inseparable from the word *enthusiasm*. You can't separate the two. There are two kinds of enthusiasm: passive enthusiasm and active, controlled enthusiasm.

Passive enthusiasm is enthusiasm that you feel but you give no expression of it whatsoever. There are times when you need to be passive with your enthusiasm, otherwise you'll disclose to other people what goes on in your mind at times when you don't want to.

A great leader or a great executive may have a tremendous amount of enthusiasm, but he'll display that enthusiasm only to whomsoever he pleases and under whatsoever circumstances he pleases. He will not just turn it on all the time, the way you and I might do. The majority of people turn on their enthusiasm and blubber over in it, but this accomplishes nothing. Controlled enthusiasm is enthusiasm turned on at the right time and then turned off at the right time. It's an important thing and your initiative is the only thing that can control that.

If you took that one subject alone, the question of how to turn on and off enthusiasm, and got it to a fine art, you could become a marvelous salesman of anything you want to sell. Did you ever hear of anybody selling anything that didn't feel enthusiasm over what he's trying to sell? Did you ever sell anything without that feeling of enthusiasm over what you were trying to do for the other fellow? You may have thought you did, but you didn't. If you didn't have that feeling of enthusiasm on your own initiative, then you didn't make a sale. Somebody may have bought something from you because he needed it and had to have it, but you had very little to do with it, unless you imparted that feeling to him.

To impart the feeling of enthusiasm to another person, especially when you're selling something, you must first be sold on it yourself. In other words, your enthusiasm starts inside of your own emotional makeup. You must feel enthusiastic, and if you open your mouth to speak, you must speak with enthusiasm. You must put some enthusiasm into the expression of your face. Put on a good, broad smile, because nobody who speaks with enthusiasm has a frown on his face. The two just don't go together.

There are a lot of things that you must learn about this business of expressing enthusiasm if you're going to make the most of it, and all of them involve your personal initiative. You've got to do it. Nobody can do it for you. I can't tell you how to be enthusiastic. I can only tell you the component parts of enthusiasm and how to express it, but the job of actually expressing it is up to you.

ATTRIBUTE #11: TOLERANCE

Let's address the subject of being open-minded. Most of my friends think they're open-minded, and I'd hate to tell them how far off they are on that because I want to keep them as friends. But who can say they're open-minded on everything, on all subjects? Not me. I'm not open-minded on all subjects. I am open-minded on a lot of subjects, the ones I want to be open-minded on.

We shouldn't have any attitude toward anybody under any circumstances unless it's based upon something to justify that attitude, or at least what we believe justifies it.

Do you have any idea how much you deprive yourselves by closing your mind against somebody you don't like, when that person just might be the most beneficial person in the world to you if you only had an open mind toward him? One of the costliest things in an industrial or a business organization is the closed minds of the people that work there. This is important for you to know. The most costly thing in any business organization or in any industry is the closed minds of the people who work there. Some people's minds are closed toward one another, closed toward opportunities, closed toward the people they serve, and closed toward themselves.

When you speak of intolerance, you often think of somebody who doesn't like the other fellow because of his religion or his politics. That just scratches the surface of the real meaning of this subject of intolerance. Intolerance extends to almost every human relationship. **Unless you form the habit of maintaining an open mind on all subjects— toward all people at all times—you'll never be a great thinker, you'll never have a great, magnetic personality, and you certainly will never be very well liked.** You can be very frank with people whom you don't like and who do not like you, as long as they know that you're sincere and that you're speaking with an open mind. The one thing that people will not tolerate is when they recognize they're talking to somebody whose mind is already closed. At that point, what they're saying has no effect whatsoever, regardless of how much value there is to it or how much truth there is in it.

There are a lot of people in this world whose minds are so definitely closed on so many things, that you couldn't crack their mind with a sledgehammer, and you couldn't get an ounce of truth in there if you lived a hundred years. They're closed up tight and hermetically sealed.

ATTRIBUTE #12: DOING MORE THAN EXPECTED

When people are asked if they're in the habit of doing more than they're paid to do, some say they do and some say they don't. Few say they *always* do. Maybe at least part of the time you're in the habit of rendering more service and better service than you're paid to render. This is something that requires your personal initiative. Nobody's going to tell you to do it and nobody's going to expect you to do it. It's entirely within your own prerogative. But, it's probably one of the most important, and one of the most profitable, sources through which you can exercise your own personal initiative.

If I had to pick out the time and the place and the circumstance under which you could make use of your personal initiative most beneficially, it would undoubtedly be in connection with rendering more service and better service than you're paid to render, because you don't have to ask anybody for the privilege of doing that. Also, if you do follow that habit regularly (not just once in a while because that's not very effective), sooner or later the law of increasing returns will pile up dividends for you, and when the dividends come back, they'll come back greatly multiplied. When you start living by this principle of going the extra mile, you can expect unusual things to happen to you, and they'll all be pleasant—every one of them.

ATTRIBUTE #13: TACTFUL DIPLOMACY

Being tactful and having a keen sense of diplomacy covers a broad area. It includes being tactful even in ordinary conversations with other people. But it's worth it because you'll get the cooperation of others more easily if you're tactful. If you tell me that I've *got* to do something, I might say, "Now, wait just a minute," because even if it is something I have to do, when put to me that way, I'm going to set up some resistance right away. But you *could* say to me, "I would very greatly appreciate it if you would do something." The difference is that you knew in the first place that you had a right to demand something of me, but you didn't put it that way.

One of the most impressive things that I learned from Andrew Carnegie at the very beginning of my association with him was that he never commanded anybody to do anything. Never. No matter who he requested to do something, he never commanded him. He always *asked* him if he would do a certain thing. He'd ask, "Would you please do a certain thing?" or, "Will you do the other thing?" You'd be surprised by the amount of loyalty that Mr. Carnegie had from his men. They'd go out of their way for him any time of the day or night because of his tactfulness in dealing with them. If it was necessary for him to discipline one of them, he usually invited him out to the house and gave him a nice five- or six-course steak dinner. He'd really put on the dog. After dinner, the showdown came when they went in the library and he'd start asking questions.

One of his chief secretaries was scheduled to become a member of his mastermind group. This boy found out that he was scheduled for promotion, and it went to his head. He commenced to run around with a bunch of highflyers in Pittsburgh, people who threw cocktail parties and such. Soon, he was taking too much liquor and staying out too late. His eyes would be hanging out on his cheeks when he'd come in the next morning. Mr. Carnegie let this go on for about three months before he invited the fellow over for dinner one evening. After dinner was over, they went into the library and Mr. Carnegie said, "Let's say I'm sitting over there in your chair and you're sitting over here in my chair.

I want to know what you would do if you were in my place and you had a man scheduled for an important promotion, and all of a sudden it seems to have gone to his head. He starts running around with fast company, staying out late at night, drinking too much liquor, and paying too much attention to everything except his job. What in the world would you do in a case of that kind? I'm anxious to know." This young man said, "Mr. Carnegie, I know you're going to fire me, so you might just as well start in and get it over with." Mr. Carnegie said, "No, if I'd have wanted to fire you, I wouldn't have given you a nice dinner and I wouldn't have brought you out to my house. I could have done that down at the office. No, I'm not going to fire you. I'm just going to have you ask yourself that question, and see whether or not you're not in a position to fire yourself. Maybe you are. Maybe you're closer to it than you realize." That man did an about-face, he did become one of Mr. Carnegie's mastermind group, and he did become a millionaire later on. It absolutely saved him from himself. Mr. Carnegie's tactfulness was out of this world. He knew how to handle men; he knew how to get them to examine themselves. It might do a lot of good if you examined yourself in connection with your faults and in connection with your virtues.

Self-analysis is one of the most important forms of personal initiative that you could possibly engage in. I never let a day go by that I don't examine myself to see where I've fallen down, where I'm weak, and where I can make improvements. Every day, I examine what I can do to render more service and better service. I've been doing this for many years, but even today I would be able to find someplace where I can improve, where I can do something better, or how I can render something more. It's a very healthy form of personal initiative, and it's a very interesting one, too, because it'll get you to be honest with yourself.

The worst form of dishonesty is creating *alibis* in your own mind to support your acts, and your deeds, and your thoughts. Instead, examine yourself, find out where you're weak, and then bridge those weaknesses, or get somebody in your mastermind alliance to bridge them for you. That's the kind of personal initiative that most people won't engage in because it involves self-analysis and self-criticism. Would you rather have someone else criticize you and point out your faults, or would you rather criticize yourself and find them?

You don't have to publicize the weaknesses that you find, and you can correct them before anybody else finds out about them. If you do, do a good job of it. But if you wait until somebody else has to call them to your attention, then they become public property. Wait for the other fellow to have to point out your weaknesses to you and they may embarrass you, hurt your pride, or even cause you to build up an inferiority complex. Personal initiative is finding out what your weak spots are, what causes you to be disliked by other people, or why you're not getting ahead as well as some other people.

Get to the point where you know you've got just as much

brains or even more than they have. A great use of initiative is to compare yourself with other people who are succeeding beyond your success. Make comparisons and analyses; see what it is they have that you don't have. You'll be surprised to find out how much you can learn from the other fellow— maybe the fellow you don't like very well, either. You can always learn something from the man who's doing better than you are doing. Sometimes, you can learn something from the fellow who's *not* doing as well as you are doing. You may find out why he's not doing as well. It works both ways.

ATTRIBUTE #14: LISTEN MORE, TALK LESS

Develop the habit of listening much and talking only when necessary. I have never heard of anybody learning anything while he's talking (except that he might learn to not talk so much). The vast majority of people do a lot more talking than they do listening. They seem dead bent on telling the other fellow off, instead of listening to see what the other fellow has to say that they might profit by. Listen much and talk when necessary. Think first and talk last.

ATTRIBUTE #15: OBSERVATION OF DETAILS

Do you have a keen sense of observation of details? Let's say you walk down State Street, or any street in front of

Marshall Fields. At the end of the block, could you give an accurate description of everything you saw in the window?

I once attended a class in Philadelphia in which the teacher emphasized the importance of observation of small details. He said it was the *little* details that made up the successes and the failures of life—not the big ones at all, but the little ones we deem unimportant or don't even observe. As part of our training, he took us out of the hall, down the street one block, across the street, up one block, and back into the hall. We passed at least ten stores, one of which was a hardware store, and in that hardware store window, there were easily five hundred articles. He asked each one of us to take a pad of paper and a pencil along (giving us a crutch for our memory, mind you) and to put down the things that we passed that we thought were important. Take a guess what the greatest number of things that any of us wrote down after going those two blocks: one block down this way, across, and up the other side. We may have passed as many as twenty stores and the greatest number of things that anybody wrote down was fifty-six. The teacher didn't have paper or pencil but he was able to list 746 things. He described each one, told what window it was in, and what part of the window it was in. I didn't accept it until after class, I backtracked him, double-checked, and verified for myself that he was 100 percent accurate. He had trained himself to observe details. Not just a few of them, but all of them.

A good executive, a good leader, or a good anything is a person who observes all the things that are happening around him, the good things and the bad things, the positives and the negatives. He doesn't just happen to notice those things that interest him, he notices *everything* that may interest him or affect his interests. Pay attention to details.

ATTRIBUTE #16: ACCEPT CRITICISM

Do you invite criticism (friendly criticism, that is) from other people? If you don't, you're overlooking one of the finest things that could possibly happen—having a regular source of friendly criticism of what you're doing in life, at least in terms of your major purpose. Invite criticism so you see the things you're doing daily that may offend other people. Of course, you think these things are all right or you wouldn't be doing them, and you'll keep on doing them until someone calls them to your attention.

You need a source of friendly criticism. I'm not talking about people who don't like you and criticize you just because they don't like you. I wouldn't let anyone like that have any effect on me whatsoever. On the other hand, I wouldn't pay too much attention to the person who gives me friendly criticism just because he loves me. You can do yourself just as much damage that way. I've heard it said out in Hollywood that when those stars begin to believe their press agents (and sometimes they do), they're just about through.

You need to have the privilege of looking at yourself

through the eyes of other people. I assure you, we all need it because, when you walk down the street, you don't look the same to the other fellow that sees you as you think you look to yourself. And, when you open your mouth and speak, in conversation or otherwise, what registers in the other man's mind is not always what *you* think is registering at all. You need criticism and you need analysis. You need people to point out to you changes you ought to make, because we all have to make changes as we go along. If we didn't, we wouldn't grow. The majority of people resent any kind of suggestion or criticism whatsoever that differs from what they're doing. They resent anything that would change their way of doing things. Consequently, they do themselves great damage by resenting it.

Get friendly criticism. Someone said that there's no such thing as constructive criticism, but I don't buy that. Not only do I think there is such a thing as constructive criticism, I also think it's absolutely wonderful. Remember that no matter what you're doing, who you are, or how well you do it, you'll never get 100 percent approval from the crowd. Don't expect it and don't be disturbed too much if you don't get it.

ATTRIBUTE #17: LOYALTY

The seventeenth attribute of personal initiative is loyalty to all to whom loyalty is due. Loyalty comes at the top of the list in my book of rules of qualifications of people that I want to be associated with. If you don't have loyalty to the people that have a right to your loyalty, you don't have anything. It doesn't matter how brilliant, or sharp, or smart, or how well educated you are. In fact, the smarter you are, the more dangerous you may be if you can't be loyal to the people who have a right to your loyalty.

Are you loyal to the people that you're supposed to be? Do you stop to think, "Well, now, do I have loyalty? Do I?" If you don't have it, think of the person in connection with which you don't have that loyalty and decide if you want to do something about it. I have loyalty to people that I don't even like because I have a sense of obligation to them. Either I am related to them from business, professionally, or they are in the family circle (and there are a few people *there* that I don't particularly like). I'm loyal to them because I have that obligation. If they want to be loyal to me, that's all right. If they don't, that's their misfortune, not mine. I have the privilege of being loyal, and I'm going to live up to that privilege because of the values I get out of it.

You see, I have to live with this fellow, Mr. Hill. I have to sleep with him and I have to look in the mirror every morning and shave his face. I have to give him a bath every once in a while. I have to be on good terms with him because you can't live with a fellow that closely and not be on good terms with him. "To thine own self be true, and it must follow, as the night the day, thou canst not then be false to any man." Shakespeare never wrote anything more beautiful and more philosophical than that. To your own self be true. Be loyal to yourself, because you have to live with yourself. And if you're loyal to yourself, chances are you'll be loyal to your friends and your business associates.

ATTRIBUTE #18: ATTRACTIVENESS OF PERSONALITY

Attractiveness of personality is necessary to induce cooperation. Is it something you're born with, or is it something that you must do on your own initiative? You can acquire it. Of the twenty-five factors that make up an attractive personality, there's only one trait that you're either born with or you're not. Only one. Personal magnetism. You can even do something about that.

You can do something about every one of the other twenty-four factors, because everyone is subject to cultivation through personal initiative. You've got to do it yourself. First of all, you've got to know how you stand on each of these points. Don't just take your own word for it. Get your wife or your husband or somebody else to tell you.

Sometimes an enemy will tell you where you fall down. Enemies are good things to have once in a while because they don't pull punches. If you'll examine what your enemies or those who do not like you say about you, chances are that you'll learn something of value. One thing you'll learn is how to make sure that whatever disparaging thing they say isn't true about you. In other words, *make sure* that whatever they say won't be true, by being so straight on the road that whatever they say about you that might be derogatory *won't* be true. That's an advantage, isn't it? Don't be afraid of enemies or people who don't like you, because they may say things that put you on the track to discover something that you need to know about yourself.

Years ago, a salesman who came to see me said that he had been with his company about ten years. During that time he had a wonderful record, received several promotions, and was making big money. However, six months prior to visiting me, his sales suddenly began to go down. Customers that used to give him their business would frown on him. I noticed he had on one of these big Texas ten-gallon hats, and so I asked him, "By the way, how long have you had that hat?" "Well," he said, "I got it about six months ago, down in Texas." I asked, "Listen, fella, are you selling in Texas?" He said, "No, I don't make Texas very often." I said, "Well, listen, wear that hat only when you go to Texas, because your other customers don't like that hat and it doesn't look good on you." He said, "Would that make any difference?" I said, "You'd be surprised what a difference it'll make to your personal appearance. Some people just won't do business with you if they don't like the way you look."

You *can* do something about your personality. You can

find out the traits you have that irritate other people and you can correct those traits. You have to make the discovery yourself, or you have to get somebody who is frank enough to do it for you.

ATTRIBUTE #19: CONCENTRATION

Develop the capacity to concentrate full attention upon one subject at a time. When you start to make a point, exploit it right down to its final analysis, make a climax, and then get on to your next point. Don't try to cover too many points at one time; if you do, you'll not cover any points at all. It's easy to make that mistake in your relations with other people, in selling, in public speaking, or whatever you're doing. It used to be one of my most outstanding weaknesses. I used to do just that very thing. Fortunately, I had a man come to me and call that to my attention, and I think no training that I ever had in public speaking was as valuable as that. And it was free. He didn't charge me anything for it. He said, "You have a wonderful command of English, you have a marvelous capacity for enthusiasm, and you have a tremendous storehouse of illustrations that are interesting. But," he said, "you have a bad habit of taking off after something out there that's not related to the point you're making, and then coming back later on and picking up the point—in the meantime, it's gotten cold." Grade yourself on that capacity to concentrate full attention upon one subject at a time. Whether you're speaking, thinking, writing, teaching, or whatever you do, concentrate on one thing at a time.

ATTRIBUTE #20: LEARN FROM MISTAKES

Get in the habit of learning from your mistakes, because if you don't learn from your mistakes, you might just as well not make them! If that isn't a truism, tell me what is. I never see a man duplicating a mistake over and over again that I don't think of that old Chinese aphorism: "If a man fool me once, shame on the man. But if he fool me twice, shame on me." There are a lot of people that should say, "Shame on me" because they just don't seem to learn from mistakes at all.

ATTRIBUTE #21: ACCEPT RESPONSIBILITY
FOR SUBORDINATES

It's important to be willing to accept full responsibility for the mistakes of one's subordinates. If you have subordinates and they make mistakes, it's you who have failed and not the subordinates. Either train him how to do the thing right, or else put him in some other job where you won't have to supervise him. Let somebody else do that. But the responsibility is yours if the person working under you is subordinate to you.

ATTRIBUTE #22: GIVE OTHERS CREDIT

Successful people have a habit of adequately recognizing the merits and abilities of others. Don't try to steal the thunder from the other fellow. If he's done a good job, give him full credit. Give him double credit. Give him more than he's entitled to rather than less. A little pat on the back has never been known to hurt anybody when you know he has done a good job.

The most successful people like recognition, and sometimes people work harder for recognition than they will for anything else. Some people are incorruptible, and no matter what you do, you can't over-flatter them. They know what their capacity is, and if you go beyond that, they begin to be suspicious of you. Most people, however, I believe are corruptible when it comes to this business of flattery. You can over-flatter them, and they will commence to believe it. Unfortunately, that's bad for them and for you, too. There was a book that was widely distributed all over this country and the central theme in that book was, if you want to get along in the world, flatter people. Flattery is not only one of the oldest weapons of the world, it's also one of the most deadly and one of the most dangerous. Now, I like approbation. I like those people that happened to know me and complimented me. I enjoyed it. But if one of them had said, "Well, now, Mr. Hill, I appreciate all that you've done for me and all that sort of thing. By the way, would you mind if I came around the house tonight? I'd like to talk to you about a business proposition," I'd have immediately suspected that he flattered me in order to get some of my time and get some benefit from me. Too much flattery or too much commendation is not so good.

ATTRIBUTE #23: THE GOLDEN RULE

Apply the Golden Rule principle in all human relationships. One of the finest things you can do for yourself is to put yourself in the other fellow's position. When you make any decision, or engage in any transaction involving the other fellow, put yourself in the other fellow's position before you make a final decision. If you do, chances are you will always do the fair thing by the other man.

ATTRIBUTE #24: POSITIVE ATTITUDE

There has already been much said about having a positive mental attitude at all times. (See Principle #7 to learn more about positive mental attitude.)

ATTRIBUTE #25: TAKE RESPONSIBILITY

Accept full responsibility for any task that you've undertaken. Don't come back with an alibi. The one thing at which the majority of people are the most adept is alibis, creating a reason why they didn't succeed, or didn't get the job done, or didn't do the thing they said they'd do. If the people who create alibis would put half as much time into *doing* the thing right, or *trying* to do it right, that they put into explaining why they *didn't*, they'd get a lot further in life and be much better off. Generally speaking, the man who is the most clever at creating an alibi is the most inefficient man in the whole works. This kind of person makes a profession of spinning alibis, or thinking them up in advance, so that if they are called on the carpet or get caught over the barrel, they have an answer.

There is only one thing that counts, and that's success. Results are what count. Results. I once wrote an epigram covering this subject that I thought was very effective. **Success requires no explanations; failure permits no alibis.** In other words, if it's a success, you don't need any explanations, and if it's a failure, all the alibis and explanations in the world won't do any good. It's still a failure, isn't it?

ATTRIBUTE #26: FOCUS ON
WHAT YOU WANT

Keep your mind occupied with what you desire, and not with what you don't. The vast majority of instances in which people engage in personal initiative are in connection with the things they *don't* want. That is where most people don't have to be taught to take the personal initiative. They really work at it, thinking about all the things they don't want, and that's precisely what they get out of life—the things that they think about, the things that they attune their minds to.

Here's where that word *transmute* can come into play. Instead of thinking about the things you don't want, the things you fear, the things you distrust, the things you dislike, think about all the things you like, all the things you want, and all the things you're going to become determined to get.

POSITIVE MENTAL ATTITUDE

One of the most important of all the principles of success is Principle #7, a Positive Mental Attitude. This is the formula with which the entire philosophy can be best assimilated and put into practical use. You cannot get the most out of the other sixteen principles without understanding and applying this one. Take this lecture to heart and truly make this principle a part of you.

In this lecture, Dr. Hill gives a number of lists of elements that go into developing and using a positive mental attitude. Write all of them down so you can refer to them.

Dr. Hill also emphasizes two things that nature discourages and severely penalizes. One is a vacuum or emptiness. The other is a lack of activity, or idleness. Consider the price of idleness: if you tied one of your arms to your side, immobilizing it for a period of time, it would atrophy, wither, and ultimately become useless. Consider the price of emptiness: if you do not take control of your power of thought, if you leave your mind vacuous and open to outside influences, it will fill up with negative thoughts, and be tossed and torn by the stray winds of circumstance and chance. An empty mind is fertile ground for the seeds of failure.

It is a great and simple truth that success attracts more success, while failure attracts more failure. With a negative mental attitude, you can believe in fear and frustration, and your mind will attract you to an experience of them. But with a positive mental attitude, you can put your mind to work believing that you have the right to achieve the riches you desire and your belief will infallibly guide you toward them.

Let me tell you something that happened last Saturday. I went down to the travel agency to get my ticket changed so I could come back on Monday instead of Sunday. When I walked in, the manager of the travel agency grabbed my hand when he saw who I was, and he introduced himself and started in to selling me *Think and Grow Rich*. While he was holding my hand and talking to me, along came a friend of his who was connected with one of the airlines. When his friend heard the name Napoleon Hill, he grabbed the other hand and started to sell me *Think and Grow Rich*. He said, "You may be interested in knowing that before I went with the airline, I had a sales organization with approximately a hundred people, and I required every salesman to have all of your books. That was a must." Well, I felt pretty good. Outside, I encountered two very nice-looking young ladies standing on the sidewalk, giving out election literature. As I passed by, one of them said, "Aren't you Napoleon Hill? I was at a woman's club about two years ago when you delivered an address. This is my cousin. Both of our husbands are very successful now due to the fact they have read your books." I went on over to my car, and a policeman was making out a ticket. After all this talk, there was a payoff. You see, I put a penny in the parking meter, thinking that twelve minutes would be all I would need on the meter. But as I stopped to bathe my vanity in all this nice conversation, when I got to the meter, a policeman was halfway finished making out a ticket. He didn't know whose car it was, but I walked up to him and said, "Now, you wouldn't do that to Napoleon Hill, would you?" He said, "Who?" I said, "Napoleon Hill." He said, "No, I wouldn't do that to Napoleon Hill, but I certainly would do it to you." I showed him my credit card and my driver's license. And he said, "Well, I'll be a monkey's uncle!" He took the ticket and tore it up and said we'd just forget about that. And he said, "You may be interested in knowing that I'm on the Glendale Police Force as a result of reading your book, *Think and Grow Rich*."

> *Nothing constructive and worthy of man's efforts ever has been or ever will be achieved, except that which comes from a positive mental attitude based on definiteness of purpose, activated by a burning desire, and intensified until the burning desire is elevated to the plane of applied faith.*

Here are five different conditions of the mind that lead to a positive mental attitude. In other words, these five are precursors to a positive mental attitude: wishes, hopes, burning desire, applied faith, and action.

#1: BEGIN WITH WISHES

Everybody has a stock of wishes. They wish for this and they wish for that and they wish for the other thing. We all have wishes. Well, nothing very much happens when you just wish for things, does it? No, nothing happens. Well, then you go a little bit further and you become curious. You put in a lot of time through idle curiosity. And do you think anything ever happens worthwhile in connection with the expression of idle curiosity? However, sometimes you can and you do consume a lot of time with idle curiosity, don't you? Sometimes, you put in a lot of time in studying what your neighbors do or not do, what your competitors do or not do, all just out of idle curiosity. That's not leading to a positive mental attitude.

#2: WISHES LEAD TO HOPE

A step above wishes is hope, when your wishes take on a more concrete form. They become hopes of achievement, hopes of attainment, hopes of accomplishment, and hopes of accumulation of things that you want. However, a hope by itself is not very effective. We all have a flock of hopes, but not all of us who have hopes have success. We just hope for success. Hoping is better than wishing. Because the difference between a hope and a wish is that hope is a beginning to take on faith. That's the idea of hope. You're transmuting a wish into that very desirable state of mind known as faith.

#3: HOPE FUELS BURNING DESIRE

At some point, you step up your mental attitude to where your hopes are transmuted into something else, known as a burning desire. There's a difference between a burning desire and an ordinary desire. A burning desire is an intensified desire based upon hope, and based upon definiteness of purpose. In this way, a burning desire is actually an obsessional desire, fueled by a motive. You cannot have a burning desire without a motive or motives back of it, and the more motives you can have for a definite thing, the quicker you will have turned your emotions into what is known as a burning desire. However, that's not enough. There's something else. There's another state of mind you must have before you can be sure of success.

#4: APPLIED FAITH

If you have transmuted wishes, idle curiosity, hopes, and even a burning desire, you have stepped all those up into something still higher, and that is applied faith. What is the difference between applied faith and ordinary belief in things?

#5: ACTION

The word *applied* might well be synonymous to *action*. You might say active faith. Applied faith and active faith are the same: faith backed by action, something that you do about it. A prayer brings positive results only when it is expressed in a positive mental attitude. The most effective prayers are those expressed by individuals who have conditioned their minds to habitually think in terms of a positive mental attitude.

Do you have any idea of the amount of time you devote each day in thinking of the negative side of things in comparison with the positive side? Wouldn't it be interesting if you kept a tabulation for two or three days of the exact amount of time you put into thinking about the no-can-do side of life and the can-do side, or the positive side and the negative side? Even the most successful people would be astounded to find out how many hours they spend each day in negative thinking. The very outstanding successes in the world are the ones that put in very little time, if any, thinking on the negative side. The great leaders put in all their time thinking on the positive side.

I once asked Henry Ford if there was anything in the world that he wanted or wanted to do that he couldn't do, and he said no, he didn't believe there was. I asked him if there ever had been. He said yes, back in the early days before he had learned how to use his mind. And I said, "Just what do you mean by that?" He said, "When I want a thing or want to do a thing, I start in finding out what I can do about it and start doing *that*, and I don't bother about what I can't do, because I just let that alone." There's a world of philosophy wrapped up in that statement. He put his mind into doing something about the part that he could do something about, and thinking about that, and not about the part that he couldn't do anything about.

I think if you put a problem—a difficult problem—to

the majority of people, they will immediately begin to tell you all of the reasons why the problem can't be solved. And if there are some things about the problem that are favorable and some that are unfavorable, most people will see the things that are unfavorable first and often never see the favorable side. I don't believe there are any problems in which you can't do something, or in which there are no favorable sides. I can't think of a single problem that I might confront that wouldn't have a favorable side to it. If nothing else, the favorable side would be that I would say that if it's a problem I can solve, I will solve it, and if it's a problem I can't solve, I'll not worry about it. But when the majority of people are confronted with difficult propositions or problems that they can't solve, they start worrying and they go into a negative state of mind. You don't accomplish anything worthwhile when you're in that state of mind.

You're only muddying the water when you make your mind negative. You never accomplish anything worthwhile.

To do anything worthwhile, you have to learn to keep your mind positive all the time. **A positive mental attitude attracts opportunities and a negative mental attitude repels them.** Do you think repelling opportunities has anything to do with your merit or right to have opportunities? Absolutely not. You may have the right to all of the good things in life. You may be entitled to them. But if you have a negative mental attitude, you will repel the opportunities leading to the attainment of those things. So your job is to keep your mind positive so it will attract to you the things that you want, the things that you desire, and the things that you are going after.

Have you ever stopped to think why prayer generally doesn't bring anything about—except a negative result? Have you ever stopped to wonder about that? I believe the biggest stumbling block of most people in all religions is that they don't understand why prayer sometimes brings the negative results, or why it generally brings negative results. You couldn't expect anything else, because there's a law that governs that. The law is that your mind attracts to you the counterpart of the things that the mind is feeding upon. There's no exception to that rule. It's a natural law and there are no exceptions for anybody. So if you want to attract (in prayer or otherwise) the things that you desire, you have to make your mind positive. You not only have to believe, but you have to put action back of that belief and transmute it into faith—applied faith. And you can't have applied faith in a negative state of mind; the two just don't go together.

People who recognize what a powerful influence one's daily environment has on the maintenance of a positive mental attitude often use constructive mottoes. Placing mottoes printed in large letters in all departments and changing them weekly *positivized* the entire industrial plant of the R. J. Letourneau Company, with two thousand employees. Those mottoes were written for a purpose. Every department in that great, sprawling plant of the Letourneau Company had those mottoes placed there regularly, sometimes daily in the cafeteria and weekly in the other departments. The mottoes were written in letters half a foot high so that you could read them all the way across the building. And believe me, every time they walked into their department, they saw that motto. By the way, we had a funny experience with them. I was standing in the cafeteria one day when a motto was placed up. The cafeteria was the place where all the men lined up to get their meals at noontime, and we could catch them all there at one time or another during the day. The cafeteria motto read, "Just remember that your real boss is the one who walks around under your hat." Now, I'd think that would be as plain as mud to anybody that would read it. It would mean that you're the real boss in the final analysis. But I heard a man let out an Indian yell and he said, "Boy, that's what I've always said. I've always known that my foreman was a louse."

STEPS FOR TRANSMUTATION

There is a method by which one may transmute failure into success, poverty into riches, sorrow into joy, and fear into faith. The transmutation must start with a positive mental attitude, because success, riches, and faith do not make good bedfellows with a negative mental attitude. The transmutation procedure is simple. Here it is, and you can very well afford to come back to this many times, assimilate it, and make it your own.

#1: When failure overtakes you, start thinking of it

as if it had been a success. To most people this seems difficult to do but it's really not. Think of it as what would have happened if it had been a success instead of a failure. See yourself in the success side of the situation, and not in the failure side. Imagine the circumstances of the failures as being a success. Start also looking for the seed of an equivalent benefit—*which comes with every failure*—and that is where you will be able to transmute the failure into success, because every adversity, every failure, and every defeat has the seed of an equivalent benefit. If you search for that seed, you will not take a negative mental attitude toward the circumstance, you will take a positive mental attitude, because you're sure to find that seed. You may not find it the first time you look for it, but eventually you will find it, if you keep on looking for it.

#2: **When poverty threatens to catch up with you, or has actually caught up, start thinking of it as riches, and visualize the riches and all the things that you would wish to do with actual riches.** Start looking for the seed of an equivalent benefit of poverty. I remember when I was a little boy sitting on the bank of the river down in Wise County, where I was born, just after my mother died and before my stepmother came along. I was hungry. I didn't have enough food. I was sitting there on the bank of the river wondering if I could catch some fish, maybe fry it, and have something to eat. I don't know what caused me to do this, but I shut my eyes and looked into the future. I saw myself going away, becoming famous and wealthy, and coming back to that very spot, charging up the river on a horse, a mechanical horse that was run by steam. I could see the steam pouring out his nostrils. I could hear his horse-shoes clicking on the rocks. It was so vivid to me. In other words, I built myself into a state of ecstasy there in that hour of poverty, and need, and want, and hunger.

Years passed, and the time came when I drove my Rolls-Royce to that very spot, the car that I paid $22,500 for. I drove my Rolls-Royce to that very spot, and I went back and imagined again that childhood scene where I had been there in poverty, in want, and in hunger. And I said, "Well, I don't know whether my imagination back in the early days had anything to do with it or not. Maybe it did." Maybe I kept alive that hope and eventually translated that hope into faith and eventually that faith brought me not only a steam horse, but something much more valuable and much more costly than a steam horse.

Look forward and imagine the things that you want to do. Transmute unfavorable circumstances and adversities into something that's pleasant. By that, I mean switching your mind away from thinking about the unpleasant things over to something that's pleasant.

#3: When fear overtakes you, remember that fear is only faith in reverse gear, and start thinking in terms of faith by seeing yourself translating faith into whatever circumstance or things you desire. I don't suppose any-body ever escapes experiencing the seven basic fears at one time or another, and most people experience them all the way through life. But if you allow fear to take possession and grip you, it will not only become a habit, it will also attract to you all of the things that you don't want. You have to learn to deal with fear by mentally transmuting it or translating it or transforming it into the opposite of fear—in other words, faith.

If you fear poverty, commence thinking of yourself in terms of opulence and of money. Think of ways and means that you're going to earn that money, acquire it, and what you'll do with it after you get it. There's no end to the daydreaming you can do; it's far better to daydream about the money you're going to have than it is to fear the poverty that you know you already have. There's no virtue and no benefit in bemoaning the fact that you are poverty-stricken or that you need money and you don't know how to get it.

There isn't anything in this world that I need that money can buy, or that anything else can buy, that I can't get if I want it. I don't think in terms of what I can't get, I think in terms of what I can get, and I've been doing that for a long time. It's wonderful to condition your mind to be positive. When the circumstances arise where you need a positive mental action, you'll be in the habit of always reacting in a positive way rather than a negative way.

You don't get a positive mental attitude just by wishing for it. You get it by weaving rope, a cord at a time, day by day, little by little. You don't just get it overnight.

HELPFUL INVISIBLE GUIDES

Create in your imagination an army of invisible guides who will take care of all your needs and all your desires—and there they are. You've heard me speak of my invisible guides, and if you weren't in this philosophy, if you didn't understand metaphysics, you'd probably say that was a very fantastic system that I've worked out. I assure you, it's not a fantastic system. I assure you that it looks after all of my needs and all of my wants. I'll admit that last week, I became a little bit careless and the guide to sound physical health let me down for a day or two. But I did something out of it. I came to his rescue. I gave him a jab in the ribs and woke him up, and believe me, I've got more energy now than I've had since we started this course. So it's a good thing that I had that little cold, because it made me express gratitude to this guide of sound physical health, not neglect him.

I fully realize that these guides are a creation of my own imagination. I'm not kidding myself or anybody else about that. But for all practical purposes, they represent real entities and real people. Each one is performing the exact duty that I assigned to him, and is doing it all the time.

GUIDE FOR PHYSICAL SOUND HEALTH

The first of these guides is the guide to physical sound health. Why do you suppose I put that as number one? What in the world could the mind do with a body that has to be supported by crutches all the time? A good, strong physical body is the temple of the mind; it has to be sound, it has to be healthy, and it has to have plenty of energy. When you turn on your enthusiasm, if there's no energy, you can't generate something out of nothing, because you've got to have a store of energy. Energy is both physical and mental in nature. I don't know of anybody who can express intense enthusiasm when their body is a series of aches and pains.

The first duty to yourself is to your physical body. See that it responds to all of your needs at all times, and does the thing that it is supposed to do. You need a little bit more help than what you can give during the day, and so when you lay your body down, nature goes to work on it, giving it a tune-up and a working over. You have to have this trained entity called the guide to sound health to do that job, to supervise it and to see that it's done properly.

GUIDE TO FINANCIAL PROSPERITY

The second most important guide is the guide to financial prosperity. Do you know of anybody that can be of great service to others without money? How long can you get along without money? You've got to have money. You've got to have a money consciousness, and this entity that you build up through this guide gives you a money consciousness.

My guide is so controlled, however, that he doesn't make money. My God, I don't permit that! I don't permit myself to become greedy, to want an over amount of money, or to pay too much for the money that I get. I pay enough, but not too much. I know people who pay too much and who also die too young because they put too much effort into accumulating money that they didn't need and couldn't use. The only purpose it serves is that it causes their descendants to fight over it after they pass on. That's not going to happen to me. I want enough, but not too much. It's my guide's business to see that I don't want too much and that I stop when I get enough.

This money-getting business becomes a kind of a vicious circle with a lot of people. You say, "Well, I'll make my first million, then I'll quit." I remember when Bing Crosby announced to his brother (who was also his manager) that when they made their first $50,000, that would be enough and they would quit. They now make over a million dollars every year and they're still struggling in the rat race and working harder than ever. I'm not speaking in a derogatory manner. Bing's a friend of mine, and I greatly admire him. I'm referring to all people who pay too much to get things that they don't need.

This is a philosophy dealing with economic success, but success doesn't require destroying your life and dying too young because you tried to get too much of anything. Stop when you get enough. Make better use of the things you have right now, instead of trying to get a lot of more things that you're not going to make any use of at all. There's a wonderful statement in the Bible. I won't translate it verbatim, but it basically says, "Not too much, not too little of anything." Not too much, not too little—just enough of everything. Learning what is enough and not too much is one of the blessings of this philosophy. It gives you a balanced life. Learn for yourself what is enough and what's too much.

GUIDE TO PEACE OF MIND

What good is it if you owned everything in the world and collected a royalty from every living person, if you didn't have peace of mind? I've had the privilege of intimately knowing the most outstanding, the most successful, and the richest men that this country has ever produced. I've slept in their houses, ate with them, known their families, their wives, and their children. And I've seen what happened to their children after they died and passed on. I know the importance of learning to live a balanced life that lets you make your occupation (or your daily labor or whatever game that you're getting joy out of) *and* have peace of mind along the way. It's not something to be abhorred or dreaded, but a sort of game you play as ardently as a man would play a game of golf or any other game that he loves.

I have always said that one of the sins of civilization is that so few people are engaged in a labor of love, a thing that they like to do. Most people are doing things because they have to eat and sleep and have clothes to wear. Let me tell you that when a man or a woman gets in a position where he or she can do a thing for the sake of love—because they *want* to do it—they're really fortunate. This philosophy leads to that very condition, but you'll never attain that position until you learn to maintain a positive mental attitude a major portion of the time.

The men that collaborated with me in the building of this philosophy represented every outstanding success in every field of their era. Out of all of those men, there was only one that I could say even vaguely approached having peace of mind along with his other successes: John Burroughs. Without doubt, he was the one that came nearest it, and the one that came next nearest to it was Mr. Edison. I would place Mr. Carnegie as number three and I'll tell you why. In the latter part of his years, he practically lost his mind trying to find ways and means of disgorging himself of his fortune and giving it away where it would do no harm. It almost drove him crazy. His major obsession in the latter part of his days was to get this philosophy well organized while he was living and into the hands of the people. He wanted this philosophy to provide them with the knowhow by which they could acquire material things, including money, without violating the rights of other people. That's what he wanted more than any other, more than anything else in the world. Unfortunately, Mr. Carnegie died in 1919, before I translated this into writing and before I wrote the first books on it. Until then, he checked (and double-checked) with me on fifteen of the seventeen principles.

There are two people that I've always regretted didn't

live to see me in the day of my triumph, because they saw me in the days of my discouragement and opposition. Those two people were my stepmother and my sponsor, Andrew Carnegie. It would have been a great joy to me—and enough compensation for a lifetime of effort—if those two wonderful people could have seen the results of their handiwork in manipulating me and directing me when I needed direction. I'm not so sure that they are not looking over my shoulder now.

Sometimes I'm sure somebody is looking over my shoulder, because I say and do things that are beyond my reasonable intelligence. I have noticed, more so in recent years than ever, that the things that I do which might be called brilliant and outstanding are always done by this man who's standing here, looking over my shoulder. In any emergency that calls for making important decisions, I can almost feel that man telling me what decision to make. I can almost turn around and imagine he's standing there in person. There is an influence there; there's no two ways about it. I could never have done what has been done in connection with this philosophy if I had nothing but the collaboration of those five or six hundred men that helped me. That wouldn't have been enough. Believe me, I have had more than that. I haven't said anything about it because I don't want to make people feel that I have been favored, or that I have anything that anybody else can't have.

My honest opinion is that I don't have anything that you

can't have. Whatever sources of inspiration I am drawing upon, you can have that same source. It's just as available to you as it is to me. I believe that with all of my heart.

GUIDES OF HOPE AND FAITH

I see these as twins, the guides of hope and faith. How far would you get in life if you didn't have that eternal burning flame of hope and faith working in your soul? There wouldn't be anything worth working or worth living for, would there?

You have to have a system for keeping your mind positive, as a resistance to all the things that can destroy hope and faith. People, circumstances, and all sorts of things you can't control pop up in your life. You've got to have a system as antidote to those things to offset them, something that you can manipulate and draw upon. I know of no better system than these eight guides that I have adopted because they work for me. I've taught them to a great many other people for whom they worked just as well as for me.

GUIDES OF LOVE AND ROMANCE

Another set of twin guides are the guides of love and romance. I don't believe that anything worthwhile can be accomplished unless you romanticize whatever you're doing. If you don't put some romance into whatever you're doing, you don't get any fun out of it. And if there were no love in your heart, you wouldn't be a human being, because the main difference between the lower animals and the human being is that humans are capable of expressing the emotion of love. Love is a great builder of geniuses and of leaders; it's a great builder and maintainer of sound health. It's absolutely true without exception that to have the great capacity to love is to have the privilege of rubbing elbows with genius. The two guides of love and romance work to keep me friendly with what I'm doing and keep me young in body and mind. Believe me, they do just that. Not only do they keep me young in body and mind, they also keep me enthusiastic, sold on what I'm doing and without any drudgery in it. In other words, there's no such thing as hard work because I don't work at anything. I play at everything I do. Everything is a labor of love.

I recognize that before you get in a position where you can economically forget about earning a living, there's something that you have to think about that maybe takes a little of the pleasure out of work. But you can develop a system that'll make everything that you do a labor of love for the time being, whether you're washing dishes or digging ditches or anything else. When I go home, I help Annie Lou wash the dishes, not because she couldn't do it but because I want to feel that I'm not too good to help wash the dishes. And I get great joy out of doing it. I'm not above working in the garden either, because if I didn't do it, Annie Lou would do it while I'm gone and deprive me of the pleasure. It gives me a nice tan and good health.

Learn to live the simple life, to be a human being instead of a stiff shirt or something else that you don't want to be (and nobody really wants to be). Learn to get love and romance into your life, and learn to have a system whereby that habit of love and romance will express itself in everything you do.

GUIDE FOR OVERALL WISDOM

The guide to overall wisdom is the comptroller of the other seven. His business is to keep them active, eternally engaged in your service. This guide adjusts you to every circumstance of your life, pleasant or unpleasant, so that you benefit by that circumstance. I can truthfully say that nothing comes to the mill of my life that isn't grist. I make grist out of everything. The more unpleasant things that come, the more grist I get out of them, because I doubly grind them to make sure they won't be anything else but grist.

Recognize that no experience in life is ever lost, whether it's good or bad. No experience is ever lost if you make the right adaptation of yourself to it. You can always profit by every experience in life if you have a system for doing it. Of course, if you let your emotions run wild and bring these unpleasant experiences into adulthood, you'll attract more unpleasant experiences than pleasant ones. But the peculiar thing about unpleasant circumstances is that they're cowardly. Get to where you will say, "Come on over here, little fellow. I've got a harness right here, and I'm going to put you to work." When they know you're going to put them to work, they find business around the corner, and they don't come your way so often.

If you fear unpleasant circumstances, they'll crowd down on you in flocks. They'll come in by the back door and the front door. They'll come when you're not expecting them or when you're unprepared to deal with them. I don't particularly invite unpleasant experiences, but if they are foolish enough to come my way, they'll find themselves ground up in my mill of life. Sure as anything, I'll make grist of them—but I'll not go down under them.

OBSTACLES TO POSITIVE THINKING

Eternal vigilance is the price one must pay to maintain a positive mental attitude, because of these unpleasant experiences and other natural opposites—the obstacles to positive thinking.

#1: Tendency of the negative self to maneuver for power over you. There are entities working in your makeup all the time, constantly maneuvering to gain power over you on the negative side of life. You have to be on constant alert to see that those entities don't take you over.

#2: Accumulated fears, doubts, and self-imposed limitations. You have to deal with them constantly lest they get the upper hand and become the dominating influence in your mind.

#3: Negative influences, especially negative people. Negative influences include people who are negative, people that you work closely with, and people that you live with—maybe even some of your own relatives. If you aren't careful, you'll respond in kind and become as negative as they are. It may be necessary for you to live in the same house with somebody who's negative, but it's not necessary for you to be negative just because you're in the house with somebody who is. I'll admit, it can be a little bit difficult for you to immunize yourself against that kind of an influence, but you can do it. I have done it. Mahatma Gandhi did it. Look what he did with immunizing himself against things he didn't want.

#4: Inborn negative traits. These are the traits you may have brought with you from birth. They can be transmuted into positive traits, once you ferret them out and find out what they are. I'm convinced that there are a lot of people who are born with natural traits of a negative nature. For instance, take a person who's born in an environment of poverty, where all of his relatives are poverty-stricken and all of the neighbors are poverty-stricken. From birth, he saw nothing but poverty, felt nothing but poverty, and heard nothing but poverty talk. That was the condition I was born in, and I know you can be born with that trait. One of the most difficult things that I had to do was to whip this inborn fear of poverty.

#5: Worry over the lack of money and the lack of progress in your business, profession, or calling in life.

You can either put in most of your time worrying over things, or you can transmute that state of mind into working out ways and means of overcoming those worries. Think about the positive side instead of the negative side. Worrying over the negative side is not going to do anything except to get you in deeper and deeper and deeper. That's all it's going to do.

#6: Unrequited love and unbalanced emotional frustrations with the opposite sex. You don't have to let unrequited love affairs destroy your balance of mind, as so many people do. It's up to you to do something about it, to maintain a positive mental attitude, and to recognize that your first duty is to yourself. Get control of yourself and do not allow anybody, emotionally or otherwise, to upset your equilibrium. The Creator didn't intend that to be done, and you shouldn't let it be done either.

#7: Unsound health, either real or imaginary. You can worry an awful lot about the things that you think might physically happen to you but never do. In the Materia Medica, we call it hypochondria—that's a two-and-a-half dollar word with the doctors. Well, it used to be two and a half dollars but now it's five dollars, and sometimes a lot more than five dollars!

You can spend an awful lot of time becoming negative if you don't have a positive mental attitude toward your health, or if you don't develop and build up a health consciousness. Think in terms of health. Your mental attitude has a tremendous amount to do with what happens to your physical body. There's no doubt about it. Try it anytime. Have you ever had the experience when you're not feeling well, and some good piece of news comes along, how quickly you snap out of it? Maybe you weren't feeling so badly, but this good news did away with the feeling that you had.

#8: Intolerance and lack of an open mind. These two things give some people a lot of trouble in maintaining a negative mental attitude.

#9: Greed for more material possessions than you need. Once again, this is about the things that you accumulate, the price that you have to pay, the things that you have to conquer in order to have a positive mental attitude.

#10: Lack of a definite major purpose.

#11: Lack of a definite philosophy by which to live and guide your life. Did you know that the vast majority of people have no philosophy to live by? Without a philosophy, they live by hook or by crook, by chance, and by circumstance. They're like a dry leaf on the bosom of the wind, going whichever way the wind blows. There's nothing they can do about it because they have no philosophy of life. They have no set of rules to go by. Trusting to luck and to misfortune, misfortune generally rules. You have to have a philosophy that you can live by. There are many fine philosophies that you can die by, but I'm much more interested in one that you can live by, and that's what we're studying here.

This is a philosophy that you can live by in such a way that the neighbors around you look upon you as someone desirable. They feel happy to have you there and you feel happy to be there. You'll not only enjoy prosperity and contentment and peace of mind, but you'll reflect that to everybody that comes into contact with you. That's the way people should live. That's the kind of a mental attitude people should live by.

#12: Letting others do your thinking for you. If you allow others to do your thinking, you'll never have a positive mental attitude because you won't have your own mind.

TWELVE GREAT AND ENDURING RICHES

Everyone desires to be rich, but not everyone knows what constitutes enduring riches. There are twelve great and enduring riches. I want you to familiarize yourself with them because before anybody can become rich, they must have a fairly well-balanced proportion of all of these twelve great riches. I want you to notice where I place money relative to its importance in regard to the others. It's number twelve, because there are eleven other things that are even more important than money if you're going to have a well-rounded-out, well-balanced life.

1: Positive mental attitude.

2: Sound physical health.

3: Harmony in human relations.

4: Freedom from fear.

5: Hope of future achievement.

6: Applied faith.

7: Willingness to share one's blessings.

8: To be engaged in a labor of love.

9: An open mind on all subjects. Tolerance toward all people.

10: Complete self-discipline.

11: The wisdom with which to understand people.

12: Money.

SELF-DISCIPLINE

The eighth principle of *Your Right to Be Rich* is Self-Discipline, but not self-discipline as you might normally think of it. Dr. Hill gives this vital asset a very specific and significant meaning: to take possession of your own mind. The only thing over which you have complete, unchallenged control is your power of thought. Developing control over yourself, developing control over your mind, focusing on the things you want, and ignoring the things you do not want are essential to achieving success. If you do not control your thoughts, you cannot control your deeds.

In its simplest terms, the principle of self-discipline teaches you how to develop control, causing you to think first and act afterward. Through the application of this principle, the power made available by each of the other principles of this philosophy becomes condensed, focused, and ready for practical application on a daily basis. The power you can unleash and the

benefits you may receive are boundless. Dr. Hill will
help you appreciate the potential that awaits you
once you understand and apply the principle of self-
discipline in your life.

The first edition of the book *Success, Unlimited* includes one
of my contributions, called "A Challenge to Life." This
challenge to life is my reaction to one of the worst defeats
that I've ever had in my entire career. It illustrates how I
transmute an unpleasant circumstance into something useful. When this circumstance happened, I had real reason to
go out and fight—I don't mean to fight mentally or orally,
but, instead, to fight physically. If I had to settle business
from behind pine trees with six-shooters, it would have
been justified under the circumstances. But instead, I elected
to do something that would damage no one and that would
benefit myself. I elected to express myself through this essay,
which says,

*Life, you can't subdue me because I refuse to take your dis-
cipline too seriously. When you try to hurt me, I laugh, and
the laughter knows no pain. I appreciate your joys wherever
I find them. Your sorrows neither discourage nor frighten me,*

for there is laughter in my soul. A temporary defeat does not make me sad. I simply set music to the words of defeat, and turn it into a song. Your tears are not for me. I like laughter much better, and because I like it, I use it as a substitute for grief and sorrow and pain and disappointment. Life, you are a fickle trickster; don't deny it. You slipped this emotion of love into my heart, so that you might use it as a thorn with which to prick my soul. But I learned to dodge your trap with laughter. You tried to lure me with the desire for gold, but I have fooled you by following the trail, which leads to knowledge instead. You induced me to build beautiful friendships, and then converted my friends into enemies so you may harden my heart. But I sidestep your fickleness by laughing off your attempt and selecting new friends in my own way. You caused men to cheat me at trade so I will become distrustful, but I win again because I possess one precious asset which no man can steal: it is the power to think my own thoughts and to be myself. You threaten me with death, but to me, death is nothing worse than a long, peaceful sleep, and sleep is the sweetest of human experiences, excepting laughter. You build a fire of hope in my heart, and then sprinkle water on the flames. But I go you one better by rekindling the fire, and I laugh at you once more. Life, you are licked as far as I am concerned, because you have nothing with which to lure me away from laughter, and you are powerless to scare me into submission. To a life of laughter, then, I raise my cup of cheer.

SELF-DISCIPLINE BY POSITIVE REACTION

It's easy to have a vengeful kind of an emotional reaction to an unpleasant experience where you've been damaged and hurt and injured by those who should have been loyal to you. However, this business of striking back at people who have injured you or tried to injure you is just a lack of self-discipline. You haven't really become acquainted with your own powers, nor your own ways and means of benefiting by those powers, if you stoop to the low level of trying to strike back at some person who has slandered you, vilified you, or cheated you in one way or another. Don't do it, because you'll only lower yourself in the estimation of yourself and of your Creator.

There's a better way to defend yourself against all who would injure you. There's a better weapon I'm trying to put in your hands. And if you'll take my word for it and never allow anybody to drag you down to their level, you'll find that this self-discipline will set the level on which you wish to deal with people. If they want to come up to your level, all right. If they don't, let them stay down on theirs. There's no sin in that. Set your own high level, and stand your ground, come what may. I have a better way of defending myself: I have a mind. I know what to do with that mind, and I never am without defense.

When our editor chose the Challenge to Life essay out of one of my books to publish in the first edition, I said, "That's fine. I want every one of the students to have a copy, because I want to tell them the story back of that essay." You may be interested in knowing that that essay was largely responsible for the late Mahatma Gandhi becoming interested in my philosophy and having it published throughout India. That essay has already influenced millions of people, and will in time be indirectly beneficial or a direct positive influence to millions of people who are not yet born. It's not the brilliance of the essay; it's the thought back of it.

When you react to these unpleasant things in life in such a way that life can't conquer you, nobody can conquer you, and when you've got laughter in your soul, you're sitting very close to the plane on which the Creator acts himself— when you've got laughter in your soul. It's a wonderful thing to have laughter in the soul and laughter on the face. You'll never be without friends, you'll never be without opportunity, and you'll never be without a means of defending yourself against people who do not know anything about laughter.

SELF-DISCIPLINE BY AUTOSUGGESTION

Autosuggestion is suggestion to self through which dominating thoughts and deeds are conveyed to the subconscious mind *as the medium by which* self-discipline becomes a habit.

The starting point in the development of self-discipline is definiteness of purpose. You'll notice that no matter what approach or angle is used, every one of these lessons includes definiteness of purpose. It stands out like a sore thumb and you can't get away from it because it is the starting point of all achievement and of everything that you do. Whether it's good or bad, you can be sure that it all starts with definiteness of purpose.

What is the reason for repetition of an idea? Why should you write out your definite major purpose, for instance, and memorize it and go over it as a ritual day in and day out? To get it into the subconscious mind, because the subconscious mind gets into the habit of believing that which it hears often. You can tell it a lie over and over again until you'll get to where you don't know whether it's a lie or not, and the subconscious doesn't, either. I know of people who have done just that thing.

SELF-DISCIPLINE FROM OBSESSIONAL DESIRE

The dynamo that gives life and action to definiteness of purpose is obsessional desire. You make a desire obsessional in the first place by living with it in your mind, calling it into your mind, and seeing the physical manifestation of it in the circumstances of your life.

Let's say you have an obsessional desire for enough money to buy a new Cadillac. Right now, you might be driving a Ford or something less than a Ford, and you want that nice, new Cadillac, but you don't have enough money to pay for it. What do you do? The first thing you do is to go over to the Cadillac agency and get one of those nice, new catalogs with all the models in it, go through it, and pick out the model you want. And every time you get in that Ford and start down the street, just before you start off, kick off the starter, shut your eyes for a few moments, and see yourself sitting in a nice, new Cadillac. As she purrs down the street as you give her the gas, imagine right now that you already have the Cadillac. Know that you own this Cadillac. You don't exactly have possession of it, but for the time being, you're there at the wheel of your Cadillac. It may sound silly, but I can assure you it's not silly. I talked myself into my first Rolls-Royce that very way.

I'll tell you how I got my first Rolls-Royce. I put myself out on a limb one evening in the Waldorf Astoria Hotel, saying that I was going to have it before the week was over (though I didn't have enough money in the bank to get it). Well, one of my students sitting right in that audience had exactly the same car that I described, even down to the orange-colored-wire wheels. He called me at my hotel the next morning and said, "Come on down, I have your car, Mr. Hill." And I went down there, he had the legal transfer made out and the keys ready to hand to me. All he wanted to show me was a little trick or two that you had to know about a Rolls-Royce in order to get the best results out of it. He took me down Riverside Drive and after we drove a little bit, he got out and shook hands with me, and said,

"Well, Mr. Hill, I'm very happy to have the privilege of letting you have this nice car." Wasn't that a wonderful thing for a man to do? Now, he said nothing about price. He didn't say, "Well, I'll tell you what I paid for it and we'll fix the price." Instead, he said, "You need it worse than I do. I don't actually need it at all. But you do need it, and I want you to have it."

Be careful what you set your heart upon through obsessional desire, for the subconscious mind goes to work on translating that desire into its material equivalent. Self-discipline cannot be attained overnight. It must be developed step-by-step by the formation of definite habits of thought and physical action. You must go through the motion of doing something about it.

You learn to become enthusiastic by acting enthusiastically. That's definite.

SELF-DISCIPLINE BY CHOOSING YOUR DESIRE

Be careful what you set your heart upon because, if you set your heart on anything and stand by that decision, you're going to get it. And before you start any obsessional desire about anything, be sure that what you desire is something that you will be willing to live with after you get it—or him or her (married people understand exactly what I'm talking about). What a marvelous thing it is to demonstrate in your own mind something that you desire above everything else, something that may even be hard to get, and then come to know after you've demonstrated it that you want to live with it the rest of your life. But be careful what you demonstrate before you start demonstrating.

You may be interested in knowing that every one of the five hundred or more men that collaborated with me in building this philosophy was immensely wealthy. I didn't pay any attention to any other kind. I was only after the ones that had made a big demonstration financially. I had no time to fool with the little boys. That wouldn't apply today, but it applied then. You may be interested to know that every single solitary one of them had an abundance of wealth but did not have peace of mind. As they demonstrated their wealth, they neglected to demonstrate along with it the circumstances of life through which they would not worship that wealth, through which it would not be a burden to them, and through which they would have peace of mind in their relationships with their fellow men. They didn't learn that lesson. If those men could have heard the remarks I made when I stepped on this stage for the first five minutes, if they could have had that lesson back in the early days before they became immensely wealthy, they would have learned how to balance themselves so their wealth would not have affected them adversely. To me, the most pitiful sight in the world is to see an extremely rich man who doesn't have anything else but monetary riches. And there are a lot of them in this world.

The next most pitiful thing is the boy or girl who has come into possession of great riches without having earned them. Your power of thought is the only thing over which you have complete, unchallenged control. In giving human beings control over but one thing, the Creator must have chosen the most important of all things—control by the power of will. This is a stupendous fact that merits your most profound consideration. If you do consider it, you will discover for yourself the rich promises available to those who become master of their mind power through self-discipline. Self-discipline leads to sound physical health, and it leads to peace of mind through development of harmony within one's own mind.

SELF-DISCIPLINE THROUGH BALANCE AND PEACE

Many of my students already know my background, and all of them will know of my background before they're through working with me. And *because* of my background, I couldn't stand up with a straight face and say that I have everything in this world that I need, or can possibly use, or can possibly wish for, and have it in abundance, if I hadn't learned self-discipline—because that's how I got it. There was a time when I had much more money in the bank than I have in the various banks I'm doing business with today . . . very much more. But I wasn't as rich then as I am today. I am very rich today because I have a balanced mind. I have no grudges. I have no worries. I have no fears.

I have learned through self-discipline to balance my life as I balance my books. I may not be entirely at peace with the income-tax man, but there is a big boy up somewhere that stands looking over my shoulder that I *am* at peace with all the time. I wouldn't be at peace with him if I hadn't learned the art of self-discipline or the art of reacting to unpleasantries of life in a positive way instead of a negative way. I don't know what I would do if somebody came up and hauled off and slapped my face real hard without any provocation. I don't know what I would do. I'm still pretty human, I think. As apt as not, I would double up my fist, and if I was close enough to him, I probably would hit him right here in the solar plexus, and he would go down with it. No doubt I would do that. But instead of doing that, if I had a few seconds to think about it, I would pity him instead of hating him. I'd pity him for being such a fool to do a thing like that.

SELF-DISCIPLINE OF CHOOSING RIGHT ACTION

There are a lot of things I used to do the wrong way that I now do the right way. Because I've learned to act the right way through self-discipline, I'm in a position to be at peace with other people, at peace with the world, and more importantly, at peace with myself and with my Creator. That's a wonderful thing to have. No matter what other kinds of riches you have, if you're not at peace with yourself, your fellow men, and those you work with, you're not truly rich. You will never be rich until you learn through discipline to be at peace with all people, all races, and all creeds. My audiences have Catholics, Protestants, Jews, Gentiles, people of different colors, and people of different races. To me they're all the same color and all the same religion. I don't know the difference and don't want to know the difference, because in my mind, there *is* no difference. I've risen above this idea of letting petty things such as racial differences anger me or cause me to feel the least bit out of step with my fellow man. I just won't let those things happen, though there was a time when they did happen.

One of the curses of the world in which we're living, and particularly this melting pot here in America, is that we haven't learned how to live with one another. We are in the process of learning, and when we are all indoctrinated with this philosophy, we'll have a better world here in the United States. I hope it'll spread into other countries, too.

SELF-DISCIPLINE BY A FOCUSED MIND

Self-discipline enables one to keep the mind fixed on that which is wanted and off that which is not wanted. At the very least, this lesson should start you on a habit or a plan whereby you occupy your mind from here on out mostly with the things you desire, and keep your mind off the things you don't desire. And if you did nothing else, all the time and all the money that you spend on this course would be paid back a thousand times over—because you'd experience a new birth, a new opportunity, and a new life. Learn through self-discipline to not let your mind feed upon the things you don't want, upon the miseries, upon the disappointments, and upon the people who injure you.

I know it's much easier for me to tell you than it is for you to do it. I appreciate how difficult it is to keep your mind occupied with the money that you're going to have when you don't have any now. How do I know it? I know all about it. I know what it is to be hungry. I know what it is to be without a home. I know what it is to be without friends. I know what it is to be ignorant and illiterate. I know all about that. I know how difficult it is when you're illiterate and ignorant and poverty-stricken to think in terms of becoming an outstanding philosopher and spreading your influence throughout the world. I know all about that, but I did it. I'm speaking now in the past tense. I did it. And if I can conquer the things that I've conquered, I know that you can do an equally good job.

You'll have to take possession. You'll have to be the person in charge. Take possession of your own mind and keep it busy, occupied with the things that you want, the things you want to do, and the people that you like, so there will be no time left to think about the things you don't want or the people you don't like.

SELF-DISCIPLINE OF FINDING GOOD

Have you ever thought of carefully examining (as near as you can without bias, that is) the people you think you don't like? The point is not to look for their faults to justify your opinion of them. That might seem the easy and natural thing, and that's what the weakling would do. But a strong person will use self-discipline to look in the life of the person he doesn't like for some things that he does like. If you'll look fairly and squarely, you will find some of those things *in every human being*. There is nobody so bad in this world that he doesn't also have some good in him. If you look for it, you'll find it. If you don't look for it, you will not find it.

This is one of the evils of this age, and maybe the evil of all ages. When we come into contact with other people, if they give us the slightest reason on earth for doing it, we not only look for all of their shortcomings, but we multiply those shortcomings and step them up into something bigger than they are. Underestimating another person is a great discredit and disservice to the person who does it. If you underestimate your enemies, they can destroy you. You may always have opposition. But you can convert a lot of that opposition—from enemies into friends—if you work on yourself first.

Don't start to work on the other fellow, trying to convert him over to your ways of thinking. Work on yourself to become charitable, to become understanding, and to become forgiving. If a person causes you an injury (an out-and-out injury without provocation, that is), you have one of the grandest opportunities in the world. In fact, you have a prerogative that he doesn't possess, because he's lost the initiative. If a person injures you with or without provocation, he's lost the initiative, and *you* have it. What is that initiative? What is it that you have that he doesn't? You have the prerogative to forgive him and pity him. That's what you have.

MENTAL WALLS OF PROTECTION

There are three mental walls of protection against outside forces that I want you to memorize. Because it's necessary to build up a way of immunizing yourself against outside influences that would disturb your mental capacity, anger you, make you unhappy, make you afraid, or take advantage of you in any way. I have this system and it works like a charm. When you have as many people knowing you all over the world as I do and as many beloved friends clamoring for appointments and so forth as I have, you'll have to have a system of choosing how many of them you'll see and how many off them you won't. That just goes without saying; you'll have to have that. Maybe you won't in the beginning. I didn't in the beginning, but I do now. My beloved friends, all over the world, would take up all of my time if I didn't have a system of keeping them from doing it. I try to keep most of them confined to dealing with me through my books. In that way, I can reach millions of them. But when they want to deal with me in person, I have to have a system for telling how many can see me in a given length of time. This system is a series of three imaginary walls, and they're not so imaginary, either. They're pretty real.

The first one is a rather wide wall. It extends way out from me. It's not too high, but it's high enough to stop anybody that wants to get over the wall and get to me with anything unless he gives me a very good reason for wanting to see him. Now, my students would never need to, because each one of them has a stepladder. They can go right over that wall without any trouble at all; they don't even have to ask me. But outsiders who are not privileged students would have to go over that wall, and they'd have to make contact in some sort of formal way. They couldn't just ring my doorbell or my telephone because my name's not listed in any telephone book. They'd have to go through some formality. Why do I have that wall? Why don't I just leave it down and let everybody come to see me, or have everybody write to me and answer all the letters that I receive from all over the world? Why don't I do that, do you suppose? You may be interested in knowing that on one occasion, I received five mail sacks full of letters. I couldn't even look at the outside of the letters, let alone open them. I didn't have secretaries enough to open all that mail, so thousands of them were never even opened. They came from all over this country. It's not quite as bad today, but the very moment I get a little publicity about something, letters come to me from all over the country. There's a write-up about me in this last issue of *Printer's Ink*, and I'm getting letters from people who knew me thirty-five and thirty-eight years ago right here in Chicago but didn't know that I was here. So we have to have a system.

When they get over the first wall, they immediately come into contact with another wall that's not so big and not so commodious, but it's much higher. In fact, it's many times as high. No one can even go over that wall with any step-ladder, not even my students. But there is a way to get over it and I'm going to tip you off to what it is. You can get over that wall easily if you either have something I want, or if you have something in common with me. Let me clarify that statement because I don't wish to convey that it's mean or selfish. I mean that you can get to me very easily if I am convinced that the time I devote to you is going to be of mutual benefit to both of us. But if it's just something that's going to benefit you and not me, chances are that you won't make it. There are exceptions, but very, very few, and I use my judgment as to what constitutes an exception. There's nothing selfish about this, I assure you—it's a necessity.

When you get over that second wall, you come in

contact with one more wall that's much more narrow. It's as high as eternity. No living person ever gets over that wall, not even my wife, as much as I love her and as close as we are together. She never gets over, and she doesn't even try, because she knows that I have a sanctuary of my soul, wherein nobody but my Creator and myself commune. Nobody. There is where I do my best work. When I go to write a book, I retire into my inner sanctuary, lay out that book, commune with my maker, and get instructions. When I come to an intersection in life that I don't understand which way to go, I go into my inner sanctuary. I ask for guidance, and I always get it. Always.

Do you see what a wonderful thing it is, to have this system of immunity? Do you see how unselfish it is? Your first duty is to yourself. Shakespeare's marvelous poetic line, "To thine own self be true, and it must follow, as the night the day, thou canst not then be false to any man." I was thrilled to the marrow of my bones when I first read that. I've read it hundreds of times and I've repeated it thousands of times. How true it is that your first duty is to yourself. **Be true to yourself. Protect your mind. Protect your inner consciousness. Use self-discipline to take possession of your own mind, to direct it to the things you want and to keep it off the things you don't want.** That's the prerogative the Creator gave you. It's the most important and precious gift of the Creator to mankind. Show your appreciation by respecting that gift and using it.

SELF-DISCIPLINE BY IMPROVEMENT

Make a list of five traits of personality in which you need self-discipline for improvement. I don't care how perfect you are, there's not a person who wouldn't benefit by doing this, if you're being perfectly honest about it. If you don't know the answers, get your wife to tell you. She'll tell you some of these things that you should put in this list. Maybe your husband will do a good job, too. In some cases, you won't have to ask the husband (because he'll tell you without it!) or the wife, vice-versa. In any case, find five things in your personality that you need to change and write them down. Right now, for the sake of experiment, write just the first one in your mind. Everyone can think of one trait of personality that they'd like to change.

You can't do anything about your defects until you take inventory of them, find out what they are, get them on paper where you can see them, and then start doing something about them. And after you discover these five traits for improvement, you can immediately start to develop the *opposite* of those traits. If you're in the habit of not sharing your opportunities or your blessings with other people, start sharing them, no matter how much it hurts. Start where you are. If you're greedy, start sharing. If you've been in the habit of passing on a little gossip to somebody, stop that for all time. Just stop it and start passing on complimentary things instead. You'd be surprised at how a man will blossom out and become a different person if you start telling him about some of the things that you know are good about him.

Don't rub it on too thick. If you do, he'll wonder what you're after. Be reasonable about it. When anybody walks up to me and shakes my hand and says, "Napoleon Hill, I have always wanted to meet you. I appreciate so much the books that you've written, and I just wanted to tell you that I have found myself. I've been a success in my profession or business, and I owe it all to *Think and Grow Rich* or to *The Law of Success*," I know that that man is telling the truth. I can tell by the tone of his voice, the look in his eye, and the way he takes hold of my hand. I appreciate it. Now, if he stood there and handed out compliments out of proportion to what I deserve, I would know right away that he's getting ready for a touch of some sort. So you do have to use discretion.

Next, make up a list of all the traits of personality of those nearest to you who need to be improved by self-discipline. You'll have no trouble at all making up that list. You'll find that one will be very easy. Notice the difference as to the ease with which you'll carry out that transaction, versus the one where you're looking into your own life for traits that need to be changed. Self-examination is a very difficult thing, isn't it? That's because we're biased in our own favor. We think that whatever we do, no matter how it turns out, since we did it, it must be right. On the other hand, if it doesn't turn out right, we always think it was the other fellow's fault. Not ours. Always.

One of these days, someone is going to walk in and tell me that they had been at odds with somebody for a long time, only to find out when they got into this philosophy that the trouble was not with the other fellow, it was with themselves. As they started through self-discipline to improve themselves, lo and behold, when they got their own house clean, they discovered the other fellow's house was also clean. That's the way it'll work out.

It's astounding how many motes you can see in the other fellow's eye when you're not looking for those in your own eye. Before anybody condemns anybody, they should go before a looking-glass and say, "Now, look here, fellow. Before you start condemning anybody, before you start passing out gossip about anybody, I want you to look yourself in the eye and find out if you have clean hands." The Bible passage says, "Let he who is without sin cast the first stone." Cast the first stone before you commence condemning other people. If you make a practice of that, you'll get to the point at which you can forgive people for almost anything.

SELF-DISCIPLINE BY THOUGHT CONTROL

Here is the most important form of self-discipline, which should be exercised by all who aspire to outstanding success: control of thought. **There's nothing else of more importance in the world than the control of your mind. If you** control your own mind, you'll control everything that you come into contact with. You really will. You'll never be the master of circumstances; you'll never be the master of the space that you occupy in the world until you first learn to be the master of your own mind. Never.

SELF-DISCIPLINE BY TAKING A STAND

You've heard me speak of Mr. Gandhi many times. He bided his time to gain freedom for India using these five principles. He had definiteness of purpose because he knew what he wanted. He used the second principle, applied faith, when he began to do something about it by talking to his fellow men, indoctrinating them with the same desire. He didn't do anything vicious. He didn't commit any acts of mayhem or murder. Third, he practiced the principle of going the extra mile. Fourth, he formed a mastermind the likes of which this world probably has never seen before. At least 200 million of his fellow men, all contributing to that mastermind alliance, focused on the main object: to free themselves from England without violence. He used the fifth principle, self-discipline, on a scale without parallel in modern times. These are the elements that made Mahatma Gandhi the master of the great British Empire. No doubt about it. Self-discipline. Where in the world would you find a man that would stand the things that Gandhi did—all of the insults, all of the incarcerations—while standing his ground and not striking back in kind? He struck back on his own ground, with his own weapons.

If you have to go to battle with somebody, select your own battleground, select your own weapons, and if you don't win, it's your own fault. You're going to have battle to do in one way or another throughout life. You're going to have to plan campaigns, put yourself across, and remove opposition out of your way. You've got to be smarter than your opposition or your enemies, and the way to do it is not to strike back on battlegrounds of their choice, with weapons of their choice. Instead, select your own battleground and your own weapons.

The time will come when this will be helpful to you. At some point, you'll have a problem to solve, somebody opposing you, or you'll need to go around somebody. You will remember that I told you to choose your own battleground and choose your own weapons. First, condition yourself for the battle, making up your mind that under no circumstances will you try to destroy anyone, or injure anyone other than what might come of defending your own rights. With that attitude, you'll win before you ever start. No matter who your adversary is, how strong he is, or how smart he is, with those tactics, you're bound to win.

Create a system whereby you take full possession of your own mind. Keep it occupied with all the things, circumstances, and desires of your choice. Keep it strictly off of the things you do not want. Do you know how you go about keeping your mind off of things you don't want? It's an elementary question, and I don't mean to insult your intelligence by asking it. I only wanted to emphasize it so that you really think about it.

SELF-DISCIPLINE OF TAKING CONTROL

I was not blessed with anything that you do not have, and maybe not half as much as some of you. My background was certainly much more difficult than that of most, and if I made the grade, I know *you* can make it. *You* have to take possession, to be in charge of your institution and your enterprise. You are an institution and an enterprise. You have to be in charge, you've got to call the shots, and you must see that they're carried out. You'll need self-discipline with which to do it. That's how you go about keeping your mind off the things you don't want, by occupying your mind and seeing in your imagination the things that you do want. Even if you don't have physical possession of them, you can always have mental possession, can't you? Unless you have mental possession of a thing first, you can be sure you'll never have the physical possession of it, unless somebody wishes it upon you or it accidentally falls off the top of a house and onto you as you're walking by. Anything that you get or acquire by desire must be created and gotten in your mental attitude first. You must be very sure about it in your mind. To see yourself in possession of it takes self-discipline.

Mastery of your own destiny is the reward for taking

possession of your own mind. Taking possession of your own mind gives you direct contact with Infinite Intelligence. You'll be guided by Infinite Intelligence. No doubt about it. When I tell you that there's someone looking over my shoulder and guiding me, I'm telling you the truth of what happens when I meet with obstacles. All I have to do is to remember that he's right there. If I come to an intersection of life and I don't know if I should turn this way or that way, or if I should go ahead or go back, all I have to do is to remember that invisible force looking over my shoulder will always point the right direction—if I pay attention to him and have faith in him. How can I make a statement like that? There's only one way, and that's by having practiced it. That's the only way I would know. I will never be guilty of telling you that anything will happen unless I have made it happen and I tell you how you can make it happen, too.

The penalty for not taking possession of your own mind, which is the penalty that the majority of people pay all through their life, is this: you will become the victim of the stray winds of circumstance, which will remain forever beyond your control. You'll become the victim of every influence that you come into contact with, enemies and everything. All these things that you don't want will sway you like a leaf on the bosom of the wind, unless you take possession of your own mind. That's the penalty that you must pay. It's a profound truth.

You have been given a means by which you can declare and determine your earthly destiny. It carries a tremendous penalty that you will pay if you don't embrace that asset and use it, and it carries a tremendous asset or reward that you will automatically receive if you accept that asset and use it.

If I didn't have any other evidence of a first cause or a Creator, if I didn't have any evidence other than what I know about this principle, then I would know there *had* to be a first cause. Because it's too profound for any human being to think out!

Giving you a great asset with a penalty if you don't accept it or a reward if you do accept it—that's the sum and the substance of what happens when you use the self-discipline with which to take possession of your own mind, to direct it to the things you want. Never mind what you want; that's nobody's business except yours. Don't let anybody come along and sell you on what you should want. Who's going to tell me what I want or what I should want? You can bet your life it's me!

It hasn't always been that way, but it is that way today. Nobody is going to tell me what I want. I'll do that. If I allowed anybody else to tell me, I'd think it was an insult to my Creator, because he intended that I should have the last word about this guy here (me, that is). Believe me, I take it.

I wouldn't choose anything that would hurt anyone else. I wouldn't do anything in this world, under any circumstances, to injure anybody or anything.

Did you know that whatever you do to or for another person, you do to, or for, yourself? It's an eternal law. Nobody can avoid or evade that law. That's why I could never be a prosecuting attorney, and it's why I'm glad that I didn't follow my inclination to become a lawyer. I had a long visit with my brother Vivian. He's a lawyer who specializes in divorce suits, especially divorce suits of very wealthy people. Let me tell you the penalty he's paid for knowing too much about the bad side of domestic relations. The penalty is that he never married, because his experience led him to the conclusion that all women were bad. He's never had the pleasure of a wife like I have. He thinks that all women are bad, because he judges them by the ones he's seen in divorce suits. It's a common trait of all of us. We judge people by the ones we know best, don't we? It's not always fair to do that. Certainly not in his case.

These are some of the vital things in life that you need to deal with. You need to understand yourself, understand people, and understand how to adjust yourself around people that are difficult to get along with. As long as you and I live, and long after that, there will always be a lot of people in this world that are difficult to get along with. We can't do away with difficult people, but we can do something about it by doing something with ourselves.

SELF-DISCIPLINE: MASTERY OVER MIND AND BODY

Self-discipline means having complete control over both the body and the mind. It doesn't mean changing your mind or your body; it means controlling it. The great emotion of sex gets more people into trouble than all of the other emotions combined, and yet it's the most creative, the most profound, and the most divine of all of the emotions. It's not the *emotion* that gets people into trouble; it's their lack of controlling it, directing it, and transmuting it, which anyone is readily able to do if they have self-discipline. So it is with other faculties of the body and the mind. You don't have to change completely. You just have to be the master. Be in control and recognize the things that you must do in order to have sound health and peace of mind. Develop daily habits by which your mind is kept busy with the things and the circumstances that you desire, and off the circumstances you do not desire. Do not accept or allow yourself to be influenced by any circumstance or thing you do not desire. You may have to tolerate it, or recognize it's there, but you don't have to submit to it. You don't have to let it conquer you or admit that it's stronger than you. Instead, prove that you're stronger than it by not submitting to it. Give your imagination a wide range of operation as to what these things are that you're going to have to deal with but that you're not going to submit to.

Build a three-wall protection around yourself so no one will ever know everything about you, or what goes on in your mind. No one wants everybody to know everything that's going on in his or her mind. On the other hand, you wouldn't want everyone to know all that you think about him or her, either. Unfortunately, there are a lot of people who make the mistake of letting *anybody* know *everything* that goes on in their mind. All you have to do is start them talking. You know the type I'm talking about. Just get them started, and you'll find out all about them, good and bad.

I did some professional work with J. Edgar Hoover on a great many occasions, and still do at times. He once told me that the fellow he's investigating is the best help to him of all. Yes, he gets more information from the guy that he's tracing than from all other sources combined. I asked, "Why?" He said, "Well, because he talks too damn much." That was his exact reply.

Tell me what a man fears and I will tell you how to master him. The very minute you find out what anybody fears, you'll know exactly how to control him (that is, if you're foolish enough to want to control anybody on that basis). I don't want to control anybody on fear, not at all. If I controlled anybody, I'd want it on the basis of love. It's too bad that the average person talks too much for his own good.

ENTHUSIASM

Many people attain some degree of success in something, but only those who acquire the habit of turning the flame of enthusiasm into a white heat of desire ever attain truly great success in anything. The ninth principle of *Your Right to Be Rich* is Enthusiasm, one of our greatest assets, the force within us that perpetually spurs us onward to do our best. What is it really? One dictionary defines it as "an absorbing or controlling possession of the mind by any interest or pursuit, a lively interest." Dr. Hill adds something more to his definition of enthusiasm. As he defines it, enthusiasm is nothing more and nothing less than faith in action.

Enthusiasm is based upon a burning desire. That's the starting point of enthusiasm and when you learn how to work yourself up into a state of a burning desire, you won't need the rest of the instructions on enthusiasm because, at that point, you'll already have the last word on enthusiasm.

BURNING DESIRE

When you really want something and make up your mind to get it, you have that burning desire. Your desire steps up thinking processes so that your imagination goes to work on the ways and means to get the thing you desire. Enthusiasm gives you a brighter mind. It makes you more alert to opportunities. You see opportunities that you never saw before when your mind is stepped up to that state of enthusiasm—a burning desire for something definite.

ACTIVE AND PASSIVE ENTHUSIASM

There are two kinds of enthusiasm: active enthusiasm and passive enthusiasm. Of these two, active enthusiasm is more effective. What do I mean by active and passive? Let me give you an illustration of passive enthusiasm.

Henry Ford was the most lacking in active enthusiasm of any man that I have ever seen. I never heard him laugh but once in his life. When he shook hands with you it was like taking hold of a piece of cold ham. You did all the shaking. He did nothing but stick his hand out and take it back when you let loose of it. In his conversation there was no enthusiasm in his voice whatsoever; there was no evidence in any shape, form, or fashion of his demonstrating active enthusiasm. What kind of enthusiasm *did* he have—because he *must have* had *some*—in order to have such an outstanding major purpose and to achieve so much success? His enthusiasm was inward, and his inner enthusiasm was transmuted into his imagination, and into his power of faith, and into his personal initiative. He operated on his own initiative, believed that he could do whatever he wanted to do, and kept himself alert and keen with applied faith through his enthusiasm. His passive enthusiasm infused the thinking inside of his own mind what it was he was going to do and all the joy he'd get out of doing it.

Long after he had "arrived" and had his problems whipped, I asked him if he ever wanted anything or wanted to do anything he couldn't do, and he said, "No. Not in recent years." (In the early days, he added, until he learned how to get or to do whatever he wanted to do, he couldn't answer me in the negative.) I said, "In other words, Mr. Ford, there isn't anything that you need or want or that you can't get." He said, "That's correct." I asked, "How do you know that's true and how do you go about making sure that whatever you want to do, you know you're going to do before you stop?" He said, "Over the years, I formed a habit of putting my mind on the can-do part of every problem. If I have a problem, there's always something I can do about it. There are many things I can't do, but there's something I can do and I start where I can do something. As I use up the can-do part of it, the no-can-do simply vanishes. It's like I get to the river or where I expect to have a bridge, and there's no bridge. I find that I didn't need the bridge because the river was dry."

ENTHUSIASM TRANSMUTES OBSTACLES

It's a marvelous thing for a man to make a statement like that. He started on his problem or his objective at a place where he could do something. And if he wanted to turn out a new model, or if he wanted to increase his production, he immediately put his mind to work on the plan in which he could do that. He never paid any attention to obstacles because he knew that his plan was sufficiently strong and definite and backed with the right kind of faith—that any opposition that he might meet would melt away when he came to it. The astounding thing was that if he took that attitude of putting his mind behind the can-do part of every problem, then the no-can-do part "takes to its heels and runs." I endorse everything that he has said because that's been my experience, too.

ENTHUSIASM OF BELIEF

If you want to do something, work yourself into a state of wild enthusiasm and go to work where you stand, even if it's nothing more than drawing a picture in your mind of the thing you want to do, and keep drawing that picture, making it more vivid all the time. Inasmuch as you make use of the tools that are available to you now, other and better tools will be put in your hands. That's one of the strange things of life but that's the way it works. Public speakers and teachers express enthusiasm by control of the voice. In fact, one of my students paid me a very high compliment when she asked if I had any voice training or voice culture or anything of that sort. I said, "No, nothing, not a thing. I had a course in public speaking a long time ago but I violate everything the teacher ever taught me. I have my own system." She said, "Well, you have a most marvelous voice and I often wondered if you trained to impart the enthusiasm or the meaning that you want to impart with it." I said, "No, the answer is this. When I say something, I believe what I'm saying. I'm sincere about it and that's the grandest voice control that I know anything about." You express enthusiasm when you know that the thing that you're saying at the time is the thing that you ought to say and the thing that will do some good for the other fellow, and perhaps for you, too.

SINCERE ENTHUSIASM

I have seen public speakers that march and prance all over the stage. They run their fingers through their hair and stick their hands down in their pockets and use all kinds of personal gestures. It distracts my attention when a speaker does that. I have trained myself to stand in one position. I never march all over the stage. I sometimes spread out my hands, but not very often. The effect that I want to give above all is the sincerity of what I'm talking about. And then, I put enthusiasm in the tone of my voice. If you learn to do that you'll have a marvelous asset.

One must feel enthusiasm before being able to express it. I don't see how anybody can express enthusiasm when his heart is breaking, when he's in distress, or in any sort of trouble that he can't throw off.

I once did a show in New York where the star of the show gave a marvelous performance, even though she learned about three minutes before she came on that her father had just dropped dead. You would never have known it. She gave the performance as perfectly as I imagine it could have been given, without the slightest indication that anything had happened. She trained herself to be an actress always, no matter the circumstances. If she hadn't trained herself to do that, she wouldn't have been an actress. An actor who can't fall into the skeleton shape of his character he's trying to portray, and can't feel the way the character ought to feel, will not be an actor. He may express the lines that are written for him, but he'll never make the right impression on the audience unless he *lives* the thing he's trying to put across.

Not all great actors are all on the stage; some of them are in private life. But the greatest actors in life are people who can put themselves into the role that they're trying to portray. They feel it, they believe in it, they have confidence in it, and they have no trouble in conveying to the other fellow a spirit of enthusiasm. This enthusiasm is a mighty tonic for all the negative influences that get into your mind. If you want to burn up a negative influence, just turn on the old enthusiasm, because the two can't stay in the same room at the time. Just can't do it. Start being enthusiastic over anything and I defy you to let doubting thoughts or thoughts of fear come into your mind while you're keyed up in the state of enthusiasm.

ENTHUSIASM IN YOUR VOICE

One should practice enthusiasm in daily conversation. Learn to turn it on or off at will. Start immediately to step up the tone of your voice when you're conversing with other people. Put a smile back of your words. Inject a pleasant tone into your voice, sometimes, by toning your voice down and not talking so loud and, at other times, by stepping it up so that they can't fail to hear you and to recognize what you're doing. In other words, learn to inject enthusiasm into your ordinary daily conversations and you'll have somebody to practice on in every person you come into contact with. Watch what happens when you start doing this. Naturally, you start changing your tone of voice. You'll deliberately intend to make the other fellow smile while you're talking to him or her and make that person like you. It's not good to put enthusiasm into telling the other fellow what you think about him if you don't think something pleasant, because the more enthusiastic you are, the less he'll like you.

When you start telling another person what you think of him for his own good, you better not be smiling. Nobody wants anybody to reprimand him, overhaul him, or tell him something for his own good, because he knows very well there's a selfish motive somewhere along the line—at least he thinks so.

Speaking in monotone is always monotonous and boresome. I don't care who's speaking, if you don't get variety, color, rise, and fall in the inflection in your voice, you're going to be monotonous no matter what you're saying, and it doesn't matter to whom you're saying it. Suppose I talked in a monotone, never changing my tone of voice. If I said exactly the same thing but didn't color my voice, do you think I would get such a rousing cheer? Of course not. I can keep you from going to sleep by rousing you with a question that you're prepared for and then letting you answer it. But getting some enthusiasm into my tone, by raising my voice and letting it back down again, keeps you jumping and guessing as to what I'm going to say next. A good way to hold an audience is to keep them guessing as to what you're going to say next. If you talk in monotones, with no enthusiasm in what you're saying, they, the listener, will be way ahead of you. He knows what you're going to say long before you say it, and he thinks that whatever it is, he doesn't want to hear it in the first place. The beautiful part about enthusiasm is that you can turn it on and off yourself; you don't need to ask anybody about it.

SHARING ENTHUSIASM

When you express enthusiasm in your daily conversations, observe how others pick up your enthusiasm and reflect it back to you. By working yourself into a state of enthusiasm, you can change the attitude of anybody—because enthusiasm is contagious. They'll pick up on your enthusiasm and reflect it back to you as their own.

All master salesmen understand that art. If they don't understand it, they're not master salesmen. They're not even ordinary salesmen if they don't know how to key up the buyer with their enthusiasm. It doesn't matter what you're selling, it works the same in selling yourself as it does in selling services or commodities or merchandise. Go into any store and pick out a salesman that knows his business. You'll recognize him because he's not only showing you merchandise, he's also giving information in a tone of voice that impresses you.

Most salesmen in stores are not salesmen at all. They don't have the first idea about salesmanship. They're what an accountant would call "order takers." Order takers are not salesmen at all. They don't sell. I've often heard them say, "I sold so much today." I heard a newspaperman talking to the man that delivers the news to him and he was telling how many papers he sold. Well, he hadn't sold any papers at all. He'd been there, of course. He had them out and people came along and bought them and laid their money down. But he didn't have anything to do with selling them just by putting the merchandise where the people could pick it up and buy it. He thought he was a salesman. In fact, he thought he was a pretty good one. You see a lot of people who'll wrap up merchandise and take your money who think they made a sale. But they hadn't made anything because you're the one that did the buying. You can't say that about a good salesman. You might go in to buy a shirt, but before you get out of there, he'll sell you some underwear, some socks, a tie, and a pair of suspenders. (He wouldn't sell me the suspenders because I don't wear them.) Just a day or two ago, a salesman sold me a belt. I didn't need a belt, but he showed me a nice one and it fitted my personality, but I bought mostly because of the personality of the man talking about it. Believe me, I'm not immune to this, either.

ENTHUSIASM THWARTS DEFEAT

When you meet with any sort of unpleasant circumstance, learn to transmute it into a pleasant feeling by repeating your major purpose with great enthusiasm. No matter what unpleasant circumstance crosses your path, instead of brooding over it or allowing it to take up your time in regret, frustration, or fear, start thinking about this marvelous thing that you're going to accomplish maybe one, two, three, four, or five years from now (or even six months or whatever it is). Start thinking about something that gets you enthusiastic. In other words, use your enthusiasm for the things you want and not for the things that you just lost through defeat.

There are a lot of people who allow the death of a loved one to drive them to distraction. I've known people to lose their minds over that. When my father passed away in 1939, of course I knew he was going to pass away. We knew what his condition was, and we knew it was only a question of time, and so I conditioned my mind so it could not possibly upset me or make the slightest impression on me emotionally.

I got a call from my brother one evening when I was at my estate in Florida. (I had some rather distinguished company there, talking about the publishing business.) The maid came in and said that my brother wanted to speak with me on the telephone, and so I went out of the room and talked to him for three or four minutes. He told me that our father had passed away and that the funeral would be that coming Friday. We chatted a little while about other things, I thanked him for calling me and went back to my company, and nobody knew that anything had happened. The members of my family didn't even know what had happened until the next day. There was no expression of sorrow, nor anything of that kind. What was the use? I couldn't save him; he was dead. Why grieve myself to death over something I can't do anything about? You might say that's hard-hearted, but that's not hard-hearted at all. I knew it was going to happen. I adjusted myself to it so that it could not destroy my confidence or make me afraid.

In matters of that kind (well, maybe not as serious as that), you have to learn to give yourself immunity against being upset emotionally. When you're upset emotionally, you're not quite sane, you don't digest your food, you're not happy, and you're not successful. Things go against you when you're in that frame of mind and I don't want things to go against me. I don't want to be unhealthy. I want to be successful. I want to be healthy. I want things to come my way and the only way that I can ensure that is to not let anything upset my emotions.

I don't think anybody can love more deeply nor more often than I have, but if I experienced unrequited love (and I have had that experience once in my life), I could let it upset me very badly. However, it didn't—because I have self-control. I won't let anything destroy my equilibrium. Nothing at all. I didn't want my father to die but, as long as he was dead, there wasn't anything I could do about it. There was no use in me dying just because he had. I've seen people do just that—go ahead and die because somebody else had died. That's an extreme illustration, but it's certainly one that's needed by everybody. We need to learn to adjust ourselves to the unpleasantness of life without going down under it. The way to do that is to divert your attention away from the unpleasant to something that is pleasant, and to put all of the enthusiasm you've got back of that other something.

It's your life and you're entitled to have complete control of it. From this day forward, your duty to yourself requires that you do something each day to improve your technique for the expression of enthusiasm, no matter what it is. I've touched upon some of the things that you could do but not all of them. Depending on the circumstances in relation to other people, you know something that you can do to step up your enthusiasm so it can be more beneficial to you and the other person.

I have an appropriate point to add here. If you have a mate and you can change your relationship with that mate so they complement you everywhere you go, you've got a fortune beyond compare, a fortune that you can't estimate, and an asset that's beyond comparison with anything else in this world. A mastermind relationship between a man and his wife can surmount, go around, and master all difficulties they may encounter. Together they join their mental attitudes and multiply their enthusiasm, turning it toward each other in places where they need it.

CONTROLLED ATTENTION

Controlled Attention, sometimes called Concentration, is the tenth principle of *Your Right to Be Rich*. It is the highest form of self-discipline because it requires coordinating all the faculties of your mind. In other words, it is organized mind power.

This principle of success concentrates all effort behind the definite major purpose of your life so you will achieve it. The essential function of concentration is to aid you in developing and maintaining habits of thought. Habits will enable you to fix your attention on any desired purpose and hold your mind there until you have achieved that purpose. Concentration is power and that power is within your grasp.

I've never known a successful person in the upper brackets of success, no matter what their calling, that hadn't had to acquire great potential powers of concentration in order to achieve their success. I'm talking about highly focused attention upon one thing at a time. You've heard people describe others (intending it to be derogatory, that is) as having "one-track minds," haven't you? Anytime someone says I have a one-track mind, I want to thank him for it, because a lot of people have multitrack minds, and when they try to run on all of them at the same time, they don't make a good job on any of them. Outstanding successes are people who have developed high capacities to keep their mind fixed upon one thing at a time.

When you have learned to concentrate on one thing at a time, you have learned to key yourself up to see yourself already in possession of the thing that you're concentrating on.

CONCENTRATION STARTS WITH A MOTIVE

Motive is the starting point of all concentration, because you don't concentrate unless you have a motive for doing it. Do you want to make a lot of money? Let's say you want to buy an estate, or a farm, and you concentrate on money in the upper brackets. You'd be surprised at how that concentration would change your whole habit and attract to you opportunities for making money that you never thought of before. I know that's the way it works because that's how it worked for me.

Years ago, I wanted a thousand-acre estate. At first, I didn't know just how much a thousand acres was, but I was concentrating on a thousand acres. Actually, the land that I was looking for cost approximately $250,000, which was a lot more money than I had at that time. Nonetheless, from the very day that I fixed my mind on the estate size that I wanted, opportunities began to open up and develop for me to get that money—in larger amounts than I'd ever gotten it before. Royalties on my books commenced to increase, demand for my lectures commenced to increase, and demands for my business counsel commenced to increase. I sold myself on the idea that I had to have the money, and I was going to get it by rendering service for it.

I got the estate. I didn't get a thousand acres, but I got six hundred acres. I told the man I was buying it from that I wanted a thousand acres. He said, "I have six hundred acres, and by the way, do you know how much six hundred acres are?" I said, "I have a rough idea. Would you mind walking around this estate with me?" We started off bright one morning with a couple of golf sticks we took along to knock the rattlesnakes with. We started around the outer edge, walking up and down the Catskill Mountains, and at noon we weren't even halfway around the property. I said, "Let's just turn around and go back. I've seen enough. Six hundred acres will be plenty." I bought the place and then the Depression came. Believe me, it was tough going but I had accumulated enough money to buy the place. I wouldn't have had it after the Depression, if I hadn't concentrated on that idea.

CONCENTRATION MOTIVATED BY OBSESSIONAL DESIRE

Concentration requires a definiteness of purpose in such proportion that it becomes an obsession. There's no use of having a motive unless you put obsession of desire or obsession of purpose in back of it. What's the difference between an ordinary purpose or desire and an obsessional desire? The word *intensity* is fitting here. In other words, to wish or hope for a thing isn't enough to cause anything to happen. However, when you put a burning desire or obsessional desire back of a thing, why, it moves you into action, attracts you to others, and attracts to you all that you need in order to fulfill that desire.

How do you go about developing an obsessional desire about anything? By thinking about a lot of things, changing from one thing to another? No, you select one thing. You eat it, sleep it, drink it, breathe it, and talk about it to anybody who'll listen. If you can't find anybody, talk to yourself. By repetition, keep telling your subconscious mind exactly what you want. Make it clear, make it plain, make it definite, and, above all else, let your subconscious mind know that you expect results.

INITIATIVE IGNITES CONCENTRATION; APPLIED FAITH SUSTAINS IT

An organized endeavor or personal initiative is the self-starter that begins the action of concentration. Applied faith is the sustaining force that keeps the action going. In other words, without applied faith, when the going gets hard (as it will, no matter what you're doing), you'd either slow down or quit. You need applied faith to keep your action keyed up to a high degree, even when the going is hard and when the results are not coming as you would like them. Have you ever heard of anybody achieving outstanding permanent success right from the start, without any opposition whatsoever? Don't look now, but I'll tip you off—nobody ever did that, and probably nobody ever will. No matter what you're doing, the going is hard for everyone.

There's tremendous amount of information in every one of these lessons that you can concentrate on. You'll have to concentrate on every one of these lessons when you come to it. Put everything else aside and concentrate only on that lesson. Add to your notes everything you can find that's related to the subject, and come back to each lesson many times. When you do concentrate on any given lesson, don't let your mind run over all the other lessons. Stick to that one lesson while you're at it.

CONCENTRATION OF A MASTERMIND

The mastermind is the source of the live power necessary to ensure success. Can you imagine anybody concentrating on the attainment of something of an outstanding nature without making use of the mastermind, and the brains, and the influence, and the education of other people? Did you ever hear of anybody achieving an outstanding success without the cooperation of other people? I never have and I have been around this success field quite a bit—at least as much as the average and maybe more than the average person—and I have yet to find anyone in the upper brackets of achievement (in any line) that didn't owe his success to the friendly, harmonious cooperation of other people. Their success largely came by means of the use of other people's brains, and sometimes other people's money (because you need to do that once in a while, too). You need the mastermind alliance in your concentration if you're aiming for anything above mediocrity.

Of course, you can concentrate on failure. You won't need any mastermind help on that—although you'll have a lot of volunteer help and a lot of good company if you just aim to fail. But if you're going to succeed, you've got to follow these regulations I'm laying down for you. You can't escape them and you can't neglect any one of them.

SELF-DISCIPLINE

Self-discipline is the watchman that keeps action moving in the right direction, even when the going is difficult. That's when you need self-discipline the most, when you meet with opposition or when the conditions and circumstances that you've got to cut through are difficult. You'll need self-discipline to keep your faith going and keep yourself determined not to quit just because the going is hard. You can't possibly get along in concentrating without self-discipline. If everything went your way, it'd be no trouble at all. You could concentrate on anything if everything was going your way and you didn't meet any difficult circumstances.

IMAGINATION

Creative vision or imagination is the architect that fashions practical plans for your action back of your concentration. Before you can concentrate intelligently, you've got to have plans, you've got to have an architect, and that architect is your imagination (and the imaginations of your mastermind allies, if you have them). What happens when you start out to do something without a definite or practical plan? Have you ever heard of anybody who had a very fine objective, a very fine purpose, or a very fine idea but it failed because he didn't have the right kind of plan for putting it over? Have you ever heard of any other kind except that? It's a common pattern for people to have ideas, but their plans for carrying them out are not good or not sound.

GOING THE EXTRA MILE

Going the extra mile is the principle that ensures harmonious cooperation from others. Going the extra mile is something you need in the business of concentrating. If you're going to get other people to help you, you've got to do something to put them under obligation to you. You've got to give them a motive. Even your mastermind allies in your own organization won't serve as mastermind allies without a motive.

FINANCIAL MOTIVE ENSURES CONCENTRATION

What are some of the motives that would get people to join you in a given undertaking? What's the most outstanding motive? There's financial gain, of course, in all business and professional undertakings. I'd say the desire for professional or financial gain is the most outstanding motive. If you're going into a business where the main object is to make money, and you don't allow your mastermind allies (or the key men and women or the people who are helping you most) to get sufficient returns, you're not going to have them very long. They'll go into business for themselves or they'll go to your competitors.

I was astounded when Andrew Carnegie once told me that he paid Charlie Schwab a salary of $75,000 a year and, in some years, a million-dollar bonus in addition to his salary. He did that for several years. To me, that was a lot of money then, and it's still a lot of money now. It made me curious about Mr. Carnegie. I wanted to know why someone of his great intelligence would pay one man a bonus of more than ten times his salary. I said, "Mr. Carnegie, did you have to do that?" He said, "No, I certainly didn't. I could let him go and be in competition with me. So, no, I didn't have to do it." There's quite a bit of meaning back of that statement. In other words, he had a good man that was very valuable to him, he wanted to keep him, and he knew that the way to keep him was to let him know he'd make more money with Mr. Carnegie than he would without him.

THE GOLDEN RULE

The Golden Rule gives one moral guidance as to the action on which one is concentrating.

ACCURATE THINKING

Accurate thinking prevents daydreaming and focuses on the creation of plans. Do you know that most of the so-called thinking is nothing but daydreaming or hoping or wishing? That's what it is. There are a lot of people in this world who spend the vast majority of their time daydreaming, hoping, wishing, and thinking about things. But they never take any physical or concrete mental action in carrying out their plans.

A long time ago, I was lecturing on this philosophy in Des Moines, Iowa. After the lecture was over, up to the stage toddles an elderly man who was decrepit and not very strong. He fished around in his pocket and brought out a great bundle of papers that had dog-ears on them. He fished among those papers and finally came up with one yellow paper. He said, "Nothing new, Mr. Hill, in what you just said. I had those ideas twenty years ago. Here they are on paper. I had those ideas." Sure he did. Millions of other people had them too, but nobody did anything about them. Nothing new in the philosophy, not a thing new in it, except the law of cosmic habit force. That's the only new thing about it, and strictly speaking, that is not new—that's a proper interpretation of Emerson's essay on compensation, but stated in terms that people can understand the first time they read it. There he was, carrying those ideas around in his pocket. He could have been Napoleon Hill instead of me, if only he'd gotten busy back before I started. One of these days some smart fellow will come along and take up right where I stop and he'll create the philosophy based on what I've done and perhaps it will be far superior. Maybe that person is here now.

LEARNING FROM DEFEAT AND ADVERSITY

Learning from defeat insures one against quitting when the going is hard. Isn't it a marvelous thing to learn beyond any question of a doubt that failure and defeat and adversity needn't stop you—that there's a benefit in every such experience?

What is the benefit to a man going through a depression, losing all of his money right down to the last penny, and having to start over again? I can tell you, because I am a man who did just that. That was one of the greatest blessings that ever came along, because I was getting just to be a kind of smarty-pants, making too much money, and making it too easily. I had to get taken back a notch. I came out fighting and I've done more good work since that time than I ever did before. Without that experience, I'd probably be up there on my estate in the Catskill Mountains instead of down here teaching.

Sometimes adversity is a blessing in disguise, and often not so disguised, if you take the right attitude toward it. You can't be whipped and you can't be defeated until you have accepted defeat in your own mind. Regardless of the nature of your adversity, there is always a seed of equivalent benefit in it, if you concentrate on the circumstance to look for the good that came of it instead of the bad. Don't spend any time brooding over the things that are lost or gone, or the mistakes that you have made, except to take the time to analyze them, learn from them, and profit by them, so that you won't make the same mistakes twice.

CONTROLLED ATTENTION

Controlled attention involves the blending and the application of many of the other principles of the philosophy. Persistence should be the watchword behind all of these principles.

Controlled attention is the twin brother of definiteness of purpose. Just think what you could do with those two principles, definiteness of purpose—knowing exactly what you want—and concentrating everything you've got on carrying out that purpose. Do you know what would happen to your mind, to your brain, to your own personality, and to yourself if you would concentrate on one definite thing? By concentrating on it, I mean to put all of the time you can possibly spare when you're not sleeping and not working. Devote all of the time that you can possibly spare to see yourself in possession of the thing that represents your definiteness of purpose. See yourself in possession of it, see yourself building plans retaining it, working out the first step you can take, and then the second, and then the third, and so on. Concentrate on it day-in and day-out, and in a little while you'll get to the point where, every way you turn, you'll find an opportunity that will lead you a little bit closer to the thing that represents your definiteness of purpose. When you know what you want, it's astounding how many things you will find that are related to exactly what you want.

When I was living in Florida several years ago, I had a

very important letter coming to the Tampa, Florida, Post Office. I knew the letter came because I talked to the National City Bank in New York. I knew that letter was in the mail and was down at the post office—and I had to have it before twelve o'clock. I called the postmaster, who was a friend of mine, and he said, "That mail is somewhere between here and your Temple Parish (which was ten miles away, since I lived out in the country). It's on Route 1 and I don't know any way you can get that letter before twelve o'clock unless you run that postman down. I'll tell you which stations to start at, because he's already passed station number nine. If you want to pick him up there, I'll give you the instructions on how to follow his route."

Well, Route 1 was the same highway I used to travel from Tampa to my home in Temple Parish. I traveled that highway every day. I didn't know there were any mailboxes on it but when it began to be important for me to observe mailboxes, I never saw so many mailboxes in all my life. Believe me, there looked to be a mailbox almost every hundred feet! They were all numbered and I was looking for the number the postmaster had given me as the one where he would probably be at that very hour and I finally caught up with him. It was on a Monday, and so he had an enormous load of mail. He said, "Man, I can't do anything about it. I don't know where your letter is and I won't know until I get rid of all this mail." I said, "Listen, fellow, I have got to have that letter. It's in there, and I have got to have it. The postmaster told me to run you down and not to take no for an answer. He said to tell you to get out and sort that mail and let me have that letter. That's what he told me, and if you don't think so, come right over here to this farmhouse and call him yourself." He said, "I can't do that. It's unlawful." I said, "Unlawful or not, I've got to have that letter now and that's all there is to it. Now listen, fellow, be a good sport. No use you and me arguing. You've got a job to do and I've got a job to do. Mine's important and yours is important. It's not going to hurt you very much to go through that mail." "Oh, hell," he said, "all right." So he went to work and the third letter that he picked out was mine. The third one. It's just one of those things, when you know what you want, somehow or other you're determined to get it, and it's not nearly as difficult to get as you thought it would be.

I often think of that experience, how indicative it is of people who know what they want and are successful in getting it. They don't let anything stop them at all. They don't pay any attention to opposition.

I've often watched my distinguished business associate, Mr. Stone, talk to his salesmen. I get a thrill every time I hear him speak, because I don't believe he knows what the word *no* means. I think he's long since believed it means yes—and the results he gets show that he believes it means yes. He can be the most definite about the things he wants of anybody I've ever known. He's the most definite about failure and in refusing to accept a turndown. When objects get in his way, he just moves right over them, around them, or blows them out of the way, but he never lets them stop him. That's concentration and definiteness of purpose put into action.

Everybody knows what Henry Ford's definiteness of purpose was. People have been riding around in a part of his major purpose every day of their lives. It was a low-price, dependable automobile. He didn't allow anybody to talk him out of it. I have heard promoters approach Mr. Ford with opportunities that seem to me most glittering. He told them that the thing he was engaged in consumed all of his time and all his effort. He was not interested in anything outside of his definite major purpose, which was to make and distribute all over the world low-priced, dependable automobiles. Sticking to that job made him fabulously rich.

I saw hundreds of people spend infinitely more money than Mr. Ford had when he started out, and they ended up in the graveyard of failure. I couldn't find a dozen people in the world today who would know what their names were. Men who were better educated than Mr. Ford, had better personalities, and had everything that he had and a lot more, except one thing. They didn't stick to the one definiteness of purpose the way he did when the going was hard.

As an inventor, Mr. Edison gives a marvelous illustration of what concentration can do. Truth be known, Mr. Edison was a genius in any sense, because when the going was hard, that's when he turned on the most steam and didn't quit.

Think of a man keeping on through ten thousand different failures as he did when he was working on the incandescent electric lamp. Ten thousand! Can you imagine going through ten thousand failures in the same field without wondering if you shouldn't have your head examined? I was astounded when I heard that and actually saw his logbooks. There were two logbooks, each with about two hundred and fifty pages, and on every page there was a different plan that he had tried, which failed. I said, "Mr. Edison, suppose that you hadn't found the answer. What would you be doing right now?" He said, "I would be in my laboratory working instead of out here fooling away my time with you." He grinned when he said it, but he meant exactly what he was saying.

INFINITE INTELLIGENCE ON YOUR SIDE

If you don't give up when the going is hard, Infinite Intelligence will throw itself on your side. You will have your faith, your initiative, your enthusiasm, and your endurance tested, but when nature finds out that you can stand the test, and you're not going to take no for an answer, it will say, "You pass. You're in."

I think that nature—or Infinite Intelligence, or God, first cause, or whatever you choose to call it—conveys information to people in simple terms, in ways they can understand. That's what this philosophy teaches. It's not like sending a high school boy or girl to the dictionary or to the encyclopedia to read about it. On the contrary, you *under-stand* it. Your own intelligence tells you the moment you come across one of these principles that it's sound. You don't need any proof; you can see that it's sound. This philosophy wouldn't be in existence today if I hadn't concentrated on it through twenty-odd years of adversity and defeat. It pays to concentrate and my own experience corroborates this—if you stand by when the going is hard, Infinite Intelligence will throw itself on your side.

I don't think that would be true in a case like that of Hitler's. No doubt he had definiteness of purpose and an obsessional desire. What was wrong with his definiteness of purpose is that it ran counter to the plans of Infinite Intelligence, the laws of nature, and the laws of right and wrong.

You may be sure that whatever you're doing will come to naught, to failure, and to grief if it works a hardship or an injustice upon a single individual. If you hope to have Infinite Intelligence throw itself on your side, you must be "right," meaning that everything you do benefits everybody whom it affects, including yourself.

Christ's whole life was devoted to concentration upon a system of living for the brotherhood of man. He didn't fare too well while he lived, but he must have been doing the right thing, because if it hadn't been right, it would have been destroyed and gone long before this. He may have only had twelve people to start but I believe what he was preaching must have been right based on what's happened since he passed on.

There is something in nature (or in Infinite Intelligence), which brings forth with every evil the virus of its own destruction. There's no exception to that. The overall plan of nature and the natural laws of the universe dictate that, no matter what the circumstance, every evil, by itself, brings its own virus of its own destruction.

Take William Wrigley for instance. William Wrigley Jr. was the first man that ever paid me for teaching this philosophy. My first hundred dollars that I ever made came from William Wrigley. Just think what that man did on a five-cent package of chewing gum. I never ride down Michigan Boulevard and see that building on the river, lit up at night, that I don't think of what concentration can do even with such a thing as a five-cent package of chewing gum.

The signers of the Declaration of Independence, George Washington, Abraham Lincoln, and Thomas Jefferson had the concentration to give personal liberties to all of the American people and, eventually, to the people of the world. It may well be that America is the cradle for the birth of freedom of mankind. I know of no other nation on the face of this earth that is concentrating upon the freedom of the individual as we're doing here in the United States. I know of no other philosophy, and no one as engaged in any other study, whose objective is to free so many people as those who are studying this philosophy.

ACCURATE THINKING

Dr. Hill's eleventh principle, Accurate Thinking, will help you penetrate the innermost secrets of *Your Right to Be Rich*. It analyzes the mystery of all mysteries, as well as the power of the human mind.

Anyone who intends to achieve any form of enduring success must learn the art of thinking accurately. He or she must understand the fundamentals of thinking, including inductive reasoning, deductive reasoning, and logic. They must learn to distinguish between important and unimportant facts, separate fact from fiction, and discern emotions vs. opinions. Ultimately, they must do their own thinking, and so must you.

Permit no one, no acquaintance, friend, relative, media expert, or authority to do your thinking for you. Remember that everything begins with an idea, a thought, and if the thought is based on faulty logic or reasoning, then the work that evolves from that thought must also be flawed. It is not easy to become an accurate thinker, but it is absolutely essential that you do so.

Accurate thinking is something everybody talks about but hardly anybody ever does. It's a marvelous thing to be able to think accurately, analyze facts, and make decisions based upon accurate thinking rather than upon emotional feelings. The majority of opinions and decisions you and I (and everybody else, for that matter) make are based upon things that we desire or things that we feel, and not necessarily upon the facts. When it comes to a showdown between the things you feel like doing and the things that your head tells you to do, which one usually wins? What's the matter with the head? Why do you suppose it doesn't get a better chance? Why isn't it consulted more? Someone once said that most people do not think, they just think that they think, and I think that just about covers it.

There are certain simple rules and regulations that you can apply to the subject of accurate thinking and this lesson covers every one of them. They will help you avoid the common mistakes of inaccurate thinking, such as snap judgments and being pushed around by your emotions. The truth of the matter is that your emotions are not reliable at all. The emotion of love, for instance, is the greatest and the grandest of all of the emotions, and yet it can also be the most dangerous. More trouble in human relationships grows out of misunderstanding the emotion of love than all other sources of difficulty combined.

THREE BASIC FORMS OF THINKING

Let's begin at the beginning on accurate thinking and see just what it is. First of all there are two kinds of thinking based upon three major fundamentals as follows.

1. **Inductive reasoning** based on assumption of unknown facts or hypotheses.

2. **Deductive reasoning** based on known facts or what is believed to be known facts.

3. **Logic** that is guidance by past experiences that are similar to those under consideration.

Of those three types of thinking that we do, which one do you think we put into operation most? Inductive reasoning, deductive reasoning, or logic?

INDUCTIVE REASONING

Inductive reasoning is based on assumption of unknown facts or hypotheses. You may not know the facts, but you assume that they exist. In fact, you create them and base your judgment on what you have created. When you do that, you must keep your fingers crossed and be ready to change your decision—your reasoning may not prove to be accurate because you're basing it upon assumed facts.

DEDUCTIVE REASONING

Deductive reasoning is based on known facts or what are believed to be known facts. This is where you have all of the facts before you and you can deduce from those facts certain things that you ought to do for your benefit or to carry out your desires. That's supposed to be the type of reasoning or thinking that the majority of people engage in, only they don't do a very good job of it.

TWO STEPS IN ACCURATE THINKING

Step #1: Separate Fact from Fiction or Hearsay. There are two major steps in accurate thinking. The first one is to separate facts from fiction or hearsay evidence. Before you do any thinking at all, you must find out whether you're dealing with facts, fiction, real evidence, or hearsay evidence. If you're dealing with fiction or hearsay evidence, it behooves you to be especially careful to keep an open mind and not reach a final decision until you have examined all the facts very carefully.

Step #2: Distinguish Important Facts from Unimportant Facts. The second step is to separate facts into two classes, important and unimportant. What is an important fact? You may be surprised that the vast majority of facts—not hearsay evidence, not hypotheses—the vast number of facts that we deal with day in and day out are relatively unimportant. When you understand what an important fact is, you'll know why.

IMPORTANT FACTS

An important fact may be assumed to be any fact that can be used to one's advantage in the attainment of one's major purpose, or any subordinate desire leading toward the attainment of one's major purpose. That's what an important fact is.

I would be remiss if I didn't say that the vast majority of people spend more time on irrelevant facts that have nothing to do with their advancement than they do on facts that would be of benefit to them. Curious people, people that meddle in other people's affairs, gossipers and all that sort of thing, put in a lot of time thinking and talking about other people's affairs. They deal with petty small-talk and petty facts—in other words, dealing with unimportant facts. If you doubt this is true, take inventory of the facts that you deal with for one whole day, and at the end of the day, sum up that inventory and see how many really important facts you've been dealing with. It would be better to do this on a Sunday or an off day when you're away from your occupation or business, because that's where an idle mind usually goes to work on unimportant facts.

ACCURATE THINKING ABOUT OPINIONS

Opinions are usually without value, because they are based on bias, prejudice, intolerance, guesswork, or hearsay evidence. It's surprising to take inventory and find out how many people have how many opinions on how many things. They have no basis for their opinions whatsoever, except the way they feel, what somebody said to them, what newspaper they read, or what influence they've come under. Most of our opinions come as a result of influences that we don't have any control over.

ACCURATE THINKING ABOUT ADVICE

Free advice, volunteered by friends and acquaintances, is usually not worthy of consideration. Why? Because free advice is rarely based upon facts and there's too much small-talk mixed up in it.

What kind of advice is the most desirable when you need advice? How do you go about getting it? The best kind of advice is from someone who is a specialist or who is known to be a specialist at the problem at hand. Go and pay him for his services. Don't go after him for free advice.

I can tell you a story about free advice.

Here's what happened to a student of mine in California. Actually, he was my friend before he was my student. For three years, he used to come over to my house every weekend and spend three or four hours with me. Now, I ordinarily would get $50 an hour, but I didn't get anything from him because he was a friend and acquaintance. He'd come over to get three or four hours of free counsel, and I gave it to him every time he came. But I knew he didn't hear a single word that I said. Not a word. That went on for three years. And finally he came over one afternoon. I said, "Now look here, Elmer, I've been giving you free counsel for three years and you haven't heard a darned thing" (but *darn*'s not the word that I used). "You haven't heard a darned thing that I've been saying! You'll never get any value out of this counsel that I'm giving until you start paying for it. We're starting a master course right away, so why don't you go ahead and join that course like everybody else, and then you'll commence getting some value." He took out his checkbook and gave me a check for the master course, and he entered the course and went all the way through it. I want to tell you that his business affairs began to thrive from that moment on. I have never seen a man grow and develop so fast. After he paid a substantial sum for some counsel, he commenced listening to it and putting it into action.

That's human nature I'm talking about. I'm telling you

it's a fact: Free advice is worth what it costs. Everything in this world is worth just about what it costs. Love and friendship, what are love and friendship worth? Do they have any price? Try to get love and friendship without paying the price and see how far you go. Those are two things that you can only get by giving them. You can only get the real McCoy by giving the real McCoy, that's the only way you can get it. If you try to mooch and get friendship and love without giving it in return, your source of supply will soon play out.

THINK FOR YOURSELF

Accurate thinkers permit no one to do their thinking for them. How many people permit circumstances, influences, radio, television, newspapers, other people, and relatives to do their thinking for them? What percentage would you say of the people permit that? I've heard some of my students say it's 97, 99, or even 100 percent. It's not quite that high, but I can tell you the percentage is way up there. Most people let other people do their thinking for them.

I have one asset of which I am proudest. Can you guess what it is? It has nothing to do with money, bank accounts, bonds, stocks, or anything of that kind. It's something even more precious than any of that. I'll tell you what it is.

I have learned to hear all evidence and get all of the facts that I can from all of the sources that are available before I put them together in my own way and have the last word in my own thinking. That doesn't mean that I'm a know-it-all, a doubting Thomas, or that I don't seek counsel. I certainly do seek counsel, but when I receive counsel, I determine how much of it I will accept and how much I will reject.

When I make a decision, nobody can ever say that it isn't a decision by Napoleon Hill, even if it's a decision based on a mistake or error. It's still mine, I did it, and nobody influenced me. That doesn't mean I'm hard-hearted or that my friends have not had any influence on me. They certainly do, but I determine how much influence they have on me and what reaction I have to their influence. I would never permit a friend to have such influence on me as to cause me to damage some other person, just because that friend wanted it done. That's been tried many times, and I would never permit that.

Do your own thinking. I think the angels in heaven sing out when they discover a man or a woman that does his or her own thinking and doesn't allow relatives, friends, enemies, or anyone else to discourage that business of accurate thinking. I emphasize this because the majority of people never take possession of their own minds. Thinking is the most valuable asset anybody has. It's the only thing the Creator gave you that you have complete control over. It can also be the one thing that people generally don't discover and use but allow others to kick around like a football (not you, of course).

I don't know why our educational system (or someone in our system of teaching or writing) has never informed people of the asset of thinking. **The greatest asset in the world—an asset sufficient unto *all* of your needs—is the privilege of using your own mind, thinking your own thoughts, and directing those thoughts to whatever objective you choose.** Yet you don't do it.

Whatever this philosophy touches, and however it begins to touch people, they blossom out as they never blossomed before. It makes a great difference when they find out that they have a mind, that they can use that mind, and that they can make it do whatever they want it to do. I won't say that they all run and immediately take possession of their mind. In fact, they rather sneak or slip in, a little at a time. But eventually, the affairs of their lives begin to change, and the reason they change is that they discover this great mind power and start using it.

PAY ATTENTION TO THE SOURCE

It's not safe to form opinions based upon newspaper reports. In fact, "I see by the papers" is the preparatory remark that usually brands the speaker as the snap judgment thinker. "I see by the papers," or "I hear tell," or "They say." How often have you heard those terms? When I hear anybody start off with, "They say so and so," I mentally pull down my earmuffs and don't hear a doggone thing they say, because I know it's not worth hearing. When anybody starts giving you information and identifies the source by saying, "I see by the papers," or they say, "I hear tell," don't pay the slightest attention whatsoever to what's said. It's not that what they're saying might not be accurate, but I know that the source is faulty and, therefore, the chances are that the statement is faulty also.

GUARD AGAINST GOSSIP

Scandalmongers and gossipers are not reliable sources from which to procure facts on any subject whatsoever. They're not reliable and they're also biased. Do you know that when you hear anybody speak in a derogatory way of anybody else, whether you know the person or either one of the persons or not, the very fact that one person speaks in a derogatory way of another person puts you on guard and gives you the responsibility of studying and analyzing very closely everything that's said? Because you know you're listening to a biased person. You know that.

The human brain is a wonderful thing. I marvel at how smart the Creator was in creating a human being, giving us all of the equipment, machinery, and mechanism with which to detect falsehood from truth. There is always something present in the falsehood that notifies the listener of it. It's something you can tell and you can feel. It's the same when someone is speaking the truth.

By the same token, what about when you hear someone overpraised by a doting or loving friend? That's a compliment and it's less dangerous to depend upon, but certainly if you want accurate facts, study the remarks of a complimentary nature just as closely as you study the others.

What if I send somebody to you for employment, send along a very laudatory letter, or get you on the telephone and give you a sales pitch about how marvelous this person is? If you're an accurate thinker, you're going to know that I'm rubbing it on pretty thick, that you'd better be very careful how much of it you accept, and you'd better do a little outside investigating. Right? I'm not trying to make a doubting Thomas out of you. I'm not trying to make a cynic out of you. I'm trying to bring to your attention the necessity of using this God-given brain that you have with which to think accurately and to search the facts (although when you find the facts, they may not be what you're looking for). There are a lot of people who fool themselves and there's no worse fooling than the fooling that one does for himself. That old Chinese proverb says, "A man fools me once, shame on the man. Fool me twice, shame on me." People just never seem to think to do a little accurate thinking or a little investigating.

You'd think bankers, for instance, would be so shrewd that a confidence man couldn't come in and take them. One of the most outstanding confidence men in the world was Barney Birch. I don't know what ever happened to him but he used to operate here in Chicago. I got acquainted with him once and interviewed him on several occasions. I asked him what type of men were the easiest victims, and he said, "Bankers, because they *think* they're so damn smart."

Maybe now you won't pay too much attention to scandalmongers and gossipers.

WISHES ARE NOT FACTS

Wishes often are fathers to facts and most people have a bad habit of aligning facts to harmonize with their desires. Did you know that? You have to look in the looking glass when you're searching for the person who can do accurate thinking. You've got to put yourself under suspicion a little too, don't you? Because if you wish a thing to be true, you'll often assume it is true and you will act as if it were. If you love a person, you'll overlook his faults. If you love him a great deal, you may never even see his faults. We need to watch ourselves with those we admire most until they have proved themselves entirely, because I have admired a great many people who turned out to be dangerous—very dangerous indeed. As a matter of fact, I think most of my troubles in my early days came from trusting people too much. When I let people use my name, they didn't always use it wisely. That happened five or six times in my life, because I trusted the people. I trusted them because I knew them, they were nice people, and they said and did the things that I liked. Be careful of the fellow that says and does the things you like, because you're going to overlook his faults. Don't be too hard on the man who steps on your corns and causes you to reexamine yourself. Don't be too hard on him, because the person who irritates you but causes you to examine yourself carefully may be the most important friend you ever had in your life.

We all like to meet and associate with people who agree with us, that's human nature. However, some people that you associate with and who agree with you (though it's all very nice and lovely) can take advantage of you, and they do. Information is abundant, and most of it is free, but facts have an elusive habit and generally there is a price attached to them. Certainly the price is unmistakably in examining them for accuracy, because that's the least you have to pay for facts.

There's a favorite question of the accurate thinker, when a thinker hears a statement that he can't accept. He immediately asks the speaker, "How do you know? What is your source of information?" If you have the slightest doubt in what they're stating, ask them to identify their source of knowledge, because it puts the person right out on a limb, and he won't be able to do it. If you ask him how he knows and he tells you, "By believing," how can you believe anything unless it is based upon something? I *believe* there's a God. A lot of people do. But I bet there are a lot of people who say that they *believe* in God but couldn't give you the slightest evidence of him if you backed them into a corner. I can give you evidence. When I say that I believe in a God, you might say, "How do you know?" I don't so much have evidence with anything in this world as much as I do with the existence of a Creator, because the organization of this universe couldn't go on and on, until the end of time, ad infinitum, without a first cause and without a plan in back of it. You know that's absolutely true. And yet, a lot of people try to prove the presence of God in devious ways that, in my book of rules, wouldn't constitute evidence at all. Anything that exists—including God—is capable of proof, and where there is no such proof available, it is safe to assume that it doesn't exist. When no facts are available for the basis of an opinion or a judgment or a plan, turn to logic for guidance. No one has ever seen God, but logic says that he exists of necessity; he has to exist or we wouldn't be here. We couldn't be here without a first cause, a higher intelligence than ourselves. We couldn't be here.

Let's talk about that thing called logic. There are times when you have a hunch; you have a feeling that certain things are true or are not true. Be careful to pay high respect to that hunch or those feelings, because that's probably Infinite Intelligence trying to break through the outer shell and let you use a little logic.

Let's say one of you got up and said, "My definite need, or major aim, is to make a million dollars this coming year." What do you think would be the first question I would ask? I'd ask, "How are you going to do it?" I want to hear your plan, and then after I hear your plan, what am I going to do about it? Am I going to accept or reject it? First, I'm going to weigh you, your ability to get a million dollars, and what you're going to give for it. My logic will tell me whether or not your plan for doing it is probable and workable and practical. That doesn't take an awful lot of intelligent thinking, but it's a very important thing to do. I'd go over it and ana-lyze your plan. I'd analyze you, your capabilities, your past experience, and your past achievements. I'd analyze the people you're going to help and the people who you'll get to help you make that million dollars. When I got through analyzing, I would be able to tell you that probably you can do it or I'd be able to point out to you that probably it would take longer than that year that you said (for example, maybe it'd take two years, maybe three). Then again, I might tell you that you probably wouldn't be able to do it at all. If my reasoning taught me that was the answer, then I'd give it to you just that way.

I've had some of my students put propositions before me that I had to turn down. I had to tell them to abso-lutely forget about it, because they're wasting their time. That's the way an accurate thinker proceeds. He doesn't allow his emotions to run away with him. If I allowed my emotions to do my thinking for me, it wouldn't matter what any of my students undertook to do. I'd tell him he could do it.

This leads to a famous quote you've seen many times. **"Whatever your mind can conceive and believe, your mind can achieve."** I don't want anybody to misread that statement, as "Whatever your mind can conceive and believe, your mind *will* achieve." I said, "It *can* achieve." Do you see the difference between the two? It *can*, but I don't know that it *will*. That's up to you; only you know that.

The extent to which you use your own mind, intensify

your faith, the soundness of your judgments, and your plans—all of these factor into what your mind can achieve. Some acid test now has to be made in order to separate facts from information. Let's see how we go about it.

SCRUTINIZE INFORMATION

Scrutinize with unusual care everything you read in newspapers or hear over the radio. Form the habit of never accepting any statement as a fact merely because you read or heard it expressed by someone. Statements bearing some proportion of fact are often intentionally, or carelessly, colored to give them an erroneous meaning. In other words, a half-truth is somewhat more dangerous than an out-and-out lie. It's more dangerous, because the half-truth is liable to deceive one who understands half of it, but thinks the whole of it is true. Scrutinize carefully everything you read in books, regardless of who wrote them. Never accept the works of any writer without asking the following questions and satisfying yourself as to the answers. That also applies to lectures, statements, speeches, conversations, or anything else. Here are the rules that I'm going to give you.

1. **Is the writer a recognized authority on the subject covered?** Is the writer, speaker, teacher, or the one making the statement a recognized authority on the subject on which he's speaking or writing? That's the first question that you ask.

YOUR RIGHT TO BE RICH

2. **Did the writer or the speaker have an ulterior or self-interested motive other than that of imparting accurate information?** The motive that prompts a man to write a book, make a speech, or make a statement in public or in private conversation is very important. If you can understand a man's motive when he's talking, you can pretty well tell how truthful he is in what he's saying.

3. **Has the writer a profit interest or other interest in the subject on which he writes or speaks?** Once you find out what a man's motive is in whatever he's doing, it's impossible for him to fool you because you'll be able to smell him out.

4. **Is the writer a person of sound judgment and not a fanatic on the subject on which he writes?** I have seen a lot of people who were overzealous to the point of being fanatic. If you wanted to judge me, for instance, you wouldn't judge me on the tie I wear, the suit I wear, or how I cut my hair, or even how I used to cut my hair. Not even on how I speak or how poorly I speak. You wouldn't judge me by any of those things. You'd judge me by how much I'm influencing people toward good or evil. That's the way you'd judge me and that's the way you would judge anybody else. You might not like a man's brand of religion or politics, but if he's doing a good job in his field, helping a lot of people, and not doing any damage, never

mind about his brand. Don't condemn him if he's doing more good than he is harm.

Before accepting statements by others as facts, ascertain the motive that prompted the statements. Ascertain the writer's reputation for truth and veracity, and scrutinize with unusual care all statements made by people who have strong motives or objectives they desire to attain through their statements. Be equally careful about accepting as facts the statements of overzealous people who have a habit of allowing their imaginations to run wild.

APPLY CAUTION

Learn to be cautious and to use your own judgment, no matter who is trying to influence you. Use your own judgment in the final analysis. What if you can't trust your own judgment? There are times when an individual can't trust his own judgment because he doesn't know enough about the circumstances he's faced with. That's when he's got to turn to somebody with broader experience or a different education or a keener mind for analysis.

By the way, can you imagine a business succeeding which is all made up of master salesmen? Have you ever heard of such a business? I have. You'd probably think it's wonderful—if there are only master salesmen, they'll bring in all the business in the world. Sure they do. They spend all the money in the world too. A million! In every organization, you need a wet blanket man, a hatchet man, and a man that will cut through the red tape (and every-thing else that gets in his way) and let the chips fall where they may. I wouldn't want to be the hatchet man, or the wet blanket man, but I'd certainly want those two in my orga-nization (if my operation was very extensive).

AVOID REVEALING THE ANSWER
YOU WANT FROM SOMEONE

In seeking facts from others, do not disclose to them the facts you expect to find. Why do I say that? If I say to you, "By the way, you used to employ John Brown and he's applied to me for a position. I think he's a wonderful man. What do you think?" If John Brown has any faults, I cer-tainly won't get them with that kind of a question, will I? If I really wanted to find out about John Brown, who used to work for you, how would I go about getting the informa-tion? In the first place, I wouldn't go about getting it from you at all. I would rather contact a commercial credit com-pany to get an unbiased report on him, because it would probably provide me facts that you'd give a credit rating company that you wouldn't give to me or anybody else.

It's surprising how much information you can get if you know the right commercial agency through which to get it. When you go to someone directly to get information about a man, unless it's very friendly and favorable, chances are you won't get the real facts, you'll get a varnished or watered-down set of facts. If you ask a man a question, don't give him the slightest idea as to what you expect the answer to be. Most people are lazy anyway, and they don't want to go to too much trouble in explaining. They'll just give you the answer they know you want. You'll be tickled to death, and go on with it, and fall down on it later.

USE A SCIENTIFIC PROCESS

Science is the art of organizing and classifying facts. That's what science means. If you wish to make sure you're dealing with facts, seek scientific sources for their testing, if possible. A man of science has neither the reason nor inclination to modify, change, or misrepresent facts. If he had that inclination he would not be a scientist; he would be a pseudo-scientist. Or a fake. There are a lot of pseudoscientists and fakes in this world who would assume to know things that they don't know.

BALANCE HEAD AND HEART

Your emotions are not always reliable. As a matter of fact, most of the time, they're not reliable. Before letting your feelings influence you too much, give your head a chance to pass judgment on the business at hand. The head is more dependable than the heart, but what makes a good combination? Balance them so both have an equal say, so to speak. If you do, it will give you comfort that you are coming up

with the right answer. The person who neglects this generally regrets his neglect.

ENEMIES OF SOUND THINKING

Here are some of the major enemies of sound thinking.

1. Emotion of love. This is the head of the list. How in
the world could the emotion of love interfere with anybody's
thinking? If you ask that, I would know right away you
haven't had many love experiences. If you ever had an experience with love at all, you know very well how dangerous it
is. It's like playing around TNT with a match in your hand.
When it starts exploding, it doesn't give any notice.

**2. Hatred. Anger. Jealousy. Fear. Revenge. Greed.
Vanity. Egotism. Desire Something for Nothing. Procrastination.** All of these are enemies of thinking. Be on the
lookout for them constantly, to be sure that you're free of
them, provided that the thinking at hand is of importance to
you, or maybe your whole future destiny depends upon your
thinking accurately. Isn't it a fact that it does? Doesn't your
future destiny depend largely on your accuracy or your lack
of it in your thinking? If that weren't true, then what would
be the use of the Creator giving you complete control over
your own mind? What good would that be? The answer is
that mind is sufficient unto all of your needs—absolutely . . .
at least in this life span. I don't know if this is true on the
preceding plane where you came from, or on the succeeding
plane where you're going. I don't know about those planes

because I don't remember where I came from and I don't yet know where I'm going. I wish I did, but I know a great deal about where I am now. I've found out a great deal about how to influence my destiny here now so that I get a lot of pleasure of it—I get joy and I can give joy. I learned how to make myself useful and justify my having passed this way. I can say that because I have discovered how to manipulate my own mind, keep it under control, and make it do the things I want it to do. I throw out the circumstances I don't want and accept the ones that I do want, and if I don't find the circumstances I want, what do I do? I create them, of course. That's what definiteness of purpose and imagination are for.

YOUR MIND: AN ETERNAL QUESTION MARK

Your mind should be an eternal question mark. Question everything and everyone until you satisfy yourself that you are dealing with facts. Do this quietly in the silence of your own mind. Avoid being known as a doubting Thomas. Don't come out and question people orally, because that's not going to get you anywhere. Instead, question them silently, in your own mind. Furthermore, if you're too outspoken or too oral about your questioning of people, it puts them on notice, they cover up, and you don't get the information you want. If you quietly go about seeking information and applying accurate thinking, you'll probably come up with the answers you need. Be a good listener, but also be an accurate thinker as you listen. Which is most profitable, to be a good speaker or a good, good listener? Why?

I don't know of any virtue (or any quality) that would help an individual get along in this world better than to be an effective and enthusiastic speaker. And yet, I would also say that it is far more profitable to be a good listener—an analytical listener—than it is to be a good speaker.

Let your mind be an eternal question mark. I don't mean that you should become a cynic or a doubting Thomas. I mean that no matter who you're dealing with, deal with them on the basis of thinking accurately. It will improve your satisfaction with every relationship you have. You'll be more successful if you're also tactful and diplomatic. You'll have a lot more substantial friends than you have by the old method of snap judgment. If you're an accurate thinker, most of your friends will be friends worth having.

INHERITED THINKING HABITS

Your thinking habits are the results of social heredity and physical heredity. Watch both of these sources carefully but particularly social heredity.

Through physical heredity you get everything that you are physically: the stature of your body, the shape and texture of your skin, the color of your eyes and hair. You're the sum total of all of your ancestors farther back than you can ever remember. You've inherited a little of their good qualities and a little of their bad, and there's nothing you can do about that—that's static, it sticks at birth.

The most important part of what you are is the result of your social heredity. This includes environmental influences, things that you have allowed to go into your mind, and things you've accepted as a part of your character. That's the important thing by far.

Your conscience was given to you as a guide when all other sources of knowledge and facts have been exhausted. Be careful to use it as a guide and not as a conspirator. Do you know people who use their conscience as a conspirator instead of a guide? They soft sell their conscience on the idea that what they're doing is right; eventually, the conscience falls in line and becomes a conspirator.

START BY EXAMINING EMOTIONS

If you sincerely wish to think accurately, there is a price that you must pay for this ability and it's a price that is not measured by money. First, you must learn to carefully examine all of your emotional feelings by submitting them to your sense of reason. That's step number one in accurate thinking. In other words, the things that you like to do best are the things that you should examine most. Make sure that they lead you to the attainment of some object, and that you'll want that object after you get it. Be careful about the thing that you set your heart on, because when you get it, sometimes you find that it's not what you wanted at all.

I could give a thousand illustrations of someone who paid too big a price for what they got. They either wanted something too badly, or tried to get too much out of it, or did get too much of it, or didn't get peace of mind, or weren't able to balance their lives along with it. The saddest thing that ever came out of my research was what I learned about the wealthy men that collaborated in building this philosophy. The fact that they didn't get success along with their money was a very sad thing to me. They didn't get success because they became too obsessed with the importance of money and power—the power the money would give them, and the money the power would give them.

BASE OPINIONS ON FACTS

You must curb the habit of expressing opinions that are not based upon facts or what you believe to be a fact. Did you know that you don't have a right to an opinion about anything—not anything at all—unless you base it upon facts, or what you believe to be facts? You have a right, of course, but I mean to say you have the responsibility of assuming what happens to you, if you express an opinion that's not based upon facts or what you believe to be facts. You can fool yourself that way, and a lot of people go through life fooling themselves by opinions that have no basis for existence. You must master the habit of not being influenced by people in any manner just because you like them, or they are related to you, or they may have done you a favor.

MANAGE OBLIGATIONS

I know that when you've gone the extra mile, you're going to put a lot of people under obligation to you, and I want you to do that. It's perfectly proper and legitimate to put people under obligation to you by helping them. No one can find any fault with that. But be careful in being influenced by people just because they have done you a favor. I'm talking now to the people for whom you've gone the extra mile. You may either be in that position, or in a position where somebody's put you under obligation, and you don't want to be. Form the habit of examining the motives of people who seek some benefit through your influence.

CONTROLLING EMOTIONS

Control both your emotion of love and your emotion of hate in making decisions for any purpose, because either of these can unbalance your thinking habits. No man ought to make an important decision while he's angry. You just shouldn't do it. In correcting children, for instance, it's a mistake to discipline children when you're angry. Nine times out of ten, you'll do and say the wrong thing, or do more harm than good. That applies to a lot of grown-ups, too. If you're really angry don't made decisions. Don't make statements to people while you're mad because that can end up doing you a lot of harm.

SELF-DISCIPLINE

There's a separate lesson on self-discipline, but self-control and self-discipline apply to this lesson, too. There are a lot of times when you need a lot of self-discipline in order to be an accurate thinker. You've got to refrain from saying and doing a lot of things you would like to say and do. Bide your time. There's plenty of time for you to plan what you're going to say and do it properly. Accurate thinkers do that. They don't just fly off of the handle, start their mouths and keep them going, like some people do. Carefully study the effect on the listener of everything before you utter the next thing. Don't make any decisions or plans until you have carefully weighed what the effect may be on yourself and on others. I can think of a lot of things I could do that would benefit me but wouldn't benefit you (and might even injure you). However, I wouldn't engage in them because I would eventually have to pay the price.

You see, whatever you do to or for another person, you do to or for yourself. It comes back to you and multiplies. That's another thing that comes under the heading of accurate thinking. After you've become thoroughly indoctrinated with this philosophy, you learn not to do anything that you don't want to come back and affect you. You learn not to think anything, say anything, or do anything that you don't want to come back and give countenance later on in life.

OPINION VS. FACTS

Before accepting as facts the statements of other people, ask yourself if their statements are beneficial. Ask them how they came by their so-called facts. When they express their opinions, ask how they know their opinion is sound. I don't want someone else's opinion, I want facts, and then I'll form my own opinion. Give me the facts and I'll put them together in my own way, says the accurate thinker.

BIAS, EXCUSES, AND ALIBIS

Learn to examine with extraordinary care all statements of a derogatory nature made by one person against others. The very nature of such statements brands them as being not without bias (and that's putting it politely). Overcome the habit of trying to justify a decision you have made that turns out to have been unsound. Accurate thinkers just don't do that. If they find out they're wrong, they reverse their decision just as quickly as they made it.

Excuses, alibis, and accurate thinking never are friendly bedfellows. I've never seen a person yet that wasn't adept at creating alibis for the things that he didn't do but should've done. Most people have a great stack of them and it doesn't take much before they'll fling them together and throw them at you. Good excuses and good alibis don't amount to a thing unless there is something behind them that's sound that you can depend upon.

If you are an accurate thinker, you will never use the terms "They say," or "I heard," or repeat others who say them. Instead, identify the original source and attempt to establish its dependability. It's not an easy matter to be an accurate thinker. There's quite a bit you have to pay in order to be one, but it's worth it. Without accurate thinking people will take advantage of you, you won't get as much out of life as you want, and you'll never be a well-balanced person.

To think accurately, you've got to have a set of rules to go by and you'll find them in this lesson. Go over this lesson, study it carefully, add some notes to it of your own, start now to do some accurate thinking. Start putting these things into practice tomorrow morning or even sooner.

Separate facts into two classes: important and non-important. If you learn to separate facts from information, this lesson alone is easily worth a thousand times as much as you have put into the entire course. Be sure that you're dealing with facts, state the facts as you're dealing with them, break them down, and throw off the unimportant facts that you've been wasting so much time with until now.

LEARNING *from* ADVERSITY *and* DEFEAT

The central theme of the twelfth principle, Learning from Adversity and Defeat, may be stated in one simple sentence: every adversity carries with it the seed of an equivalent or greater benefit. Pain, failure, setbacks, defeats, losses—misfortunes we all must suffer—are simply a part of the human condition. No one wins all the time. Those who succeed are those who do not let adversity stop them. They persevere. They view hardships as tests that permit them to build their strength to even greater dimensions and carry on. Remember this critical point: defeat is never the same as failure unless and until it has been accepted

> as such. Once again, this principle is presented in a context of a test in which you will evaluate yourself as to how much or how little the major causes of failure are part of your life.

No one likes to undergo adversity, unpleasant circumstances, or defeat. After careful consideration of real circumstances and the laws of nature, I believe it was intended that we all should undergo adversity, defeat, failure, and opposition. People do not like defeat or adversity, and yet I'm compelled to tell you that had it not been for the adversity that I went through during the early part of my life, I wouldn't be standing here talking to you tonight. I wouldn't have completed this philosophy that reaches millions of people all over the world. It was out of the opposition that I met with that I grew the strength, the wisdom, and the ability to complete this philosophy and take it to the people in the shape that it's in now.

If had my choice, there's no doubt that I would have made it easier for myself, just the same as you would from here on out. We're all inclined to find the line of less resistance. Did you know that picking the line of less resistance is what makes all rivers, and some men, crooked? That's right, yet it's a very common habit for us to do that. We don't want to pay the price of intense effort, no matter what we're doing. We like to have things come the easy way. The mind is just like any other part of the physical body. It atrophies, withers away, and becomes weak through disuse. One of the best things that can happen to you is to meet with problems, circumstances, and incidents that force you to think, because without a motive, you might not do much thinking anyway.

FORTY MAJOR REASONS FOR FAILURE

There are forty major reasons or causes of failure—more than twice as many causes of failure as there are principles of success. There are seventeen principles of success, some combination of which is responsible for all successful achievements, and more than forty major causes of failure. The forty I talk about are not all of them; they're just the major causes.

IMPORTANCE OF KNOWING YOUR WEAKNESS

Self-examination is one of the most profitable things that you can indulge in. Sometimes you don't want to do it but it's a very necessary thing for us to know ourselves as we are—especially our weaknesses.

In sharing this philosophy of success, it is necessary to tell you the things that you should do and also the things you should not do. Grade yourself as I go along and comment on each one of them. Grade yourself from zero to one hundred. If you're 100 percent free of any one of them, grade yourself 100 percent. If you're only 50 percent free, grade yourself 50 percent. And if you aren't free at all, grade yourself 0. When you're through, add the total and divide it by forty to get your general average on controlling the things that cause men and women to fail.

#1. DRIFTING WITHOUT DEFINITE PLANS

If you don't follow that habit of drifting, if you make decisions quickly, lay out plans and follow those plans, know exactly where you're going and are on the way, you can grade yourself 100 percent on this one. However, be careful before you mark your grade, because it's the rarest thing in the world that anybody would grade himself 100 percent on this one. To do that, you really have to be organized and you really have to be prepared.

#2. PHYSICAL HANDICAP

I may not need to make any comment about an unfavorable hereditary foundation at birth. On the other hand, it could be a cause of failure, or it could also be a cause of success.

Some of the most successful people I have ever known were handicapped by bad afflictions at birth.

#3. MEDDLESOME CURIOSITY

Without curiosity, we'd never learn anything; we'd never investigate anything. But the wording, as "meddlesome curiosity," involves other people's affairs, something that doesn't really concern you, right? If you're not guilty of that, you'll grade yourself 100 percent. Or will you? As you grade yourself, go back to your past experiences and determine to what extent you have control of this weakness.

#4. LACK OF PURPOSE

Lack of purpose specifically refers to lacking a definite major purpose as a lifetime goal. If you lack this, here's a mighty good place to rate yourself 0.

#5. INADEQUATE EDUCATION

One of the most astounding things that I have discovered is that there is very little relationship between schooling and success. I want you to think about that one. Some of the most successful people I have ever known have been people with the least amount of formal education or formal schooling.

A lot of people kid themselves into believing that they're failures because they don't have a college education. If you come out of college with the feeling that you should be paid for what you know instead of what you do, then that college education hasn't done you much good. Wait until you meet that old man destiny standing just around the corner with a club (and it's not stuffed with cotton). Sooner or later, you'll find out that you're not going to be paid for *what you know*, you're going to be paid for *what you do with what you know* or *what you can get other people to do.*

#6: LACK OF SELF-DISCIPLINE

Lack of self-discipline is generally manifested by excesses in eating, drinking, and indifference toward opportunities for self-advancement and improvement. Lack of self-discipline. I hope you can grade yourself very high on this one.

#7: LACK OF AMBITION

Lack of ambition is an inability to aim above mediocrity. How much ambition do you have? Where are you going in life, what do you want out of life, and what are you going to settle for? There was a young soldier I came across just after World War I who said he just wanted a sandwich and a place to sleep that night, but I wouldn't let him do it. I talked him into settling for a higher rate than that, and the result was that he became a multimillionaire within the next four years. I hope I'll have as much success with you in stepping your ambition up to where you're not willing to settle for a penny. Aim high. It's not going to cost you anything to aim high. You may not get as far as you aim, but you can certainly get farther than if you don't aim at all. Get your sights raised up. Be ambitious and be determined that you're going to become in the future what you have failed to become in the past.

#8: POOR HEALTH

Ill health is often due to wrong thinking and improper diet. People have a lot of alibis on account of ill health, I can assure you. They have a lot of imaginary ailments (they call it hypochondria in the Materia Medica). I don't know to what extent you've been coddling or babying yourselves on this, that, and the other imaginary aliments. If you have, grade yourself pretty low on that one.

#9: UNFAVORABLE CHILDHOOD

What about unfavorable environmental influences during childhood? Once in a great while you'll find that the influences upon a person during childhood are of such a negative nature that a person will go all the way through life with those negative influences. I'm quite convinced that if I had been permitted to continue in my childhood as I started out, before my stepmother came into the picture, I really and truly would have become a second Jesse James—only I would have been able to shoot faster and straighter than he did.

#10: LACK OF PERSISTENCE

Lack of persistence is failing to follow through with one's duties. What is it that causes people to fail to follow through when they start something? What's the main reason why people do not follow through, do the thing right, and see that it's done right? Lack of motive, that's the answer. They don't want to do it badly enough. I'll follow through on anything that I want to follow through on, but if I don't want to follow through, I can find a lot of alibis to keep from doing it. Is it profitable for you to get in the habit of following through when you undertake something, or is it profitable to permit yourself to be sidetracked? How do you rate on that one? Do you follow through or are you easily sidetracked? Are you easily dissuaded from doing a thing when somebody criticizes you? Believe me, if I had been afraid of criticism, I never would have gotten anywhere in life. In fact, I got to where I really courted criticism because it put the fight in me; when that fight was in me, I did a much better job and I carried through better.

There are a lot of people who fail because they lack that driving force that causes them to carry through, especially when the going is hard. No matter what you're doing, you're going to run into that period when the going is hard. If it's a new business, you'll probably need finances you don't have in the beginning. If it's a profession, you'll need clients you don't have in the beginning. If it's a new job, you'll need recognition with your employer that you don't have—you have to earn that recognition. You need follow-through in the beginning, when the going is always hard.

#11: NEGATIVE ATTITUDE

People can have a habit of negative mental attitude, a habit of keeping their mind negative all the time. Are you preponderantly negative most of the time or are you preponderantly positive? When you see a doughnut, what do you see first? Is the first thing you see the hole or the doughnut? Of course, you don't eat the hole, you just eat the doughnut. But a lot of people who come across a problem are like the fellow who sees the hole in the doughnut and growls about it because it takes out so much cake. They don't see the doughnut itself. This is a negative mental attitude.

What is the result of a person who has the habit of allowing his mind to become negative and remain negative? You can't put him in jail for it. You can't sue him for it. A negative mind repels people. A positive mind attracts . . . what? It attracts people who harmonize with your positive mental attitude and your fine character. Just like that old saying, "Birds of a feather flock together," negative birds flock to the negative mind, and positive birds flock to the positive mind.

Who has control over your mind? Who determines whether it's positive or negative? I want you to grade yourself on the extent to which you exercise that prerogative—the most precious thing you have or ever will have. The only thing you have complete unchallenged control over is the right to make your mind positive and keep it that way, or allow the circumstances of life to make it negative. You have to work to keep your mind positive. Why? With so many negative influences around you—so many people, so many circumstances—you'll become negative if you let yourself become a part of those circumstances instead of creating your own in your mind. If you have a very clear concept of the difference between a negative mind and a positive mind, can you picture what happens in the chemistry of the brain when your mind is positive or when it's negative? Have you noticed the difference between your achievements when you are afraid and the achievements when you are not afraid (whether in selling, teaching, lecturing, writing, or anything else)?

I first wrote *Think and Grow Rich* while I was working for President Roosevelt during that bad depression, which was during his first term. I wrote it in that same negative mental attitude that everybody else was in (in other words, my negative attitude was unconsciously forced upon me by the masses). Several years later when I got that book out and read it, I recognized it was not a salable book because of its being negative. A reader will pick up exactly the mental attitude that a writer is in when he writes a book, no matter what kind of language or terminology he uses. Without changing a word in the book, I sat down at my typewriter when I was in a new frame of mind. I was "up on the beam," as we say—100 percent positive—and I typed that book in *that* frame of mind and that's the thing that made that book click. You can't afford to do anything when you're negative. Anything you do that you expect to benefit you, anything that you expect to influence other people—if you want to get people to cooperate with you, if you want to sell people something, or if you want to make a good impression upon people, don't come near them until you're in a positive frame of mind.

Grade yourself accurately on this one. Grade yourself on the *average* state of mind that you maintain, not just on your state of mind at any given time. Here's a good rule to go by to determine whether or not you are more positive than you are negative: observe how you feel when you wake up in the morning and get out of bed. If you're not in a good frame of mind, I can tell you it's because a lot of thought habits that preceded that hour (the day before, perhaps) had been negative. You can make yourself very ill by allowing your mind to become negative and it will reflect itself the next morning. When you come out of sleep, you're just fresh from coming out of the influence of your subconscious mind. Your conscious mind had been off duty all night, and when it goes back on duty, it finds a mess there that you've got to clean up. But, the subconscious mind's been stirring all night long. If you wake up full of joy and you want to get going on what you're going to do today, chances are you've been pretty positive the day before, or maybe several days before.

#12: UNCONTROLLED EMOTIONS

Emotions are both negative and positive. Have you ever realized that it's just as necessary to control your positive emotions as it is your negative ones? Why? Why in the world would I want to control the emotion of love, for instance? One woman answered, "Love can get you in hot water. It can *scald* you." (She must have had some experience with that.) How about the emotional desire for financial gain? Do you need to control the desire for money? You're not afraid of getting too much, are you? Maybe getting it the *wrong* way, or working your emotion up to where you want to get *too* much. I met a lot of people who had too much money for their own good, especially people who got it without earning it or people who inherited it.

Would you be interested in knowing why they call me Napoleon? I'm going to tell you because it makes a good point here. Since I was the eldest son (or the first child), my father named me after my great-uncle, Napoleon Hill, of Memphis, Tennessee, who was a multimillionaire cotton broker. I suppose my father hoped that when Uncle Napoleon died, I would get some of the money. Well, he died and

I didn't get any of the money, and when I found out that I was not going to get any of it, I felt very bad. After I swapped some of my youth for wisdom and observed what happened to the ones who *did* get it, I was thankful—eternally grateful—that I didn't get a dime of it because I learned a better way of getting it for myself than having it given to me.

#13: SOMETHING FOR NOTHING

The desire for something for nothing, or the desire for something for less than its value, is actually the desire for something without being willing to give adequate compensation for it. Are you ever troubled with that tendency? Who of us hasn't been at one time or another? You can have a lot of faults, but you want to find out what they are and start getting rid of them—that's why we're making this analysis. This is your chance to come face-to-face, be trial judge, defendant, and prosecutor all at one time. You get to make the final decision. Far better for you to find your faults than it would be for me to find them for you. Because if you find them, you're not going to spend any alibis; you're going to try get rid of them.

#14: INABILITY TO MAKE DECISIONS

Do you have a habit of reaching decisions promptly and firmly? Or do you reach decisions very slowly, and after you reach them, do you allow the first person that comes along to reverse you? Do you allow circumstances to reverse your decision without a sound reason? To what extent do you stand by your decisions after you make them? What circumstances would cause you to reverse a decision you made?

You should hold an open mind on that subject at all times. Never make a decision and say, "That's it and I'm going to stand by it forever," because something might develop later on that would prompt you to reverse that decision. Some people are stubborn. Right or wrong, once they've made a decision, they die by it. I've seen a lot of people who would rather die than reverse themselves or have somebody reverse them on a decision. Of course you're not like that. Not if you're really indoctrinated with this philosophy. You may have behaved like that once, but you're not like that now (or you're not going to be like that after this).

#15: EXCESSIVE WORRY

This is a wonderful world we're living in. I'm glad I'm here. I'm glad I'm doing what I am, and if unpleasant circumstances cross my path, I am very glad for that, too, because I'll find out whether I'm stronger than the circumstances or not. As long as I can conquer them and go over them, I'm not going to worry about circumstances. I won't worry about things that oppose me; people that don't like me, people who say mean things about me. I'd worry if people said mean things about me and, after examining myself, found out they were telling the truth. As long as they're not telling the truth, I can stand back and laugh at them for how foolish they are and how much damage they're doing to themselves.

#16: POOR CHOICE OF SPOUSE

Here's a honey: number sixteen—the wrong selection of a mate in marriage. Don't be too quick to grade yourself on that one. If you made a 100 percent mistake on that, look around before you grade yourself and see if you can't do something about correcting that mistake, maybe resell yourself. I've known of that being done, haven't you? There are some people who believe all marriages are made in heaven, and it'd be a wonderful thing if they were, but I've seen some that were not made in heaven. I don't know where else they might have been made, but they certainly weren't made in heaven.

I've also seen business marriages or business relationships that were not made in heaven, and I've helped to correct a lot of those in which business associates weren't working together in a spirit of harmony. Believe me, no business on the face of this earth can succeed unless the people at the top level, at least, are working in harmony.

There's no household or home that can be a joy, or a place that you want to go, unless there is harmony at the top. That harmony starts with loyalty, dependability, and ability. That's how I'd evaluate people. If I want to select a man or woman for a high position, the first thing I would look for is whether that person was loyal to the people to whom he owed loyalty. If they didn't have loyalty, I wouldn't want him or her on any terms whatsoever. The next thing I would look for would be dependability, whether or not you can depend upon him to be at the right place at the right time and to do the right thing. After that would come ability. I've seen a lot of people who had great ability but they were not dependable, not loyal, and, therefore, very dangerous.

#17: OVERLY CAUTIOUS

Number seventeen is having overcaution in business and professional relationships. Have you seen people so cautious that they wouldn't trust their own mother-in-law? I knew a man who was so cautious that he had a special wallet made with a little lock put on it. He hid the key in a different place every night, so that his wife couldn't go through his trousers and take money out of his wallet. Wasn't he a honey? I bet his wife loved him.

This is about overcaution in business and professional relationship, and lack of all forms of caution in all human relationships. Have you seen people like that? They just didn't have any caution. Some people start their mouths going and go off and leave them. Never mind what they're going to say, nor what the effect will be on other people. You've seen people like that, haven't you? They have no caution whatsoever— no discrimination, diplomacy, or consideration of what they do to other people through their words. I've seen people with tongues that were sharper than an unused double-edged Gillette blade. I've seen people who would sign anything a salesman put in front of them, not even reading it. They wouldn't even read the big type, let alone the little type. Have you seen people like that?

Of course you're not like that. You know you can be overcautious and you can be under-cautious. The happy medium is found in the lesson on accurate thinking where you carefully examine things you are going to do before you do them, not afterward, and where you evaluate your words before you express them, not afterward.

#18: OVERLY TRUSTING

It know it might be a little bit difficult for you to grade yourselves accurately on this one. To be perfectly candid with you, it would be a little difficult for me to grade myself accurately on seventeen and eighteen, because there've been a lot of times in my life when I wasn't cautious at all. I think most of my troubles in my early days came through my trusting too many people. I let somebody come along and flatter me into using the name Napoleon Hill, and he'd go out and flim-flam a lot of people—all in the name of Napoleon Hill. That happened several times in my life before I tightened up and became cautious. That can happen to a lot of people you know, but on the other hand, I wouldn't want to become so cautious that I didn't trust anybody for anything. You'd get no joy out of living if you did that.

#19: POOR CHOICE OF ASSOCIATES

How many times have you heard of people getting into trouble because they were associated with the wrong kind of people? I've never seen a youngster in my life that became bad or went wrong, where the reason couldn't be traced back to the influence of some other person. Not once have I ever known a youngster to go wrong or to get into bad habits unless somebody else influenced them.

#20: WRONG VOCATION

Number twenty is the wrong selection of a vocation or a total neglect of a choice of a vocation. About ninety-eight people out of every hundred would grade 0 on that one. Of course, students of this philosophy who have been indoctrinated by lesson number one on definite major purpose would grade much higher than that. Give yourself a grade 0 or 100 percent on this one, not halfway. You either have a definite major purpose or you don't have it. You can't grade 50 or 60 or any other amount on this one, or on definiteness of purpose. You either have a major purpose or you don't have it.

#21: LACK OF CONCENTRATION

Lack of concentration of effort is like having divided interests. You don't split your interests or divide them over a lot of different things. One person is not strong enough to do this. Life is too short to ensure your success unless you learn the art of concentrating everything you've got on one thing at a time. You also have to follow through on that one thing and do a good job.

#22: FAILURE TO BUDGET MONEY

It might be difficult for you to grade yourself on number twenty-two: lack of a budget, control over income and expenditures, and having a systemic way of taking care of your income and your expenditures. Do you know how the average person manages the question of a budget? He manages it by being well over on his expenditures, depending on the amount of credit that he can get from other people. When the credit shuts down on him, then he more or less slacks off, but until that happens, he'll run wild with spending.

A good business firm would go bankrupt quickly if they didn't have a system of control over income and expenditures. That's what a comptroller in an organization is for. (Usually called a wet blanket, every successful business of any size has to have a wet blanket.) A man who controls the assets of the company keeps the numbers from getting away at the wrong time and the wrong way.

#23: FAILURE TO BUDGET TIME

Time is the most precious thing that you have. Of the twenty-four hours in every day, each person generally devotes eight hours to sleep, eight hours to make a living, and another eight hours to free time.

As Americans, we have the freedom to do anything we want with those "free" eight hours. You can sin, spend, establish good habits or bad habits, reeducate yourself, and so forth. But what are you actually doing with those eight hours? That's going to be the determining factor on how you grade yourself on this particular question. Are you budgeting the use of your time to the best advantage? Do you have a system of actually making all of your time count? The first sixteen hours is taken care of automatically, but the other eight hours is not. It's flexible and you can do what you want with it.

#24: LACK OF ENTHUSIASM

Without doubt, enthusiasm is among the most valuable emotions, provided that you can turn it on and off, like a water spigot or an electric light. If you can turn on your enthusiasm when you want to and turn it off whenever you want to, you can grade yourself 100 percent on this one. Lack of the ability to do that would grade you somewhere toward that little zero.

How do you go about controlling your enthusiasm? Have you ever thought about your willpower? What it was placed there for? You have a power of will and what's the purpose of that power of will? It's for discipline to make your mind whatever you want it to be and form whatever habits you want.

I have never been able to determine in my own mind which is worse: no enthusiasm at all (like a cold fish), or red-hot enthusiasm (that's out of control). They're both bad. If somebody made me mad right now, I could turn off my enthusiasm just like that and turn on something else. That might be much more appropriate (provided that I kept bad language out of the picture, that is). But there was a time when I could turn on the anger much more quickly than I could turn on enthusiasm, and I couldn't turn off anger nearly as easily. That's something you will have to overcome, the ability to turn on or turn off any of your emotions.

#25: INTOLERANCE

Intolerance is a closed mind based on ignorance or prejudice, in connection with religious, racial, political, and economic ideas. How do you rate on that one? It would be a marvelous thing if you could rate 100 percent and honestly say that you have an open mind on all subjects, and toward all people, at all times. However, if you could say that, you'd probably not be human—you'd be a saint.

I suppose there are times when you can make up your mind to be open-minded on all these things, at least for a little while. I know I can, at least for a little while. However, if you can't grade 100 percent, and can't honestly say you are open-minded toward all people, at all times, on all subjects, what is the next best thing to do? We're tolerant some of the time, of course. The more you try to be tolerant, you'll eventually get to where you'll be in the habit of tolerance instead of intolerance.

When the vast majority of people meet other people, they immediately begin to look for the things that they don't like in the other people, and they *always* find things they don't like. But there's another type of person, and I notice that this other type of person is always much more success-ful, much more happy, and much more welcome when he comes around, or when he meets a person. Whether it's an acquaintance or a stranger, the first thing he does is not only to look for things that he likes in that person, but also to compliment them, either by saying or doing something to indicate that he recognizes their good qualities (instead of the bad ones). I get a great feeling when somebody walks up to me and says, "Aren't you Napoleon Hill?" and I say, "Yes, I'm guilty." "Well, I want to tell you, Mr. Hill, how much good I got out of your book. I just thrive on it, I love it, and it does me a lot of good." I enjoy it, unless of course they rub it on too thick (and you can do that too, you know). My point is, I've never seen the person that doesn't respond in kind if you compliment that person. As bad natured as they are, even a pussycat will curl up his tail and begin to purr if you stroke him on the back. Cats are not very friendly, but you can make them friendly if you do what cats like.

#26: UNCOOPERATIVE

Uncooperative means failure to cooperate with others in the spirit of harmony. I suppose there are circumstances in which failure to cooperate would be justified. Or are there? There are a lot of circumstances where you fail to cooperate. I often come into contact with people who want me to do things that I can't possibly do for them. They want my influence, want me to write letters of recommendation, or want me to make telephone calls for them. I don't do any of those things, or cooperate in any way, unless I'm sold on what I'm cooperating with, and with whom I'm cooperating. You might want to be like that, too.

#27: UNEARNED RICHES

Do you have possession of power or wealth not based on merit or what you've earned? I hope you won't have any trouble grading yourself on this one.

#28: LACK OF LOYALTY

Another reason for failure is that lack of a spirit of loyalty for those to whom it is due. If you have loyalty in your heart to those to whom loyalty is due, perhaps you can grade 100 percent. Unless you practice that all the time, you wouldn't grade 100 percent; you would grade something lower than that.

Incidentally, if you grade yourself less than 50 percent on any of these, put a cross mark there and go back and study that particular point. You should have all of these causes of failure at least 50 percent under control. If it falls below that, you've reached the danger point.

#29: UNSOUND OPINIONS

Do you have the habit of forming opinions that are not based upon known facts? Grade yourself on the extent to which you do that. If you grade below 50 percent on this one, begin to work on yourself right away—stop having opinions unless you base them on facts or what you believe to be facts.

When I hear anybody expressing an opinion on something that I have reason to believe he knows nothing about, I always think of that story of two men who were discussing Einstein's theory of relativity. They got into a hot argument about it and one of them says, "What does Einstein know about politics anyway?" He thought he understood relativity, didn't he? There are people like that, who have opinions about everything. They could run the country better than Eisenhower's running it. They could tell J. Edgar Hoover a few things about his job. They could always work their friends over and improve them. However, if you examine them very carefully, they're generally not doing too well themselves.

#30: UNCONTROLLED EGO

Egotism is a wonderful thing and vanity is a wonderful thing. If you didn't have a little vanity, you wouldn't wash your neck, or your face, or have your hair curled, or marceled (or whatever it is that women do to their hair). You have to have a little vanity, a little pride, but you can have too much. I think lipstick is a wonderful thing, if it doesn't get on my shirt, but there's such a thing as too much lipstick. Rouge on the face is a wonderful thing too, but nature is a pretty good old hand at painting faces just right. When I see a sixty- or seventy-year-old woman painting her face up to look like a sixteen-year-old, I know she's fooling herself and nobody else—because she's certainly not fooling me.

The ego is a marvelous thing. A lot of people need a buildup in their ego, because they have allowed the circumstances of their life to whip them down until they've got no fight left in them, no initiative, no imagination, and no faith. Human ego is a wonderful thing when you have it under control and don't allow it to become objectionable to other people. I have yet to see a successful person that didn't have great confidence in his ability to do anything he started out to do. One of the purposes of this philosophy is to enable you to build your ego up to where it will do anything you want it to do, no matter what it is. Some people's egos need to be trimmed down a little bit (and even need a little squishing, if you know what I mean), but I'd say even more need a buildup of their ego.

#31: LACK OF IMAGINATION

I have never been able to determine exactly whether this great capacity for vision and imagination is an inherited quality or an acquired quality. I think perhaps in my case it was inherited, because I had a lot of imagination back to the earliest days that I can remember. That was one of the things that got me in difficulty in other things—I had too much imagination and didn't steer it in the right direction.

#32: UNWILLINGNESS IN GOING THE EXTRA MILE

When you develop the habit of going the extra mile, you'll get joy out of doing it, and chances are good that you'll put a lot of people under obligations to you—willing obligations, that is—because they won't mind being under obligations to you on that basis. If you have enough people obligated to you, there's no reason why you can't make legitimate use of their influence, education, ability, and whatnot to help you succeed in whatever you're doing.

Do you know how to get anybody to do whatever it is you want him to do? Do something for him first. How easy is it to do something nice for another person, without even having to ask him? When there's a long list of people who are standing ready as an army to help you when you need help, how do you cultivate that army before the time of need? You can't just go the extra mile this minute, and the next minute turn right around and ask the person to whom you rendered that service to render you twice as much service. You can't do it that way, because it won't work that way.

You've got to build up something called goodwill in advance. Again, the timing has got to be right. There are a lot of people who will go the extra mile only for the sake of expediency. They do it just to put you under obligations. They don't time it well enough to allow you to forget about it, so to speak. Then, they'll turn right around after having done you a favor, and ask you for two or three favors. Have you ever had that experience? Have you ever seen someone make that mistake?

If I had to select one principle with which you could do the most with the most people, I'd say it was this principle: going the extra mile. That's the one thing that anybody can control, if they want to. You don't have to ask anybody for the privilege of going out of your way to be nice and to be of help. But, the very moment you start doing it, you'll probably create contrast, because most people are not doing that.

#33: DESIRE FOR REVENGE

Have you ever had a desire for revenge for real or imaginary grievances? Which is worse, desire for revenge for a real grievance (such as an injury somebody inflicted upon you) or for an imaginary grievance? Think that one over.

What happens to you when you have an expression of revenge, a desire for revenge for any reason whatsoever? Does it hurt the fellow? The point is that the desire for revenge hurts yourself. Revenge makes you negative and poisons your mind. It even poisons your blood if you maintain that desire long enough, because any kind of a mental attitude will get into your blood—and interfere with your sound health.

#34: ALIBIS

Do you know people who have a habit of producing alibis instead of satisfactory results? To what extent do you immediately begin to look for an alibi when you make a mistake, do something that doesn't turn out right, or neglect to do the thing that you should have done? How often do you say, "It was my fault, I'll admit my duty." Or, do you begin to conjure a set of alibis to justify what you've done or neglected to do? The point is to grade yourself on the preponderance of your habits on this subject.

If you're an average person, you look for an alibi to justify what you do, what you refrain from doing, or neglect doing. If you're not an average person (and I'm sure you'll not be if you become properly indoctrinated in this philosophy), you will not look for alibis. You know alibis weaken you; alibis are a crutch to lean on. Instead, you'll face the music, acknowledge your mistakes, acknowledge your weaknesses, and acknowledge your errors. After all, self-confession does something wonderful to the soul.

When you really know what your faults are and confess them honestly, you don't have to spread them to the whole world, but rather, confess where confession is necessary. I had a student come into my office a few days ago and make a confession that's going to be of more use to her than anything that's happened since she was a very small girl. Previously, this student was suffering because she had not yet learned how to distinguish between her needs for things and her rights to have them. Have you ever thought about that? She needed things very badly and she was willing to get them the wrong way, but a lot of people make that mistake. They cannot tell the difference between things they need and the things that they have a right to get.

#35: LACK OF DEPENDABILITY

Though this one might be hard for you to grade yourself on, generally speaking, you know whether you're dependable, or whether your word is dependable. You know whether your performance and your occupation or your job is dependable. You know whether your relationship to your family, your wife, your husband, or your children is dependable. You know whether you're a dependable family man or woman. You know whether you're dependable or not with your credit relations, or with people from whom you buy things on credit.

Isn't it wonderful to have dependability among your friends? You always know exactly where they are and where they are always going to be, regardless of what happens. Isn't it wonderful to have dependability among your loved ones, when you know they are not going to let you down on any score, at any time, or for any reason? If you have a half dozen people like that in your life—absolutely dependable under all circumstances—how lucky you are. I'd say that if you have three people like that in an entire lifetime, you're indeed fortunate.

With as many people as I know all over the world, I'm not so sure I can count on all ten fingers the people in my life who are dependable under all circumstances. Dependability, what a marvelous thing it is.

#36: LACK OF RESPONSIBILITY

Lack of responsibility is an unwillingness to assume responsibilities commensurate with one's desire for compensation. In other words, you desire the good things of life—a good income, a nice home, a nice car, and a wardrobe of nice clothes—but you're unwilling to assume the responsibilities that entitle you to those things. How do you grade yourself on that? Are you willing to assume the necessary responsibilities to be entitled to all the things you want to get out of life? That's what you're grading yourself on.

#37: FAILURE TO HEED YOUR CONSCIENCE

How often do you fail to obey your conscience when it's advantageous to do so? Are there times when you tell your conscience just to step aside for a few moments? You tell your conscience, "Don't look right now," because that little business transaction you want to attend to seems a little bit off color. Did you ever do that? I think you could do that a few times and get away with it, but if you got in the habit of it, you would convert your conscience into a conspirator that would endorse all of the mean things that you might ever want to do. And that would be bad.

Conscience was given by an all-wise Creator, so that you would always know what is right and what is wrong without having to ask anybody. If you're on good terms with your conscience, and really respond to it under every circumstance and let it be your guide, then you are a very fortunate person and you have been using your conscience properly. But, if there are times when you waver in indecision, and make your conscience step aside, then you will grade yourself low and begin to work on that score.

I think it's a marvelous thing that the Creator gave each

individual a sort of judge advocate to sit over all of his acts, all of his needs, all of his thoughts, and tell him when he's right and when he's wrong.

#38: INABILITY TO RELEASE WHAT YOU CANNOT CONTROL

Now, about the habit of unnecessary worrying over things one cannot control. How are you going to grade on that? If you can't control the thing that you're worrying over, what can you do about it? You can adjust yourself to that thing that you can't control, and do it in a positive mental attitude so as to not let it get you down. Or you can transmute that worry into something you can control.

#39: ACCEPTING TEMPORARY DEFEAT AS FAILURE

Do you know the difference between failure and temporary defeat? Have you ever thought about that? First of all, failure is only failure when you accept it as such, regardless of the conditions. It's temporary defeat, perhaps, but certainly not failure. If you were selling and you took no for an answer every time you heard it, you'd never make a living selling. It's just easier for people to say no than it is to say yes. They don't mean it at all, they just mean that they have not yet been broken down by a good salesman. Temporary defeat and failure.

Who determines whether a circumstance is a temporary defeat or failure? Who determines that? That's right: you're the one who determines that.

#40: LACK OF FLEXIBILITY

How are you at adjusting to the varying circumstances of life? One reason for failure is a lack of flexibility of your mind.

Do you know sometimes it's necessary for you to go along with unsavory bedfellows, people that you don't like? You go along with them until such time as they drop out of your life. Of course, you could have it out with them right up front, but if you do that, you'll often get the worse out of it. You can wear them out, or work them to death by going along with them for a time. If you make an incident out of everything that you do with people you dislike, why you'll always be in difficulty. On the other hand, you can let these things, or things that are food for incidents, pass by.

Time is a wonderful cure, a wonderful agent. The greatest doctor on the face of the earth is time—Old Mother Time, or is it Father Time, whichever it is. In any case, there are a lot of things in this world that can be cured only with time.

There are people who fret themselves to death. They wear themselves out making incidents out of very silly, small, and unimportant things that come up every day in their lives. Not a day goes by for any of you that you couldn't make an incident out of something or make an unpleasant scene with someone, if you allow yourself to do it.

As a student of this philosophy, maybe you'll grade yourself about 80 percent on this one. In connection with flexibility, most of the time you adjust yourself to circumstances you don't like without going down under them, and without making an incident out of them.

You might have a very peculiar cause of failure that I haven't mentioned here at all. It would be most interesting to see what it is, if you do have one, because I have given you a pretty good catalog here of the things that cause people to fail. The most important thing about this list of forty things that causes people to fail is that you can do something about each one of them right now. Isn't that true? What would be the use of my having you make this analysis if you couldn't do anything about it?

You can eliminate every one of these causes almost instantaneously. Some will take a little time to develop more positive habits. For the most part, you can wipe every one of them out of your character overnight, by determining to do so, and determining to develop a more agreeable set of circumstances.

You can eliminate these causes of failure no matter what adversity you've had in your life. Go back over the last ten years and look at every unpleasant circumstance you've ever had. Search now for that seed of equivalent benefit that was there, even though you didn't find it and didn't use it at that time. It's very difficult to find the seed of an equivalent benefit in an unpleasant circumstance, while a wound is still open and hurting. There again, timing is important. But, if you give it a little time, and make up your mind that you're not going to go down under the circumstance, and then go back and evaluate it carefully, you will find that you will have learned something of benefit from it.

COOPERATION

In the sixteenth century, the great writer John Donne penned the immortal words, "No man is an island." Perhaps those very words inspired Dr. Hill to count Cooperation as one of the backbones of his philosophy. Also referred to as teamwork, cooperation is the thirteenth principle.

How can such a simple, obvious thing be so important? Consider this: very few, if any, substantial or lasting achievements have been, or ever will be, made by one man or one woman working alone. We all need others. Even the proverbial lone-wolf inventor needs other people with production experience to manufacture and package the invention he's created during years of isolation in his basement or attic. To get his invention to his customers, he needs marketers to advertise and promote it as well as salesmen and retailers to offer it.

What human organization do you know—a home,

school, government, or industry—that can truly succeed without its members working harmoniously together toward a common goal? Cooperation is such a powerful idea because it involves the development and utilization of a particular aspect of the human spirit. A part of our spirit recognizes the oneness of people and the fellowship of all humankind. True cooperation allows no room for selfishness or greed.

There are two kinds of cooperation, one based upon force or coercion and the other based upon voluntary action (and driven by motive).

FORCED COOPERATION

Most circumstances of cooperation are based upon some form of force or coercion. For instance, most employees cooperate with their employer, but there's a certain amount of coercion in it. There's a fear that if they don't cooperate, they'll not have their jobs anymore. Of course, there are circumstances in which the employees' cooperation with the employer has made it so beneficial that they do it willingly.

Any kind of cooperation that's forced or coerced, or based on any type of coercion, is not desirable. People only cooperate on that basis as long as they have to, and when they get to the point they don't have to do it any longer, they kick over the traces.

VOLUNTARY COOPERATION

Relatively speaking, there's a small percentage of employers throughout the United States who understand the advantage of having their employees cooperate with them on a willing basis. There's friendliness in those companies, and it's based upon benefits that they extend to their employees.

COOPERATION VS. THE MASTERMIND PRINCIPLE

Cooperation is different from the mastermind principle when that cooperation is based upon coordination of effort, or when it doesn't necessarily involve the principle of definiteness of purpose or the principle of harmony. For instance, an army of men working under their superior officers in the military service represents a tremendous amount of cooperation, but it doesn't necessarily mean that there's harmony, or that they like what they're doing. There's a certain amount of enforced coercion; they're doing what they have to do. Sometimes they like to do it, but sometimes they don't like to do it.

It's true that willing cooperation is *part* of the mastermind principle, the medium by which great personal power may be attained. No one has ever acquired such power without the aid of these two—the principles of cooperation and mastermind—making them both indispensable.

Cooperation is indispensable in four major relationships: in the home, in one's job or profession, in social relationships, and in supporting our form of government and free enterprise. If every citizen cooperated in those four areas, this would be a better country than we have now.

EXAMPLES OF COOPERATION NOT BASED ON MASTERMIND PRINCIPLE

Let me give you examples of cooperation that do not involve the mastermind principle: 1) Soldiers, working under army regulations; 2) employees, working under rules of employment; 3) government officials, working under laws of the nation; 4) professional men (such as lawyers, doctors, and dentists), working under rules of ethics of their profession; 5) citizens of a nation, living under a dictator.

HOW THE MASTERMIND PRINCIPLE ADDS
POWER TO COOPERATION

Cooperative effort assumes great power when the principle of cooperation is combined with the mastermind principle, which involves harmony and a shared motive. I'll explain this by using the example of government officials, when working in harmony with and supported by a majority of the people.

During Roosevelt's first term in office, the emergency of an economic depression supplied motives for harmony—a desire for economic recovery for all people. I have never seen a finer illustration of power attained through a combination of the principles of cooperation and the mastermind than I witnessed in the Roosevelt administration. We all had a motive in getting behind the president, and that motive was self-survival. We were in danger; there was an emergency. We had to close ranks and get behind the president, whether we agreed with his political principles or not, and we did that. We did it on a grand scale for a time, but as soon as the emergency passed or was softened, the combination of the mastermind principle and cooperation began to disintegrate. Before Roosevelt finally got out of office, there was an upheaval, a lack of harmony, and a lot of other things that caused a lot of people worry and annoyance, not to mention loss.

Employers and their employees can have a motive such as that which inspired harmony in the Arthur Nash Clothing Company, when the company faced bankruptcy. During the time I was publishing *The Golden Rule* magazine, I got a "Hurry up!" call from Mr. Nash, of the Nash Clothing Company in Cincinnati. He wanted me to come over to Cincinnati and see him, and when I got over there I found he was in trouble. He was bankrupt. For no reason that he could explain, his business, which had been going profitably for years, suddenly became unprofitable, and the business dropped off to where they didn't have enough to pay the payroll.

As I went over the situation with Mr. Nash, I said, "There is only one thing that can save your business. You have to work out a plan whereby the employees will take a new lease on life, put their heart and soul in the business, and help you save the business." We worked out such a plan whereby, at the end of the year, in addition to their regular salaries, they would receive a bonus consisting of a percentage of the profits. There were quite a lot of details that I'll not go into, but that was the sum and the substance of it.

Mr. Nash called all his employees together, got up, and told them what he had in mind. He said, "First of all, I think I should tell you all that the company's bankrupt. We don't have enough money to pay this coming week's salary or payroll." He said, "For a long time, this business has been going downhill. I noticed the employees were losing interest, and the enthusiasm that used to prevail is no longer here. The spirit of the thing's gone, and unless we can recapture that spirit, that willingness of enthusiasm for everyone to jump in and do something, why we're all in the same boat, which is namely bankrupt. But, I have a plan and I think it'll work because it's based upon the Golden Rule.

"Here's the plan. You'll come down Monday morning and start in on a *new* basis—the same mental attitude that you were in ten years ago when we were thriving. I'll pay your wages as soon as we can make the wages, including the back wages that I'll not be able to pay you this coming week. If we make a go of it, at the end of the year, we'll divide the profits on a basis that'll give you the same standing as a stockholder in the company. I'm going to leave the room so you can talk it over frankly and decide what you want to do. When you want to see me, you send for me."

He and I went to lunch, and after about an hour, the messenger came over and pulled him away from the luncheon. They went back and Mr. Nash was told what had happened. The employees all got together and decided not only were they going to accept his proposition, they also had an idea of their own. They came in the next day—with their savings. Some of them had money in old socks, some of them in tin cans, some of them in savings accounts. They laid $16,000 in cash on his desk and said, "There it is, Mr. Nash. If that's the way you feel about us, this is the way we feel about you. We earned this money down here just as much, but if it will do any good, use it. When you can pay it back, pay it back. And if you can't pay it back, that's all right, too."

Every one of those employees found the spirit of real cooperation. The company began to thrive, and before Mr. Nash died some ten years later, it became the most prosperous mail order clothing business in the whole United States. As far as I know, it still is that today, despite the fact that he's gone. Imagine the same business, at the same location, making the same kind of clothes, with the same people doing the work—failing one day and starting to succeed on a grand scale the next day. What happened was a change of mental attitude. What caused them to change the mental attitude? It wasn't fear that they'd lose their jobs. It was a motive. Mr. Nash had inspired them with his sincerity and he had a purpose in making that kind of an offer. They were touched by it. They knew it was sincere, and they made up their minds they were going to be just as a good a sportsman as he was. They were not going to let him outdo them.

THE POWER OF MOTIVE

When you get any group of people together on the basis of motive, I don't care what their problems are; they'll meet those problems successfully. They always do. The Rotary Clubs and their members throughout the world give us a marvelous illustration of the mastermind principle and the harmony in the ranks. I belonged to the first Rotary Club ever organized in Chicago. I was a member of the original group Paul Harris organized. The original purpose included building up his legal practice in a way that wouldn't violate his ethics, but we finally outgrew that purpose. The purpose of the Rotary Club that exists now is based on the idea of developing fellowship among the members. The Rotary Club spread all over the world and it's become an outstanding influence for good wherever it has touched.

You don't do anything in this world without a motive; there must be a motive to inspire everything that you do. The only person that does anything without a motive is an insane person, because he doesn't really have to have a motive.

MOTIVE #1: OPPORTUNITY

The opportunity to get increased compensation and promotion is one of the most outstanding motives for gaining friendly cooperation. Whenever that motive has been put into use in any business, there's always a very beneficial and a very profitable return.

MOTIVE #2: RECOGNITION

Being recognized for personal initiative, a pleasing personality, or outstanding work is a strong motive to inspire cooperation. Give a person recognition when he does a good job; say so, and do something about it.

I know an employer who has the birthdays of his employees, their wives, and all of their children. On their birthday, they get a present and a card personally signed by him. In this way, he's made his organization into one great big family. As he has built himself up in the hearts of those people, you can just imagine what that does to each person.

MOTIVE #3: PERSONAL INTEREST AND HELPFULNESS

A powerful motive for gaining friendly cooperation is to take an interest in the problems of people that you're associated with, or working with, and help them solve their problems. A lot of people say, "My problems are mine but the other fellow's problems are his." I'm not interested in that. You have the right to do that if you want to. But I can tell you that attitude won't be beneficial to you, and it won't be profitable either. If you want to have a lot of friends and a lot of cooperation, you'll make it your business to look around and, wherever you can, start being of help to people.

MOTIVE #4: FRIENDLY COMPETITION

You can create a system of friendly competition between departments, and between individuals within the same department. In either case, the system is based on friendly cooperation. In a sales organization, for instance, if you can have one group competing with other groups in the same organization (on a friendly basis, that is), they'll all strive to do their very best in order to win. They'll do it because of good sportsmanship. Good sales managers often set up that kind of motive to inspire their salespeople to do better jobs.

MOTIVE #5: FUTURE BENEFIT

The hope of future benefits, in the form of some yet unattained goal, can often be obtained by mutual cooperation. Maybe there's something that you want to accomplish with a group of people, and it can only be accomplished by everyone pulling together, in the same direction, at the same time, with a spirit of harmony.

We could mention other motives. There may be a particular case in which you need the cooperation of somebody and know what kind of a motive you could plant in the mind of that person to get that cooperation. You know the cooperation you want (and hope to benefit by) can't be gotten by force or coercion, because if you get it by that method, sooner or later the cooperation will play out and turn into resentment.

FOUR WAYS TO BUILD COOPERATION
THROUGH MOTIVES

Andrew Carnegie's method of inspiring cooperation was based on four principles. First, he established a monetary motive through promotions and bonuses. That was one of his most potent and influential motives in getting men to cooperate. All the men who worked for Andrew Carnegie knew that they had the potential of becoming an exceedingly wealthy executive. They'd seen one man after another do that very thing: start at the bottom ranks and climb right on up to the top.

His second method of getting cooperation was his question system. He never reprimanded any employee personally but, through carefully directed questions, allowed the employee who deserved it to reprimand himself (or herself). If he wanted to reprimand or discipline someone, he'd call him in and start asking him questions which could only be answered one way—the way Mr. Carnegie wanted them answered. That was very smart. If he wanted a fault brought out, he'd let the man bring it out himself, by asking questions that would force him to bring out the fault. He'd also use it to get the person to admit a lie, which the man wouldn't want to do, especially when he knew that Mr. Carnegie knew what the lie was. That was one of the things that indicated what a smart man Mr. Carnegie was. He knew how to get the best results out of people without unnecessarily attacking them or offending them.

The third motive Mr. Carnegie used was that he always had one or more men in training for his job. Just think about an employer that has a number of men standing training for his job. You don't think they would be disloyal, do you? You don't think they'd lie down on the job, refuse to do their best work, or neglect to go the extra mile, do you? They'd be very silly if they did. Mr. Carnegie knew how to hang out plums for people to reach for, so to speak, and because he kept the plum just a little bit ahead of the reach of the man, he caused that man to grow stronger and build a longer arm for reaching it. That was much better than throwing fear into a man's heart, of losing his job or something of that sort, as so many other employers had done.

Fourth, he also never made decisions for his employees but encouraged them to make their own decisions, and be responsible for the results thereof. I think it's a wonderful thing that he would not make decisions for his executives, his under-executives, or anyone in training for executive jobs.

THE POWER OF DECISION

I was in the office of Mr. Iris H. Curtis, owner of the *Saturday Evening Post*, who was also one of the contributors to this philosophy, when his son-in-law Edward Bok came in. After he apologized for interrupting our meeting, he said, "I must speak with Mr. Curtis because I need an answer immediately." I noticed he had a telegram in his hand as he hurriedly explained to his father-in-law that there was a problem in buying the supply of paper that they were going to need for the whole next year. As you can imagine, it took a tremendous amount of money to buy paper for *Ladies' Home Journal*, *Saturday Evening Post*, and *Country Gentleman* magazines. He told his father-in-law what the problem was and the three things he thought they could do about it. Then he said, "What I want you to tell me is, which one shall I do?" Would you be interested to know what Mr. Curtis said to him? After he briefly analyzed each of those three solutions and considered their good points and their bad ones, Mr. Curtis said, "This is your responsibility. That's my answer. It's your responsibility to determine which one of the plans you're going to adopt." After Mr. Bok thanked him and left, Mr. Curtis said, "If he makes the wrong decision, it'll cost us nigh unto a million dollars." I said, "Why didn't you give him the right decision?" He said, "If I had, I'd ruin a good executive. That's why I didn't." Mr. Bok did become a good executive. He made *Ladies' Home Journal* the outstanding magazine of its time. He didn't do it by having his father-in-law make decisions. He made them himself.

Mr. Carnegie taught people to make decisions and be responsible for the decisions when they made them. That's important. Our American system of free enterprise gets friendly cooperation as long as the basic motive of profit is intact and not interfered with by outside influences. If we took away the profit motive, it would take the roof off our whole system of free enterprise. Certain pressure groups are trying to do that very thing all the time—take away the profit motive. You have to have a motive for everything you do, and we believe that the United States has a system of free enterprise based on the finest combination of motives that exist anywhere in the world.

I don't know what you think about this philosophy up until this point, but I want to tell you something. If you get 50 percent of the benefits that are available to you out of this philosophy—not a hundred but just fifty—you can so thoroughly change your lives that the year that's ahead of you can be the most outstanding year of your life. From here on out, for the rest of your life, you can enjoy a controlled destiny, one that you hew out for yourself—where you'll find happiness, pleasure, contentment, security, the friendship and the goodwill of people around you—because you'll create circumstances leading to that end.

PRINCIPLE #14

CREATIVE VISION
or IMAGINATION

Men and women who have cultivated and used the great gift of Creative Vision—or Imagination—are responsible for the benefits of civilization as we know them today. Examples of this principle are all around us, though perhaps one of its clearest illustrations may be found in the film *2001: A Space Odyssey*. In one particular scene near the beginning of the movie, an apelike creature tosses a bone into the air, and as it spirals skyward, the film transports us tens of thousands of years forward, and the flash of sunlight on the bone becomes the shine of a soaring spacecraft high above the earth.

Creative vision brought into being the motion picture project itself, the screen on which you see that scene, the videocassette player, and television set with which you may have watched it at home. Creative vision also originated everything that was used to make the motion-picture: the actors' costumes, the spacecraft models, the sets, the microphones, and the cameras. Of course, it was through creative vision that writer Arthur C. Clarke crafted his classic novel, and it was through creative vision that Stanley Kubrick turned that book into a landmark film.

That single scene epitomizes the power of the principle of creative vision as well. These lectures also epitomize the great philosophy by Napoleon Hill, the man who exercised his creative vision to bring it to us.

The imagination is the workshop wherein is fashioned the purpose of the brain and the ideals of the soul. Someone said that, and I don't know of a better definition.

TWO KINDS OF IMAGINATION

There are two forms of imagination. The first one is synthetic imagination, which consists of a combination of recognized old ideas, concepts, plans, or facts that are arranged in a new combination. New things are few and far between. As a matter of fact, when you speak of somebody having created a new idea or anything new, chances are a thousand to one that it's not anything new but merely a reassembling of something that's old that's gone before.

The second form of imagination is the creative imagination. It operates through the sixth sense, has its basis in the subconscious section of the brain, and serves as the medium by which completely new facts or ideas are revealed.

Any new idea, plan, or purpose brought into the conscious mind, which is repeated and supported by emotional feeling, is automatically picked up by the subconscious brain and carried out to its logical conclusion, by whatever natural means are practical and convenient.

I'll repeat part of that statement so you can see a very important point in it—any idea, plan, or purpose that is brought into the conscious mind and is repeated and supported by *emotional feeling.* In other words, ideas in your mind that do not have your emotion, enthusiasm, or faith will seldom produce any action. In order to get action, you've got to get emotion into your thoughts, you've got to have enthusiasm, or you have to have faith.

SYNTHETIC IMAGINATION

Here are some examples of applied synthetic imagination. Let's first consider Edison's invention of the incandescent electric lamp. You may be interested to know there is nothing new about Edison's electric lamp. Both factors that were combined to make up the incandescent light were old and well known to the world long before Edison's time. It remained for Thomas A. Edison to go through ten thousand different failures before he found a way to marry these two old ideas and bring them together in a new combination.

As most of you know, one of these ideas consisted in the fact that you could take and apply electrical energy to a wire, and at the point of friction, the wire would become hot and make a light. A lot of people found that out before Edison's time. Edison's problem was in finding some means of controlling that wire, so that when it was heated to a white heat, it would make a light and it wouldn't burn up.

He tried all of these experiments—ten thousand, to be exact—and none of them worked. Then one day, as he lay down for one of his customary catnaps, he turned the problem over to his subconscious mind, and while he was asleep, the subconscious mind came up with the answer. I've always wondered why it was that he had to go through ten thousand failures before he could get his subconscious mind to act and give him the answer. He already had half of the idea, but after he woke up from that catnap, he knew that the solution to the other half of his problem consisted in the charcoal principle.

To produce charcoal, you put a pile of wood on the ground, set it on fire, then cover it over with dirt, allowing just enough oxygen to percolate through to keep the wood smoldering, but not enough to permit it to blaze. It burns away a certain part of that wood, and the part that's left behind is called charcoal. You know, of course, that where there is no oxygen, there can be no combustion. Taking that concept with which Edison had long been familiar, he went back into the laboratory, took this wire that he had been heating with electricity, put it in a bottle, pumped the oxygen out, and sealed the bottle, cutting off all oxygen, so no oxygen could come in contact with the arc. Then, when he turned on the electrical power, it burned for eight and a half hours. To this day, that's the principle upon which incandescent electric lamps operate. Have you ever noticed that if you drop one of those lightbulbs, it pops like a gun? Do you know why? It does that because all of the air has been drawn out of it. No oxygen is allowed inside that bulb, because if it were, the filament would quickly burn up. That's an example of two old and simple ideas brought together through synthetic imagination

Examine the operations of your imagination or the imagination of successful people. In a large proportion of the cases, I think you'll find that synthetic imagination, and not creative imagination, was used. The ideas of rearranging old ideas and old concepts can be very profitable.

You may have discovered that there's only one new principle in this philosophy that you're studying (the law of cosmic habit force). In other words, everything here is as old as mankind, and I've only made one contribution that you may not have been familiar with before. What did I do? I used my synthetic imagination and I reassembled existing ideas. In other words, I started out with the salient things that go into the making of success, and I organized them in a way that they had never been organized before in the history of the world. I organized them in a simple form, where you or anyone else can take a hold of them and put them into practical use.

I often wonder why somebody else smarter than I didn't think of that long before I did it. When we get a hold of a good idea, we're always inclined to go back and say, "Why in the world didn't I think of that?" Or, when you do get it, you think, "Why didn't I get it a long time ago, when I needed the money?"

Henry Ford's combination of the horse-drawn buggy and the steam-propelled threshing machine is nothing other than the use of synthetic imagination. He was inspired to create the automobile the first time he saw a threshing machine outfit being pulled along by a steam-propelled engine. There it went down the highway: a threshing outfit with a machine attached to the locomotive of the steam engine. When Mr. Ford observed it, right then and there he got the idea of taking that same principle and putting it onto a buggy (instead of the horse). His "horseless buggy" was eventually known as the automobile.

CREATIVE IMAGINATION

Now let's look at examples of creative imagination. Basically, all new ideas originate through single or mastermind application of creative vision. What does that mean? It generally means that when two or more people get together and begin to think along the same line, in the spirit of harmony (and with the kind of enthusiasm that all the people in the group begin to get when they're working with ideas), out of that group will come an idea pertaining to the thing that they're discussing. In other words, if they go into that discussion for the solution of a major problem, somebody will find the answer, depending on whose subconscious tunes in to the infinite storehouse and picks the answer out first. The answer doesn't always come from the smartest, most brilliant, or best educated man of the group. As a matter of fact, it often comes from the least educated and the least brilliant person in the group.

Let's look at some examples of creative imagination, such as the scientific discovery by Madame Curie. All Madame Curie knew was that, in theory, there must be some radium somewhere in the universe. She hoped it would be on this little ball of mud that we call the earth. See, she had a definite purpose. She had a definite idea. She worked it out mathematically and determined that there was radium somewhere. Nobody had ever seen any, produced any, or found any.

Imagine Madame Curie trying to find radium and compare it to the proverbial story about the person looking for a needle in a haystack. In comparison with her task, I'll take the needle and haystack anytime. By now, I think you might have an idea how she went about searching for it. You don't

think she went out with a spade digging in the ground looking for it, do you? Oh no, she didn't do that. She wasn't that
foolish.

She conditioned her mind to tune into Infinite Intelligence, and Infinite Intelligence directed her to the source.
It's the exact process you use in attracting riches or in attracting anything else you desire. First, you condition your mind
with a definite picture of the thing you want. You build it
up, and support it with the faith and belief that you're going
to get the thing you want, and keep on wanting it even
when the going is hard.

The radar and the radio, for example, are by-products
of creative imagination and the Wright brothers flying
machine. Nobody had ever created and successfully flown a
heavier-than-air machine until the Wright brothers produced theirs. The Wright brothers had no encouragement
from the public when they announced that they were going
to fly the machine. Until then, they hadn't flown it successfully, but they were going to demonstrate it again at Kitty
Hawk, North Carolina. When they announced that to the
press, the newspapermen were so skeptical, they wouldn't
even go down there. Not one single solitary newspaperman
went there for the biggest scoop in the last hundred years.
They were smart-alecks, wise guys who knew all the answers.
How often does that happen when somebody comes up with
a new idea? There are always people who don't believe it can
be done because it's never been done before.

There is no limitation to the application of creative

vision. The person who can condition his mind to tune in to Infinite Intelligence can come up with the answer to anything that has an answer. Anything, no matter what it is.

Look at Marconi's invention of wireless communication and Edison's talking machine. Before Thomas Edison's time, nobody had ever recorded or reproduced sound of any kind. Nobody ever did that, or anything even resembling it. As far as I know, there hadn't even been any talk about it, or stories written about it, and yet Edison conceived that idea, and almost instantaneously. He took a pencil and a piece of paper or an envelope out of his pocket, and drew a crude sketch of what later became Edison's Incredible Talking Machine, as they called it. It's the one that had a cylinder on it, you know, and when they tried it out, the thing worked the very first time.

It was quite a contrast from his earlier experiences. You see, the law of compensation paid him off for those ten thousand failures, when he thought he was working on the incandescent electric lamp. Don't you see what a generous, and fair, and just thing the law of compensation is? Where you seem to be cheated in one place, you'll find it'll be made up in some other place, in proportion to your efforts, whatever they may be. That works with penalizing, too. Maybe you escape the cop at one corner because you run a red light. Maybe you escape him again, too. But, the next time, he'll catch you on two or three counts. You'll find he eventually catches up with you. Well, somewhere out in nature, there's a tremendous cop and a tremendous recording machine. It records all of our good qualities and all of our bad ones, all of our mistakes and all of our successes. Sooner or later, they all catch up with us.

Let's look at creative vision in evaluating the great American way of life. We still enjoy the greatest privilege of freedom and greatest opportunity for riches mankind has ever known. However, we need to use vision if we are to continue to enjoy these great blessings. If you looked back to see what traits of character have made our country great, here they are. First of all, the leaders who have been responsible for the American way of life made definite application of the seventeen principles of the science of success with emphasis on the following six. At that time, they didn't call these principles by these names, though they were probably conscious that they were applying these principles. One of the strangest things about all of the successful people that I've worked with is that not one of them could sit down and categorically give me a step-by-step modus operandi about how he succeeded. By sheer accident, mind you, they stumbled upon these principles listed here.

In fact, I want you to go back and measure the fifty-six men that signed the Declaration of Independence by these six principles. See if you can trace the application of these principles to their act: 1) Definiteness of purpose, 2) going the extra mile, 3) the mastermind principle, 4) creative vision, 5) applied faith, 6) personal initiative. They made way for the American way of life. They did not expect something for nothing. They did not regulate their working hours by the time clock. They assumed full responsibilities of leadership, even when the going was hard.

Looking back over the past fifty years of creative vision, for instance, we find that Thomas A. Edison, through his creative vision and personal initiative, ushered in the great electrical age. He gave us a source of power the world had not previously known. Think of how one man ushered in a new age—the great electrical age—without which all of this industrial improvement that we've had—all the radar, all the television, all of the radio—would not be possible. What a marvelous thing one person did to influence the trend of civilization all over the world. What a marvelous thing Mr. Ford did when he brought in the automobile. He brought the back woods and Main Street together, he shortened distances, and he improved the value of lands by causing marvelous roads to be built through them. He gave employment directly and indirectly to millions of people who would not have otherwise had employment. Now, millions of people have businesses supplying the automobile trade. Wilbur and Orville Wright changed the size of the earth, so to speak, shortening distances all over the world—just those two men, operating for the good of mankind. Andrew Carnegie, through his creative vision and personal initiative, ushered in the great steel age that revolutionized our entire industrial system and made possible the birth of myriad industries, which could not exist without steel. He was not satisfied with the accumulation of a vast fortune of his own. He raised scores of his associate workers into sizeable fortunes they could not have accumulated without Carnegie's aid. He finished up his life by inspiring the organization of the world's first philosophy of personal achievement, which makes the know-how of success available to the humblest person. What a marvelous thing one man can do, operating through one other man.

When you begin to analyze it, you see what can take place when one individual gets together with another individual and forms a mastermind alliance. They begin to do something useful. There's nothing impossible for two people working together in the spirit of harmony under the mastermind principle. Without that alliance, even if I'd had a hundred lives to live, I could never have created this philosophy. However, the inspiration, faith, confidence, and go-ahead spirit I got by having access to a great man like Mr. Carnegie enabled me to rise up to his level, something I never could have done without this mastermind principle and creative vision. There have been times, if I had listened to what would seem to be logic and reason, I would have quit this philosophy and gotten myself a job, as one of my former relatives said she thought I should have done. I could have gotten a job as a nice bookkeeper somewhere, bringing in seventy-five dollars a week. I'd have been very secure and it would have been wonderful to be at home every night (well, most every night), and everything would have been lovely. Believe you me, I had to fight that argument for quite a while, but I did fight it successfully.

I saw bigger things in life. I began to use not only my

synthetic imagination but also my creative imagination (and particularly the latter). It enabled me to pull aside the curtain of discouragement and despair, look into the future, and see there what I now know is taking place all over the world as a result of my having passed this way. All of that through creative vision! How marvelous to be able to tap that thing called creative vision and through it to tune into the powers of the universe. I'm not making a poetic speech, I'm citing science, because everything I'm saying is practical, and is being done, and it can be done by you.

Here is a brief bird's-eye view of what men and women with creative vision and personal initiative have given us. First of all, the automobile, which has practically changed our entire way of living. Those of you who have been born in the last twenty-five, thirty, or even forty years have no concept of what the vibrations of this nation were under the horse and buggy age, in comparison with today. In those days, you would walk down the road, or could ride down the road—safely. Problem is you can't even cross the street where there's a policeman watching in safety, unless you are very alert. The whole method of transportation and the whole method of doing business changed as a result of that one thing called the automobile. Airplanes now travel faster than sound and have shrunk this world to where peoples of all countries know one another better

Maybe the Creator intended it this way. Instead of these worries and things that we've been having in the past, maybe reducing the world in size would bring the people of all nations within traveling distance, so they would become better acquainted, and finally be neighbors or brothers— under the skin as well as on the skin. If the brotherhood of man ever takes place, it'll be because of these various marvelous things that the imagination of man has uncovered and revealed, bringing us together in ways that make it more convenient for us to assemble and to understand each other all over the world.

You can't carry on a war with a person that you are doing business with each day. You can't fight with the neighbor that you're living by each day and have any peace of mind. Try to get along with the people that you have to come into contact with. You'd be surprised at how many good qualities there are in people you previously didn't like, when you come to know them as they are.

Have you ever considered the radio and television, which give us the news of the world almost as fast as it happens? Without any cost to us, they provide the finest of entertainment to the log cabins of the mountain country and the city mansions alike. It's quite an advance from the days when Lincoln learned to ride on a back of a wooden shovel in a one-room log cabin. It's quite a way from the mountains of Tennessee, and the backcountry of Virginia, where I was born (at that time, only famous for mountain feuds, corn liquor, and rattlesnakes).

You can turn a little knob and tune in the finest operas, the finest music, and the finest everything. You can know what the world is doing almost as fast as it's doing it. You know, if we'd had those conveniences when I was growing up, I doubt if I would have made my first definite major purpose that of becoming a second Jesse James. I probably would have wanted to become a radio operator or something of that sort. My, how all this has changed everything for those mountain people down there, throughout the country, and throughout the world. Just think of all the things the mind of man has brought forth to introduce people to one another.

SOUND HEALTH

In many ways Napoleon Hill's philosophy was ahead of its time. This is particularly true in the area of health. Long before it was fashionable to do so, Dr. Hill was speaking of the body-mind link and of these two parts of ourselves as inseparable. He pointed out how anything that affected one must affect the other. At first, many looked at this concept somewhat skeptically. Now we know beyond a doubt that we are body-mind creatures. To function at our best, we must follow the mandate of the fifteenth principle of *Your Right to Be Rich*, the maintenance of Sound Health.

Let us emphasize that this lecture is presented as Dr. Hill always presented it, with this caution: always check with your physician before beginning a program of exercise, diet, or medication. The thrust of this lecture is not to advocate any specific form of medical treatment, but to help you stay healthy through basic proven attitudes and behaviors.

Moderation in all things is recommended: not drinking too much or overeating, and balancing diet, work, and play. There are many more aspects involved, but all of them involve the exercise of another principle: self-discipline. Dr. Hill's premise was that sound health can largely be maintained by simply taking control of ourselves—thinking and living in a positive manner. Only recently have we learned how correct he was. We are discovering some of the ways illness is caused: our own destructive behaviors, poisons we ingest in our diet and from our industries and environment. Certainly, influences beyond our control can make us ill, but there is much we can do to prevent illness from striking us down.

It's wonderful to have a system whereby you can get this old physical frame in fine condition, to do anything you want to do and how you want to do it. If I hadn't had a system for keeping myself healthy and full of energy, I couldn't have done the amount of work that I have all these years, and I couldn't do the amount of work I'm doing now.

As a matter of fact, with the healthy condition of my physical body, I can run rings around people half my age who don't have the system that I have. I have to keep myself in that condition for several reasons. In the first place, I enjoy living better and if I want my body to respond if I make demands on it for enthusiasm, the physical basis has to be there for that enthusiasm. I don't want to get up in the morning ailing. I don't want to look in the glass and see my tongue all coated. I don't want my breath to smell bad. That's not good, is it? There are ways and means of avoiding all of that, and I hope that you get suggestions out of this lesson that'll help you keep your physical body in fine condition.

A MENTAL ATTITUDE OF HEALTH:
HEALTH CONSCIOUSNESS

Let us place mental attitude—or health consciousness—at the head of the list, because without thinking and acting and being in terms of health, chances are you're not going to be healthy. I never think of ailments, as a matter of fact; I can't afford ailments. I just can't afford them. They take up too much of my time. They hurt my mental attitude too much. And, you might ask, "How can you help having ailments?" I have them, and you may have them now, too, but when you get through with this lesson, you're not going to have them as often as you did before, because here is a way of controlling ailments. Notice that every one of these things in connection with conditioning your mental attitude is something that you can control if you want to.

MENTAL HEALTH #1: CONTROL FAMILY AND OCCUPATIONAL STRESS

Griping or complaining about your family relationships or occupational relationships hurts your digestion. You might insist that certain circumstances in your family make it necessary to complain. If that's the case, it's better for you to change the circumstances so you won't have any circumstances to complain about.

The reason I mention family relationships and occupational relationships is because that's where you spend most of your life. If you're going to allow those relationships to be based upon friction, misunderstandings, and arguments, you're not going to have good health, you're not going to be happy, and you're not going to have peace of mind. If there's any hatred in your life, you must get rid of it. No matter how much a person deserves to be hated, you can't afford to do the hating. The reason you can't afford it is because it's bad for your health. It hurts digestion and produces stomach ulcers. Worse than that, it produces a negative mental attitude that repels people instead of attracting them to you. You certainly can't afford that. It attracts reprisals in kind, because if you hate people they'll hate you. They may not say so but they will.

MENTAL HEALTH #2: ELIMINATE GOSSIP

Eliminate gossip or slander from your life. That's a hard one to comply with because there's so much wonderful material to gossip about in the world. It seems a pity to cut yourself off from all that pleasure, doesn't it? Gossip or slander attracts reprisals and also hurts the digestion. Instead, let's transmute that desire into something that's more profitable to you.

MENTAL HEALTH #3: CONTROL FEAR

There must be no fear because it indicates friction in human relationships and also hurts the digestion. Any fear in your makeup most definitely indicates something in your life that needs to be changed or altered. I can truthfully say that there isn't anything on the face of this earth, nor in the universe, that I fear. Nothing at all. I used to fear just about everything the average person fears, but I had a system for overcoming those fears. If I had a fear now, do you know what I would do about it? I'd have it out with myself. I'd eliminate the cause of that fear. No matter what it would take, or how long it would take, I would eliminate the cause of fear. I simply will not tolerate fear in my makeup.

You can't have good health, prosperity, happiness, or

peace of mind if you're going to fear anything—even death most of all. Personally, I'm looking forward to death with a great anticipation. It's going to be one of the most unusual interludes of my whole life. As a matter of fact, it'll be the last thing I'll experience. Of course, I'm putting it off for a long time. I've got a job to do and all that, but when the time comes, believe me I'm going to be ready. It's going to be the last thing I'll do and the most wonderful thing of all, because I'm not afraid of it.

HEALTHY THOUGHTS CREATE A
HEALTHY BODY

The way you use your mind has more to do with your health than all of the other things combined. You can talk all you want about germs getting into the blood, but nature has set up a marvelous system of doctoring inside of you, and if that system is working properly, the resistance within your physical body will take care of all those germs. Nature has a way of keeping your body healthy through resistance; it keeps the germs down so they cannot multiply. The minute you become worried, or annoyed, or fearful, it breaks down that body resistance and those germs multiply by the billions and trillions and quadrillions. The next thing you know, you really are sick.

PHYSICAL HEALTH ACTION #1: EAT WITH PEACE OF MIND

Don't allow worries, arguments, or unpleasantness at mealtime. Did you know that the average family selects mealtime as the time to discipline the husband, wife, children, or whatever the case may be? That's the one time you can get them all together, when they're not inclined to run away while you're giving them a tongue lashing. They will stand, or sit, and eat while you're saying your piece, but if you could see what happens to the digestion or the bloodstream of someone who eats while they're undergoing punishment, you'd know that's the wrong time to do it. The thoughts you have while you're eating go into the food you eat and become part of the energy that goes into your bloodstream.

PHYSICAL HEALTH ACTION #2: EAT IN MODERATION

Overeating creates too much work for the heart, the lungs, the liver, the kidneys, and "the sewer system." Most people eat twice as much as they really need. Think about how much money you'd save on grocery bills, especially with prices the way they are. It's astounding how many people overeat. If you're doing manual labor outside, you might need heavy, substantial food. A man who's digging ditches has to have a certain amount of meat and potatoes, or something equal to it, but a man or woman doing office work, or

YOUR RIGHT TO BE RICH

spending all day in a store or a house, for instance, doesn't have to have the same amount of food.

PHYSICAL HEALTH ACTION #3: EAT A BALANCED DIET

A balanced diet includes fruits, vegetables, and plenty of water (or the equivalent of water in some form of juices). In California, I follow a system of making sure at least one meal a day is nothing but "live" food—vegetables, berries, nuts, melons, and things of that sort. It includes food that is considered alive, and nothing that's been canned or processed in any way, shape, form, or fashion. When I follow my established diet at home, I notice all the difference in the world in my energy. I can't do that here in Chicago. They'd think I was nuts if I went into a restaurant and ordered that kind of a meal. As a matter of fact, I doubt if I could get that kind of a meal in Chicago.

PHYSICAL HEALTH ACTION #4: EAT SLOWLY

Eating too rapidly prevents proper mastication. I can get away with it, because I have a good, strong, vital body, but I don't suggest you try it. I'm sure you know a lot of people who do it, but eating too rapidly shows that you've got too much on your mind, you're not relaxing, and you're not enjoying yourself.

A meal should be a form of worship. Your thoughts should be on all of the beautiful things that you want to do, your major purpose, or the things that please you most. If you're engaged in conversation with someone else while you're eating, it should be a pleasant conversation, not a fault-finding fishing job. If a man's sitting across the table from a beautiful woman, I don't see why he doesn't talk about her beautiful eyes, her hairdo, her lipstick, or any of the things that women like to have you talk about. Even if you're sitting across the table from your wife, it would do you both a world of good.

PHYSICAL HEALTH ACTION #5: AVOID SNACKING BETWEEN MEALS

Don't eat candy bars, peanuts, or snacks between meals; don't drink too many soft drinks. If you want to take a drink, you might as well get a hard one, because it'll do you some good. I mean something like water, for instance. (I shook you up on that one, didn't I?)

I've seen office girls make a whole lunch out of candy bars, snacks that they get out of the newsstand, and a bottle or two of Coca-Cola. A young person's stomach can stand that for a while, but if your body is not being treated properly, sooner or later, nature makes you pay up for that kind of mistreatment of your stomach. It would be far better if an office worker got a head of lettuce, put salad dressing on it, and ate that. It would also be good to have some fruit or grapes, because anything you can get at the fruit stand would be far better than eating candy bars.

PHYSICAL HEALTH ACTION #6: CONTROLLING LIQUOR (AND CIGARETTES)

Liquor in excess is taboo at all times—except after six o'clock. I admit that was meant to be funny. I don't mean *exactly* what was said here. In excess, liquor is taboo at all times, but liquor in a reasonable amount is . . . reasonable. I can take a cocktail or two, but more than that and I might commence to say things maybe I shouldn't say or do things I ought not do. Neither would do me any good.

I like to be in control of my mind all the time. What's the sense of pickling your stomach and your brain so that you're not yourself? People find out too much about you that you don't want them to know. In addition, you look silly, don't you? Don't you think that a person whose tongue has been loosened up with liquor makes a spectacle of himself? That doesn't do him very much credit, no matter who he is.

If I go into a home (as I often do) where they're taking cocktails, I don't say, "Oh no, thank you, I don't touch the stuff." I take the cocktail and, if I'm not in the mood to drink, I wait until nobody's looking and I sit it down somewhere. Sometimes I just carry it around. I once carried a cocktail around one whole evening before I got a chance to sit it down. As soon as I got a chance, I dumped it into the sink. They thought I drank it, but I didn't because I was to make a speech that night. It would have been silly to get all caught up with liquor before making a speech. Whether it's liquor, or smoking, or anything else, keep it in moderation.

If you take it instead of it taking you, that wouldn't be too bad, but the better plan is to get over using it at all.

PHYSICAL HEALTH ACTION #7: RELAXATION AND PLAY

Balance all work with an equivalent amount of play, because you need play to ensure sound health. That doesn't mean you should play an *equivalent* number of hours, because it just doesn't work out that way. Believe me, I can work one hour and yet only five minutes of playing can offset my work time. When I write, I'm up on another plane entirely. It's so intensely hard on the physical constitution that forty minutes is all I can stand of it. But after I go sit down at my piano and play for five or ten minutes, I've completely balanced off all that intense activity I've been engaged in.

PHYSICAL HEALTH ACTION #8: GET ENOUGH SLEEP

Sleep eight hours out of every twenty-four, if you can find time to do it. Getting good sleep is a mighty fine habit to get into. I mean get in there and lie down. Don't turn and twist and groan and snore and all that sort of thing. Lie down and sleep peacefully. Get in such good rapport with your own consciousness and your neighbor's that you don't have anything to worry about. When you hit that old pillow, you can go right smack to sleep.

ELIMINATE WORRY

Train yourself not to worry over things you can't remedy. It's bad enough to worry over the things you can remedy; I wouldn't worry over them any longer than it took me to remedy them. Some time ago, one of my students asked if I spent time worrying over people who came to me with their problems. I said, "Other people's problems? I don't worry over my own problems, why should I worry over somebody else's problems?" It's not because I am indifferent—I'm far from indifferent. In fact, I am very sensitive to the problems of my friends and my students, but not sensitive enough to let them become my problems. They're still your problems. I'll do all I can to help you solve them, but I don't absorb them and take them over myself. That's not my way of doing it and don't you get into that habit either. There are a lot of people who not only make room for all of their own problems, but they also take on the problems of all their in-laws, relatives, friends, the neighborhood, and sometimes the problems of the whole nation. Worry was made for somebody else, not for me.

You don't have to go looking for trouble; it will find you in its own way. The circumstances of life have a queer way of revealing to you the thing you're searching for. If you're looking for faults in other people, or looking for trouble, or looking for things to worry about, you'll always find them.

If you're looking for things to worry about, you don't have to go very far; in fact, you don't have to go out of your house.

ELIMINATE HOPELESSNESS

A person without hope is lost. However, sound health inspires hope and hope inspires sound health. Now, what do I mean by hope? I mean hope of some yet-to-be-obtained objective in life, something that you're working toward, something that you're trying to do and you know you're going to do it.

Don't worry because you're not doing it fast enough. A lot of people who want to make a lot of money and get rich are so impatient that they become nervous; they work themselves into a fury because they don't get the money fast enough. Sometimes this desire to get money quickly influences people to get it the wrong way, and that's not good.

Develop hope by daily prayer, not for more blessings but for those you already have (such as freedom as an American citizen). What a marvelous thing it is to express prayer every day in one form or other. In your own words—or in your thoughts without any words at all—express prayer of appreciation for the freedom that you enjoy as an American citizen. Be thankful for the freedom to be ourselves, freedom to live our own lives, freedom to have our own objectives, freedom to make our own friends, freedom to vote as we please, to worship as we please, and to do pretty much anything else we please. We're free to abuse ourselves by wrong living, if we want to. We have the privilege of acting on our initiative in a job that is secure from war hazards at the present time. (At least we think there's not any danger of war at this time. There might be some time later on, but right now there isn't.) We are free with the opportunity to secure economic freedom according to our talents, free to worship in our own way. Free to practice sound physical and mental health. We are free to use the time that lies ahead of us—free to control our future—in any way. Think of how marvelous it is that you are master of the time that still lies ahead of you.

The richest part of my life and my achievements are still ahead of me. I'm still just a youngster in the school of my profession. In fact, I'm only going to kindergarten. But since I'm going to do some really good work before I pass on, I'm making better use now of my time than I used to. Time is a precious thing. In fact, I evaluate it in terms of minutes now.

PAIN IS NATURE'S MESSENGER

A headache is nature's way of warning you that something needs correction. If you think of it that way, the headache is a wonderful thing. We couldn't get along without headaches, and we'd die too young if we did, because a headache is nothing but nature telling you that there's trouble somewhere and you'd better get busy and do something about it.

Did you know that physical pain is one of the most miraculous and marvelous things of all of nature's creations? Physical pain is a language that every living creature on earth and people of every nationality understand. The language of pain is the only universal language. Every living creature begins to do something when physical pain begins to clamp down on it. Pain is a form of warning and takes no prerogatives of any sort, at any time. That's a bad habit. Sound health does not come from bottles, but it may come from fresh air, wholesome food, wholesome thinking, and wholesome living habits—all of which is under your control.

Fat people may be good-natured, but they generally die too young, and I don't like to see people die too young. Fasting is one of the secrets to my marvelous health. I have no ailments and lots of energy because twice a year I go on a ten-day fast. I spend ten days without any food of any nature whatsoever. For two days, I condition my physical body through preparation by fruits, fruit juices, nothing but live vital elements going into the body. Then, I go on my fast of water, taking in nothing but just plain water, as much water as I can drink. Sometimes I put a few drops of flavoring or lemon juice or something in it, just enough to take the flatness out of water. (Believe me, when you're fasting, water will taste mighty flat.) For the first days after my fast, I eat very light and very little, maybe only a small bowl of soup (with no grease in it) and a slice of whole-wheat bread on that first day. You don't have to start fasting just because I said so. In fact, you don't have to fast at all, but if you do, you should learn how and why to do it under the direction of a doctor or somebody skilled in fasting. I once recommended a fast to one of my students who was about seventy-five pounds overweight. She said, "Fast for ten days? I'd starve to death the first day if you took food away from me." Not only do I believe she meant it, I think she probably would. If a person got lost in the woods, not only would they be scared to death, but I also suspect they could starve to death in two or three days. There is tremendous therapeutic, spiritual, and economic value in learning *the art of fasting.*

ENJOY YOUR WORK

Work must be a blessing because God provided that every living creature must engage in it in one way or another or perish. Isn't that a marvelous way to think about work? The birds of the air and the beasts of the jungle neither spin, nor sow, nor reap. Nevertheless, they have to work before they can eat just the same.

Work should be performed in the spirit of worship, and as a ceremony. It's wonderful to look at your work as the rendering of useful service, not in terms of what you're getting out of it but in terms of the people that you're helping as a result of what you are doing. When you're engaged in a labor of love—doing something for somebody just because you love that person or he's a friend of yours, and not doing it for money—you never feel tired doing that kind of work. It does something for you. You get your compensation as you go along. This business of going the extra mile is a wonderful part of this philosophy. It makes you feel better as you go along doing it. You feel better toward yourself, better toward your neighbor, and it gives you a better standing in the world of your health. When work is based on the hope of achieving some definite major purpose in life, it becomes voluntary service, a pleasure to be sought, and not a burden to be endured. Work with a spirit of gratitude for the blessings it provides. For the sound physical health, economic security, and the benefits it may provide one's dependents, embellish your work with love.

BUILD FAITH

Learn to commune with Infinite Intelligence from within and adapt yourself to the laws of nature all around you. The greatest system of therapeutics that I know of is an abiding and an enduring source of faith. If any ailments creep in, I know of no better medicine to take than faith.

CREATE GOOD HABITS

All habits are made permanent and work automatically through the operation of the law of cosmic habit force, which demands that every living thing will take on and become a part of the environmental influences in which it exists. You may fix the pattern of your thought habits and your physical habits, but cosmic habit force takes these over and carries them out. Understand this law and you will know why the hypochondriac enjoys poor health.

BUDGET TIME
and MONEY

Years after Napoleon Hill developed his philosophy of achievement, philosopher Buckminster Fuller
coined a famous phrase, which later became the title
of one of his books, *Spaceship Earth*. Fuller envi-
sioned our entire planet as a kind of spaceship hur-
tling through the universe. Like a spaceship, he
reasoned, our planet contains a finite amount of
resources, and we have to manage and make the
most of these resources if we are to survive, let alone
prosper. Years before Buckminster Fuller developed
the phrase Spaceship Earth, Napoleon Hill coined the
sixteenth principle of *Your Right to Be Rich*: Budget
Time and Money. Hill and Fuller are two great minds
sharing the same idea: that there is only so much of
anything to go around—time, money, the resources
of our planet.

What do you do with the resources at your disposal? How well do you use the seconds, minutes, hours, days, years that are given to you? How much of your resource of time is wasted? The money that you earn, how well do you use it? How much goes to pay for your residence, your clothing, and the food on your table? How much goes toward recreation? How much do you save, if any? How much of your financial resources is wasted? If you answer those questions with absolute honesty, you may not like the answers, but answering them honestly may be the only thing that will lead you to make the most of your resources from now on. Simply because you're human, your resources are, and must be, finite. If there's only so much of you to go around, how do you apportion yourself? How can you best distribute yourself to make the most of what you have to offer your family, your occupation, your country, and your world? To these questions and more, Dr. Napoleon Hill offers some guidelines and answers.

If you ever want to have financial security in this world, there are at least two things you must do. You've got to budget your time (how you use your time) and budget your money (how you manage your expenditures and your receipts), according to a definite plan.

Let's address time first. You have twenty-four hours divided into three eight-hour periods. You don't have much control over the eight hours for sleep, because nature demands it. You don't always have too much control over the eight hours that you put into work, either. Even if you're working for yourself, you still don't have too much control, because you have to be there to work. However, there are eight hours that are yours to do with what you wish, even waste them if you want to. You can play, work, enjoy yourself, relax, or develop yourself by taking courses of instruction, reading, or anything you want. Therein lies the greatest opportunity of the whole twenty-four hours.

In the days when I was doing my research, I worked sixteen hours a day, but it was a labor of love that I was engaged in. I reserved eight hours a day for sleep and the other sixteen I worked. I spent part of the time training salesmen in order to make a living, but most of the time I was doing research, getting this philosophy ready to give to the world. Had it not been for the fact that I had at least eight hours of free time of my own, I never could have done the necessary research. With those eight hours of spare time, you can practice developing all of those habits that you choose (through the law of cosmic habit force). You don't necessarily have to follow my plans, but you'll get some mighty good ideas in the lessons on applied faith, cosmic habit force, and mastermind. When you work out a plan of your own, it'll be better than if I give it to you verbatim and you just follow what I tell you. Let's return to the suggestions for budgeting of time, budgeting of income and expenses.

BUDGETING MONEY FOR LIFE INSURANCE

Consider your monthly or weekly amount of income. Use a budgeting book and make this your first entry. Whether you have a family or you don't, life insurance is an absolute must—you cannot afford to be without it. If you brought five children into this world to whom you're responsible for an education, it's up to you to insure yourself so that if you pass out of the picture and there's no longer any income, they'll have enough money to educate themselves. If you've married a wife that's dependent entirely upon you, it's up to you to carry enough insurance to give her a down payment on a second husband if you should pass out of the picture.

Life insurance gives you such wonderful protection in case you are taken away from your source of production. This is important for a family man or a man that is in business where his services are a large portion of the assets. There are men who are considered "key" men if their being taken away would pose a tremendous loss to the business. Men like that should always be insured for a large sum of money, enough to fill the chasm that's left after they are gone.

BUDGETING MONEY FOR FOOD,
CLOTHING, AND HOUSING

The next thing to budget is a definite percentage of income for food, clothing, and housing. Now, don't go out and blow the works. By that I mean you can go down to the grocery store and spend five times as much as you actually need, if you don't have a system to go by. Believe it or not, I do the shopping at our house, not Annie Lou. That way I get what I want. I learned a great deal about shopping by following the housewives that I knew. I found out who were good shoppers and asked them questions, and I can tell you there were a lot of things that I didn't know about buying food and handling food after you buy it. When I go over to one of those big supermarkets in California, I always pick out the most likely housewife, follow along behind her, and start asking her questions. You'd be surprised at how cooperative they are, telling you what you should do and what you shouldn't. For food and clothing, I must say we don't have a budget for this. I buy whatever strikes my fancy, but I also happen to be in a position where a budget on food and clothing is not necessary. There was a time when it was necessary, and I imagine in the lives of most people, it is necessary to have a budget for these things.

BUDGETING MONEY FOR INVESTMENT

Set aside a definite amount for investment, even if it's only as small as a dollar a week or even fifty cents a week. It's not the amount that's important, it's the habit of being resourceful and frugal. It's wonderful to be frugal and not waste things. I've always admired anybody that doesn't waste things. My grandfather used to go around picking up old nails and strings and pieces of metal. You'd be surprised by the collection of things he had. My frugality never ran to that extent . . . it ran more to a Rolls-Royce and six-hundred-acre estates. No matter how much of this philosophy you have, if you don't have a system for saving a part of what goes through your hands, it makes no difference how much goes through, does it? And, if you don't have that system, it will all go through. Whatever amount remains after you have taken care of those three items should go into a current checking or spending account for emergencies, recreation, education, and etcetera that can be drawn upon. You might call it a petty cash account, for things you don't budget. If you're really frugal, you'll let it get up to a pretty good size; you won't keep it down too low all the time. It's nice to know that you have a good nest egg lying in the bank, in your savings account. No matter what happens, you can always go down there and get the money. You may not need it, and the chances are it'll put you in that frame of mind where you won't have to go down and get it. But if you don't have it there, believe me, you'll have a thousand needs and you'll be afraid.

Perhaps the thing that gives me the most courage to speak my peace, be myself, and demand that people keep off of my toes, is the fact that I no longer have to worry where my money's coming from. I have no money worries. As a matter of fact, I don't have any worries at all. People try to worry me sometimes, but it's like Confucius says, "When rat tries to pull cat's whiskers, rat generally winds up in honorable cat's belly."

Develop a system of trapping a little percentage that goes through your hands. It's not the amount as much as the fact that you're establishing frugal savings habits. If your wages or income is so low that you can't cut your expenses any further and you can only take 1 percent off the top (that is, one cent out of every dollar), take that one cent and put it away in some place where it's hard for you to get at it. I'm a great believer in having money invested in the investment trust where they represent a great variety of well-known stocks so that if one goes bad, it doesn't affect your investment at all. There are a lot of those investment trusts, some good and some not so good, but if you want to invest in an investment trust, you ought to go to your banker or somebody that is acquainted with them. Don't try to do an investment like that on your own judgment. As a rule, most individuals are just not qualified for doing that, but if you get some of your money working for you, you'd be surprised at what a nice game it is. You know that you're setting aside a certain amount every month or every week, and that amount is beginning to work for you. This business of trapping the money is my way of telling you to get it into a place where you can't reach down in your pocket and get it.

Whenever I go to the bank, I get some pocket money, and no matter what amount I get, I take a twenty-dollar bill, wrap it up, and put it in that little special pocket in my wallet. If I ever happen to run out of money, I'll always have twenty dollars. The other day I needed it, too. It came in very handy. Otherwise, I'd have had to cash a check with somebody who didn't know me too well and I wouldn't have wanted to do that. Saving money is a very difficult thing for most people because they don't have any system to go by.

BUDGETING TIME FOR YOUR PROFESSION OR OCCUPATION

First of all, on the choice of a profession or occupation, how much time are you giving to that? How much thought and time have you given to the question of getting yourself adjusted in an occupation or a business or a profession that can be a labor of love?

You can grade yourself on all of these, from zero up to one hundred. Of course, you're not giving 100 percent of your time on this first item. But if you haven't already found the profession or occupation that can constitute a labor of love, then you should put in a lot of time searching until you do find it.

BUDGETING TIME FOR CAN-DO THINKING

How much time do you spend on the can-do sort of thinking and how much do you spend on the no-can-do? In other words, how much time do you put into thinking about what you desire or what you don't desire? Have you ever stopped to take inventory and see how much time you put into things that you don't desire in life: fear, ill health, frustration, disappointment, or discouragement? I'll bet you'd be surprised. If you had a stopwatch, you could record the time that you put in every day worrying about things that might happen to you but never do.

You'd be surprised as to how much of your time goes a little here, a little there, and a little over to that other place. Next thing you know, a predominantly good portion of your time is being spent thinking about things you don't want—unless you have a budgeting system, whereby you keep your mind definitely fixed on the things that you do want.

BUDGETING TIME FOR GRATITUDE

I have three hours set aside for meditation. Three hours for silent prayer and meditation. It doesn't make any difference what hour. When I go home from these lectures, no matter what hour I get home, I usually put in three hours of meditation expressing gratitude for the marvelous opportunity that I have had to minister to other people. If I don't get it in at night, I spend some time during the day expressing gratitude. Do you know that the finest prayer in this world is not to pray for something? Pray for what you already have. Divine Providence, I ask not for more riches but more wisdom with which to make better use of the riches that I already have. What a wonderful thing that is! All of you have so many riches. You have health, you live in a wonderful country, you have wonderful neighbors, and you belong to a wonderful class (*to the class of students in these lessons by Napoleon Hill*). Think of all the things you have to be thankful for.

Think of the things that *I have* to be thankful for. As I stand here and tell you that I have everything in this world that I want, there would be something wrong with this philosophy and me *if I weren't rich*. Wouldn't there? I'd have no right to teach it to you whatsoever, if I couldn't say that about myself. I can be the master of my fate and the captain of my soul because I live my philosophy. I designed it to help other people, too, because under no circumstances would I do anything to intentionally hinder, bend, harm, or endanger another person.

BUDGETING TIME FOR RELATIONSHIPS

How much time do you put into business and personal relationships? How much do you spend on public relations or goodwill-building in your relationships with other people, whether in your business or in your job? You must spend at least some time cultivating people, because if you don't, you're not going to have the friends you really want. Out of sight, out of mind. I don't care how good the friend is, if you don't keep contact he'll forget about you. You've got to keep contact.

One of these days, I'm going to make up a series of postcards that only take two cents each to mail. I'll have a beautiful motto of friendship on each one. That way, my students can mail one a week to each of their friends, just to keep in contact. That wouldn't be a bad idea for a business or a professional man, either. Nothing would hinder a professional man from building up a wonderful clientele by doing that very thing. He wouldn't violate the ethics of his profession by doing it, and there'd be no commercial angle to it, either. All he has to do is to send one a month (that's twelve cards a year), with the right kind of message on the back of it, and sign it himself. Believe me, that would the best way to build up his practice.

BUDGETING TIME FOR HEALTH

How much time are you putting into the physical and mental health habits that build a health consciousness? A health consciousness doesn't just grow without some effort.

COMMIT TO LIVE YOUR RELIGION

How much time do you put into living your religion? I'm not talking about believing in it. I'm not talking about going to church and putting a quarter in the basket now and then (anybody can do that). I'm talking about *living it*—in your bedroom, your drawing room, your kitchen, at your place of business, and in your office. That's what I mean about how much you're living your religion. When you grade yourself on that, that's the place to grade yourself, not by how much you go to church, because chances are you go to church once a week or maybe more (with some religions you have to go more), because it's not how many times you go that counts. It's not how much you contribute to the church in the way of money. It's what you do *to live that religion*. That's the thing that counts every day of living. Any of the religions are wonderful if people live by them instead of just believe in them. I don't know of a religion on the face of this earth that wouldn't be wonderful if only people would live by it.

It may seem trite to ask you to grade yourself on how much time you're spending on living your religion, but unless you're very different from most people I know, you need to reflect on this subject.

BUDGET TIME FOR IMPROVEMENT
AND ADVANCEMENT

How do you use your spare time? There's where you really need to examine yourself and give an honest account. How much of that eight hours of spare time do you devote to some sort of advancement of your interests, improvement of your mind, or benefiting by (joining a professional or civic) association?

REVIEW: HOW THE OTHER PRINCIPLES
FIT THIS ONE

A Definite Plan. Do you have a budget system for how you spend your money? If you haven't got a system, work one out. You can make that system flexible if you want, so you can cheat a little bit one week and pay it back the next week.

Accurate Thinking. In budgeting your resources, how much time do you spend learning how to think accurately and put your thoughts into action? How much are you doing to put the principle of accurate thinking into actual practice? Remember, that principle is about thinking accurately, doing your own thinking, and making use of the power of thought (whether controlled or uncontrolled). Are you controlling your thoughts or are your thoughts uncontrolled? Are you letting the circumstances of life control you or are you trying to create circumstances that you can control? Remember that you can't control all of them, nobody can, but you certainly can create some circumstances that you can control.

Have you thought about the privilege of voting? "I guess I'll not go to the polls today; the crooks are going to run the country anyway and my little vote's not going to count." Do you say that or do you say, "I have a responsibility and I'm going to go to the polls and vote because it's my duty to do that." Put a little time in on what you do? A lot of people don't and that's why there are so many crooked politicians and others in public office that shouldn't be there. Too many decent people don't vote.

Improving Relationships. Are your family relationships harmful or are they harmonious? Have you set up a mastermind relationship or are you letting that principle slide by? How much time do you budget to develop and improve your family relationships? Do something to get started. Sometimes, somebody has to give in. If the wife won't give in and start something, why don't you gentlemen? And vice versa. If your husband doesn't start a little masterminding, why don't you? Why not make it interesting for him? I'm sure you made it interesting for him before you married him, or he wouldn't have married you. Why not start over and renegotiate your marriage relationship? Imagine what wonderful things this could do to your relationship. Improving relationships will pay off in peace of mind, dollars and cents, friendships, and in any way you measure it.

Going the Extra Mile. In your job or business or your profession, are you going the extra mile and do you like your work? If you don't like your work, find out why. If you're going the extra mile, how much are you going the extra mile? Are you doing it in the right mental attitude? I don't care who you are or what you're doing, if you always make it your business to go the extra mile with everyone, you will have so many friends that when the time comes for whatever it is you want to carry out through them, they'll be at your beck and call.

I'll never find a better relationship than I have with the people in my classes. I work at it, I want to earn it, and I want to deserve it. The result is that people don't just applaud with their hands, they applaud with their hearts, and that's the kind of applause I appreciate.

LAW *of* COSMIC HABIT FORCE

The seventeenth and final principle of *Your Right to Be Rich* is the Law of Cosmic Habit Force, and this particular principle presents us with a paradox. On the one hand, some of Dr. Hill's students have said that this is the most difficult principle to understand. On the other hand, it is perhaps the simplest principle of all. Perhaps the paradox lies in the fact that cosmic habit force is so obvious; it surrounds and permeates everything in the cosmos: the sweep of the galaxies, the ebb and flow of the tides, the rhythm of the seasons. As the saying goes, it can be easy to overlook the obvious. Simply put, cosmic habit force is the law through which the balance of the universe is maintained in orderliness—through established habits.

If the universe is a company, then cosmic habit force is its comptroller. That's the big picture. The small picture is how this principle affects you. The reason cosmic habit force is so important to you is that through it, you create the individual habits that become a fixed part of you—habits that can be positive or negative. You must learn the secrets of cosmic habit force and how to apply its power to your physical and mental behaviors. The power is there and, whether you know it or not, you are using it every day. How you use it will lead you to failure or to success.

If you're a student of Emerson, and you've read his essay on the law of compensation, you'll get the sum and substance of this lesson much more quickly and you'll also get more out it (than those who aren't familiar with it). Over a period of ten years, I read Emerson's essays, especially the one on compensation. When I finally interpreted what he was talking about, I decided that one day I would rewrite that particular essay so that men and women could understand it the first time they read it. This lesson is that rewrite.

carried on according to a system. If the Creator had to hang out those stars and watch them every night, he would be a very busy fellow. He's not going to do that. He's got a better system that works automatically.

WORK WITH LAWS TO CREATE SUCCESS

If you learn what those laws are, you can adapt yourself to them and profit by them. If you don't learn what they are, through ignorance or neglect you'll suffer by them. The majority of people don't realize that there is a law of cosmic habit force. Do they go through life using this marvelous law to bring prosperity and health and success and peace of mind? No. Instead, they experience poverty, and ill health, and frustration, and fear, and all of those things that people do not want, because they keep their mind on those things. The cosmic habit force simply picks up those habits of thought and makes them permanent. That's where I come along and break them up with this science of success philosophy and that's just why you're here.

Mr. Stone and I had a very charming lady in our office last week. She wanted to sell us some space in a book that she was getting out based upon the birth dates of people. She wanted to know my birth date, but Mr. Stone didn't let her get very far with her story. He told her he would have nothing to do with any system or book that presupposed their birth date had anything to do with what happened in one's life. He said, "I can't speak for Napoleon Hill but that's my decision," and I said, "Well, you just made my speech, Mr. Stone." To the woman, I said, "I don't care what star you were born under. I don't care what unfavorable circumstances you may have met with in life, and I don't care what happened to you in the past. I do know that if you will follow my instructions, you will get from where you are now to where you want to go, and you'll get there easily. I know that, and I know that you can set up habits that will make your success so easy, you'll wonder why in the world you worked so hard in the past and didn't get so far."

Most people work harder at failing in life than I work at succeeding—a lot harder. It's much easier to succeed when you learn the rules. There's a lot more pleasure in it than in failing, and you are not going to succeed unless you understand this law of cosmic habit force. Start building habits that lead to where you want to go. All actions—and reactions—of matter are based upon the fixed habits of cosmic habit force. Have you ever stopped to think of that? The very smallest particulars of matter all exist as a result of habits that are fixed upon.

CONTROLLING HABITS

Thought habits of individuals are automatically fixed and made permanent by cosmic habit force. Think about that. Thought is not fixed, but a habit of thought is automatically fixed. Another way of saying this is this: the thoughts that you give expression to are going to be *fixed into habits*. You don't need to worry about this. As long as you keep your mind on the things that you want to become a habit, cosmic habit force will take over from there. The individual creates the pattern of his thoughts by repetition of thought on a given subject. The law of cosmic habit force takes these patterns and makes them permanent (unless they are broken up or changed by the will of the individual). What a terrible thing if we couldn't break habits.

When I see the number of people smoking cigarettes, I'm beginning to think maybe they can't break that habit. When I see all the publicity that the magazines and newspapers give about the high death rate in lung cancer due to cigarettes, I wonder whether or not people can break the cigarette habit. If you want to go ahead and get lung cancer by smoking, that's your business. There's nothing more for me to say about it. However, I want to give you a little test that might be helpful. If you can't start out tomorrow morning and prove your willpower stronger than a little pinch of tobacco and a little piece of silk paper, then you'll want to begin working on your willpower right away and reeducating it. When I quit smoking, I laid my pipes down and told Annie Lou to take them and throw them away because I wouldn't need them anymore. She said, "I'll put them away until you call for them," but I said, "Throw them away. I'll not be needing them anymore." Habits? If you can't get control of the habit of smoking, it's going to be very difficult for you to get control of other habits, like fear and poverty and everything else you allow your mind to dwell upon.

When I have some enemies to deal with, I always take the biggest guy first, because when I lick him then the rest put their tails between their legs and run. If you got some habits you want to break, don't start with the little easy ones; anybody can do that. Start with the big ones, the ones that you most want to do something about.

Take that pack of cigarettes that you have in your handbag or in your pocket. When you go home, put it up on the dresser and say, "You may not know it, but I'm more powerful than you are, and I'm going to prove it by not going into that package again. I am going to let it sit there for forty days, after which I won't need cigarettes anymore." I'm not talking against the cigarette business, and I don't have any stock in the cigarette companies. I'm just giving you some ideas through which you must start testing your capacity to build the kind of habits that you want by starting with the tough ones.

Here's another habit. Go on a week's fast, that's a whole week without any food. Tell your stomach that you're the boss (it may think it's the boss, but you're the boss). Don't do this on your own, do it under the directions of a doctor, because fasting is not child's play. Get control over your stomach and you'll be surprised at how many other things you have control over.

How in the world can we expect to be successes in this world if we're going to allow all these merriment habits to take hold of us and rule our lives? We can't expect to be successes. We have to form our own habits long enough until cosmic habit force takes them up automatically.

HABIT OF HEALTH CONSCIOUSNESS

Now let's return to the question of how the individual may apply the law of cosmic habit force. Let's look at physical health, for instance. The individual can contribute to the healthful maintenance of his physical body by establishing habit patterns. If you want to prove the effectiveness of this law of cosmic habit force, this is a mighty fine place to start because I don't know of anything people want more than a good strong physical body that responds to every need in life. Without it, I couldn't do the kind of work that I do. I couldn't write the inspirational books. I couldn't deliver inspirational lectures if I didn't know that when I put my foot on the gas, there's going to be power there. No matter how steep or how long the hill, I know that I've got plenty of power to go the full distance because I keep my body in that kind of condition.

Your thinking is the place to start in applying cosmic habit force for the purpose of developing sound health. A positive mind leads to the development of a health consciousness. Do you know what I mean when I talk about a health consciousness, or a prosperity consciousness, or any other kind of a consciousness? It's a continuous awareness of the condition you want. A health consciousness is a predominating tendency of your mind to think about health, and not about disease or ailments.

Everyone will tell you all about their medical operations. Just six months ago, a good friend of mine visited me after he came out of the hospital. Let me tell you, he described his operation so vividly, I could feel the surgeon's scalpel turning in my back. I finally turned around and rubbed my back, because it actually began to hurt back there where he was describing. Fortunately, I got myself under control, but I didn't ask him to come back and see me again.

Most people don't like to hear you talk about your ailments. They're not interested in your ailments, and you ought not to be either, except to get rid of them, and the best way to get rid of them is to form a health consciousness. Think in terms of health, talk in terms of health, look in the glass a dozen times a day and say, "You healthy man!" or, "You healthy woman!" Talk to yourself, and you'll be surprised at what'll happen.

The positive mind leads to the development of a health consciousness, and cosmic habit force carries out the thought patterns to their logical conclusion. However, it will just as readily carry out of the picture of an ill-health consciousness created by the thought habits of the hypochondriac, even to the extent of producing the physical and the mental symptoms of any disease on which the individual fixes his thought habits through fear. I'm saying that if you think about certain ailments or disease long enough, nature will actually simulate them in your physical makeup.

There was an old elderly lady in the mountain section of Wise County, Virginia, where I lived as a small boy. She used to come over to my grandmother's house every Saturday afternoon, sit on the front porch, and entertain us all afternoon with operations of herself, her husband, what her husband died with, what her mother died with, what two of her children died with, and so on. After about three or four hours of this, she ended up saying, "I know that I'm going to die of cancer," and put her hands on her left breast. I saw her do that a dozen times. I didn't know what cancer was at the time. About ten years later, my father sent me a copy of the county paper and I saw an announcement of Aunt Sarie Ann Steve's death, from cancer of the left breast. It seems she finally talked herself into it. That's not an exaggerated case at all. It just happens to be one of the cases that I know about. You can talk yourself into a headache, you can talk yourself into a bilious condition, and you can talk yourself into anything. You can think yourself into any malady, if you allow your mind to dwell upon the negative side of your physical body. Thinking is important.

THOUGHT HABITS WHILE EATING

The mental attitude and the thought patterns established while eating (and also during the following two or three hours, while the food is being broken down into liquid form for introduction into the bloodstream) may determine whether the food entering the body is suitable for the maintenance of sound health. In fact, your mental attitude when you're eating becomes part of the energy that goes into your bloodstream. If you don't know that, you'd better learn about it, because it does. You can't afford to eat when you're disturbed, and you can't afford to eat when you're too tired physically. Sit down, rest, and relax when you eat. As a matter of fact, eating food should be a form of religious exercise. It should be a religious ceremony. When I get up in the morning, the first thing I do is to go out to the kitchen and squeeze a great big tall glass of orange juice. I worship every ounce of that orange juice as it goes down. I don't just drink it all down at once, I let it go a little at a time and worship every mouthful of it. If you think I'm kidding, perish the idea because I'm telling you something very important about your eating. If you get into the habit of blessing your food, not only when you sit down at the table but as it goes into your body, it'll go a long way toward keeping you healthy.

THOUGHT HABITS ABOUT WORK

With your work, mental attitude becomes a vital ally; a silent repairman works on every cell of the body while one is engaged in physical action. Therefore, work should also become a religious ceremony, surrounded by only positive thoughts. One of the tragedies of civilization is the fact that so few people in the world are engaged in the labor of love, that is, doing the thing they want to do because they want to do it, and not just because they have to eat and sleep and wear some clothes.

I hope and pray that before I cross over to the other side, I will have made valuable contributions to mankind, such that individuals may find a labor of love in which to make a living and earn their way. What a grand world this would be if it weren't for some of the people who live here. It's not that there's anything wrong with them, it's just their habits that are wrong. They think wrong, and that's what's wrong. Let them think in terms of good health, opulence, and plenty. Let them think of fellowship and brotherhood instead of stirring race riots, setting a man against man, brother against brother, nation against nation, and thinking in terms of war instead of cooperation.

There's plenty in this world for everybody, including the squirrels, and animals, and birds. If only some people didn't try to get too much while trying to keep other people from getting enough through wrong thinking. I honestly don't want any advantage or benefits of any nature that can't be shared everywhere and with all people. I don't want anything that I can't share with people. I want no advantage over other people, save only the opportunity of sharing my knowledge and my ability to help them help themselves.

The famous Mayo Brothers discovered four vitally important factors that must be observed to maintain sound physical health. There must be an equal balance of the thought habits of work, play, love, and worship. Isn't that interesting? That's according to the great Mayo Institute, where they have had thousands of people pass through their clinic. They found out that when those four things are out of kilter, the imbalance almost invariably results in some form of physical ailment.

Here is one of the major reasons for adopting and following the habit of going the extra mile. This habit not only benefits one economically, but it also enables one to work with a mental attitude that leads to sound physical health. When you do something out of the spirit of love, or out of the spirit of desire to help other people, and not out of a selfish desire, it tends to give you better health and builds up better health habits. Conversely, consider the person who has the habit of griping and who performs all work grudgingly and in a negative frame of mind. Nobody wants to work with him or employ him. The fellow who gripes while working not only damages himself, he also damages everybody around him.

Mr. Andrew Carnegie told me that one single negative mind in an organization of ten thousand could more or less discourage the mind of everyone there, within only two or three days. He wouldn't even have to open his mouth or say anything. Just releasing thoughts would affect everyone. Go into a home where's there fighting between members of the family, and you know it the moment you cross the threshold. I can tell when I get in the front yard whether I want to go in or not, or whether it's safe to go in or not.

We have an experience in our home that makes me prouder than anything else. Almost invariably, when a person walks into our home for the first time, they look around and make a compliment. For instance, an outstanding publisher came to see me not long ago and when he walked into our living room he said, "What a beautiful home." He looked around again and probably noticed that it was just an ordinary home after all, not anything outstanding. Then he said, "The word *beautiful* is not just the word I want." He said, "It's the way I feel when I come in here. The vibrations are good." I said, "Now you're getting hot. You're talking right up my alley."

This home is constantly charged and recharged with positive vibrations. Nothing inharmonious is permitted inside this house. Even our little Pomeranian dogs have picked that up. They respond to the vibrations of the home, they can tell a person that's not in harmony with our home the moment they come in, and they don't like that kind of a person. Sparky will go up and sniff a person and if she's pleased with that harmonious atmosphere, she'll go over and kiss his hand. If she's not pleased, she finds that he's not in harmony, she'll bark at him and back away. I didn't teach her that, either; it was her own idea.

Homes, places of business, streets, and cities all have their own vibrations, made up of the dominating thoughts of those who work and go that way. If you go down Fifth Avenue, New York City, it doesn't matter how much or how little money you've got in your pocket; if you walk by those big, prosperous stores like Tiffany's, you'll catch the feel of that crowd and you'll feel like you're prosperous, too. On the other hand, go just four blocks in the other direction to Eighth Avenue or Ninth Avenue in Hell's Kitchen. I defy you to walk one block there without feeling like you're as poor as a church mouse even though you may have all the money in the world.

ECONOMIC AND FINANCIAL BENEFITS OF HABIT THINKING

Let's consider the economic and financial benefits of working with the principle of cosmic habit force. First of all, remember definiteness of purpose.

> *Through a combination of these principles of success, one may condition his mind and body to hand over to cosmic habit force the exact picture of the financial status he wishes to maintain, and these thoughts will automatically be picked up and carried out through their logical conclusion by this law of nature which knows no such reality as failure.*

HABIT OF THINKING WHAT YOU CAN DO

I've probably had more opportunities to study successful people at close range than any other man living today. I have observed that they constantly think in terms of things they can do, never in terms of things they can't do. I once asked Henry Ford if there's anything he wanted to do that he couldn't do. He said, "Why, no. I don't think about the things

I can't do. I think about the things I can do." The majority of people are not like that. They think and worry about the things they can't do. Consequently, they can't do them. In other words, they think about the money they don't have, and worry about it. Consequently, they don't have it, and never get it. Money is a peculiar thing, isn't it? It doesn't follow the fellow who doesn't believe he's got a right to get it. I wonder why that is? Money is an inanimate thing; I don't believe it's the fault of the money. No, the fault's not there, it's in the mind of the person who doubts that he can get it.

I notice that when a student of mine starts believing that they can do things, it starts to change their entire financial condition. And when they don't believe they can do things, they don't do them. The whole purpose of this philosophy is to induce my students to build up habits of belief in themselves and in their ability, to direct their minds to whatever they want in life, and to keep their mind off the things they don't want.

If you don't know much about Mahatma Gandhi, it'd be a good idea for you to get a book and read up on his life. There's a man who didn't have anything to fight the British with, except his own mind. He didn't have any soldiers, money, or military equipment. He didn't even own a pair of breeches. Yet he put to test the great British Empire, with nothing more than his mind power, resisting them, not wanting them, and not accepting them, until the British finally got the big idea to pick up and get out. It's surprising how many individuals do that when you set your mind against them. You don't have to say anything and you don't have to do anything. You just have to say in your own mind, "I don't want that person in my life" and eventually they'll get out—sometimes very quickly.

This mind power stuff is very powerful, potent, marvelous, and profound once you become acquainted with it and start using it. This is the medium by which one's thought habits may be controlled until they are taken over by cosmic habit force. I want to call attention to the fact that no one has ever been known to become financially independent without having first established *a prosperity consciousness*, just as no one may remain physically well without having first established *a health consciousness*.

GET IN THE HABIT OF THINKING WHAT YOU WANT

I remember so well that when I started out with Andrew Carnegie, my greatest difficulty was forgetting that I was born in poverty and illiteracy and ignorance. It took me a long time to forget the little mountain hut in the mountains of Wise County, Virginia, where I was born. It was a long time before I could forget about it or get it out of my system. When I would start to interview an outstanding man, I'd always think, "Oh well, I'm so insignificant." I guess I thought I ought to be ashamed and afraid because I remembered where I came from. I remembered my poverty. It was a long time before I could shake that poverty off. But I finally did it.

I began to think in terms of opulence. I began to say, "Why wouldn't Mr. Edison want to see me, and why wouldn't Mr. Wanamaker want to see me? I'm just as big in my field as he is in his." I not only felt that, but I saw the day when I made it come true. It's an achievement when you can reach out and influence the lives of millions of people all over the world. It's an achievement that never would have happened if I hadn't changed the thoughts of Napoleon Hill. My biggest job was not getting in to see the men of affairs and to get their collaboration. That was easy. My biggest job was to change the habits of thinking by Napoleon Hill.

Had I not changed those habits, the books I wrote that have inspired millions of people would never have had the effect that they had, because when an author writes a book or makes a speech, the exact mental attitude that he's in when he's writing or speaking is conveyed to his audience. Nothing could keep one's audience from picking up his thoughts. You get an impression about that writer as you read their book. You couldn't possibly read one of my books and not know I'm dealing with principles as fundamental as Infinite Intelligence itself. You don't need anybody to prove it to you; you just know it. Before I could write those books, I had to completely build over my thought processes and my habits of thinking. I had to learn to keep my mind on the things that were positive, and keep it there constantly.

EXCESSIVE THOUGHTS AND FIXATION

Did you know that each one of you came over to this plane with a marvelous doctoring system of your own? Much the same way a chemist breaks up food and deliberately takes out of it the things that nature needs, if you think right, eat right, exercise right, and live right, the chemist doctor inside you does everything automatically. It's a system that nature gave you for balancing everything that you need to keep your body in fine condition all the time. But, you have to do your part.

NEGATIVE FIXATIONS

Fixation, or excessive thought, is wonderful if it doesn't happen to be a negative fixation. Here are fixations of fear: limitation thoughts about the things that you can't do, the fear of criticism, or the fear of anything else. If you want to make use of fixation and benefit by the law of cosmic habit force, work on the fixation of faith. Applied faith is a fixation you can tie to, because faith is knowing that when you reach out for the things you need, you'll always find them, and if they're not where you thought they were, they'll be close at hand. By all means cultivate that kind of fixation. Don't let it get away from you by neglect.

REPETITION CREATES A HABIT

How do you go about creating a fixation or thought habit? Repetition. Apply it in everything you do, and think, and say. Repetition. You may remember the Coué formula, "Day by day, in every way, I'm getting better and better." Millions of people all over this country were saying that and it didn't amount to a tinker's damn unless the person saying it believed it. It wasn't what he said that counted, it was what he thought while he was saying it. There were a lot of people that said it over and over again and then finally turned thumbs-down on it. It didn't work for me because I didn't believe it in the first place, so you can understand why it didn't work. It makes no difference what formula you use, or whether you use any oral formula at all, as long as your thought patterns are positive, you've got to repeat them over and over again.

Make a habit of thinking in positive terms until the cosmic habit force picks up your mental attitude and makes the circumstances of your mind predominantly positive, and not predominantly negative. The majority of people's minds are predominantly negative all the time. You want to make the mind predominantly positive all the time so, no matter what you want, you can turn on the power and get some response from Infinite Intelligence. Infinite Intelligence is not going to do anything for you while you're in a state of anger, no matter how much right you have to be angry. Infinite Intelligence is not going to do anything *for you*, but she's going to let you do something *to yourself* if you keep yourself in a state of a negative mind. You can't afford to entertain any action, expression, human relationships while you're in a negative mental attitude, and the best way to keep from being in the negative mental attitude is to build up positive habits and let cosmic habit force take over and make them predominant in your mind.

MORE NEGATIVES TO AVOID

Here are the negatives that you should avoid making into fixations: poverty, imaginary illness, and everyday garden-variety laziness. Do you know what a lazy man is? He's a man who hasn't found a labor of love. There are no lazy people except those who haven't found what they like to do. Of course, some of them are pretty hard to please. They go through life and have an alibi for why they don't like this and don't like that. As a matter of fact, they don't like anything, period. They are lazy. Other negatives are envy, greed, anger, hatred, jealousy, dishonesty, drifting without aim or purpose, irritability of mental attitude in general, vanity, arrogance, cynicism, sadism, and the will to injure others. Those things can become fixations in the lives of most people, but as a student of this philosophy, you can't afford to have that kind of a fixation. You just can't afford it, it's too expensive.

POSITIVE THOUGHT HABITS

Here are positive thought habits that you *can* afford to have (and you can't afford to not have them). The definiteness of a major purpose in life heads the list. Make it a fixation by all means. Eat it, sleep it, and drink it. Every day, indulge in some act that leads in the direction of your overall major purpose in life. More positives include faith, personal initiative, enthusiasm, willingness to go the extra mile, imagination, the traits of a pleasing personality, accurate thinking, and all the other traits of individual achievement in this philosophy.

Turn those positive thought habits into fixations so that they dominate your mind—you live by them, think by them, act by them, and you relate yourself to people by them—you'll be surprised how quickly your life will change in these ways:

- People who have tried to injure you will (of their own accord) fall away and become ineffective.
- You'll become very potent and attract new opportunities.
- You'll solve your problems quickly when they arise.
- You'll wonder why you didn't do this before—why you worried over your problem, and why you just didn't get busy and dissolve it, or solve it.

REPETITION AND ACTION

On every one of those positive thought habits, you'll notice every one is under your control—and subject to your control—as a result of repetition of thought. All you have to do is keep repeating it over and over and over again, and put some action behind the thought.

Word without deeds is dead. Engage in some sort of action. One should develop fixations, but one should also take care to see that they are fixations on something one wants, not that which one does not want. Isn't it a strange thing that the majority of people go through life getting everything they don't want and very few things that they do want? A lot of people don't get the mate in marriage that they really want (after they get him or her and find out that's the case, that is). I know a lot of people who don't get out of their jobs, or profession, what they want.

How does a professional (such as a dentist, lawyer, doctor, or engineer) attract wonderful patients, meaning they are agreeable to get along with, they pay their bills promptly, and that sort of thing? The answer is to be that way himself. In other words, the effects start with the professional man himself. His own mental attitude toward his clients or patients determines what they do toward him. It's true, whether or not the person happens to be a merchant, a man or a woman in a job, or any other person whatsoever. *If you want to reform people, don't start with other people, start with you.* Get your mental attitude right and you'll find that the others will fall in line. They can't help it. If your mind is positive, the negative-minded person can't influence you in the least. A positive-minded person is always the master of the negative-minded person, if the positive person exercises his right to be positive.

We are what we are today because of two forms of heredity. One of them we control outright and one of them we do not control at all.

PHYSICAL HEREDITY

Through physical heredity we bring a little sum total of all of our ancestors. If we happen to be born with nice brain power or nice well-developed bodies, that's just fine. Unfortunately, if we happen to be born with a hunchback or some affliction, there's not much we can do about that. In other words, we have to take "as is" what physical heredity hands us.

I know a man who lost the use of his legs through polio and he ran a peanut stand two blocks away from the White House. However, right inside the White House was a man with the same affliction who was running the biggest nation in the world. That man made an asset out of his affliction instead of a liability.

SOCIAL HEREDITY

Social heredity consists of all the influences in your life after you were born (and maybe dating back to the prenatal stage before you were born). These influences include things you hear, things you see, things you are taught, things you read, and legions of other things too numerous to mention. These influences have the greatest impact on what happens to us through life. However, equally important to what we get out of our environment is *how much we control it.*

It's a good idea for all of us to go back and reexamine the things we believe and find out what right we have to believe them. Where did we get our beliefs? What is there to support those beliefs? I don't think I have any beliefs that are not supported by good sound evidence, or least what I believe to be evidence. I didn't arrive at that open-minded state of tolerance overnight. I used to be as intolerant as the next person, but I realized it was bad for me, and certainly not good for my students, to have a closed mind about anything.

CONCLUSION

This concludes Dr. Hill's entire presentation of his philosophy. To realize its greatest contribution to the science of success, and the greatest potential for your own success, consider reading it again and again and again. Go over and over the materials in this program until they become second nature to you and an authentic part of you.

This presentation of Dr. Hill has an historic character to it. These lectures are akin to a snapshot taken in Chicago in the spring of 1954. However, the philosophy is not static in the way a snapshot is. Dr. Hill's philosophy is every bit as alive, and vital, and viable today as it was when he created it so many years ago. It will work for you as it has worked for millions who have lived by its teaching and profited from it.

Millions more people will live and profit from these valuable teachings in the future. You are one of those people, a student of this science of success. You can put its power to work every day and achieve riches in every aspect of your life—personal and professional—that you always dreamed of. You're already ahead of the pack, because you've done something most people will never do, by taking the first and biggest step of your life. You've begun a new path. Joy, fulfillment, and achievement lie before you, and we wish you well in your journey.

INDEX

INDEX